COVENANT & CONVERSATION:
A WEEKLY READING OF THE JEWISH BIBLE
GENESIS: THE BOOK OF BEGINNINGS

Other works by the author

Rabbi Jonathan Sacks

COVENANT & CONVERSATION

A Weekly Reading of the Jewish Bible

GENESIS: THE BOOK OF BEGINNINGS

Maggid Books & The Orthodox Union

Covenant & Conversation
Genesis: The Book of Beginnings

First edition 2009

Maggid Books
An Imprint of Koren Publishers Jerusalem Ltd.

POB 8531, New Milford, CT 06776-8531, USA
& POB 4044, Jerusalem 9104001, Israel
www.korenpub.com

ISBN 978 1 59264 020 1, *hardcover*

A CIP catalogue record for this title is
available from the British Library

Printed and bound in the United States

This publication was made possible with the kind support of the
Raphael and Linda Benaroya Foundation

לעילוי נשמת

בננו יקירנו מחמד לבנו
דוד ז"ל **בן רפאל ולינדה (יפה)** הי"ו
נלב"ע י"ג כסלו תשס"ח

מו"ר אבינו
יעקב בן רפאל וז'ולי ז"ל
נלב"ע י"ז אב תשס"ה

מרת אמנו
רחל בת יום טוב ורוזה ז"ל
נלב"ע כ"ו אדר תשס"ז

In loving memory of

Our beloved Son
David ben Raphael and Linda

Our beloved Father
Yaakov ben Raphael and Julie

Our beloved Mother
Rachel bat Yom Tov and Rosa

To our daughter Gila and
our son-in-law Elliott

יְשִׂישׂ עָלַיִךְ אֱלֹהָיִךְ. כִּמְשׂוֹשׂ חָתָן עַל כַּלָּה

May God rejoice in you
As you rejoice in one another.

– J.S.

Contents

Living with the Times: The Parasha

We must live with the times," the Rebbe said.

The disciples, sitting around the table, eagerly awaiting the master's words, were perplexed. "Live with the times? Isn't that what the enemies of faith are always saying – The past is dead; long live the future? Surely we believe the opposite, that God's word is eternal, that certain things do not change, that values and principles and laws are constant. To be a Jew is to be beyond time. What then does the Rebbe mean when he says, We must live with the times?"

"What I mean," said the Rebbe, "is that we must live with the *parashat hashavua*, the weekly portion of the Torah."

Like so many Jewish stories, ancient and modern, this one, told of the sixth Lubavitcher Rebbe, contains hidden depths. Wherever they are throughout the world, Jews read a weekly portion of the Mosaic books – the *parashat hashavua*. It forms the music of the Jewish year. Autumn is Genesis (*Bereshit*) with its tales of beginnings, the birth of the world, of humanity and of the Jewish people. Winter is Exodus (*Shemot*), the story of exile and redemption, slavery and freedom and the beginning of the long journey through the wilderness in search of the Promised

Land. Spring is Leviticus (*Vayikra*), with its laws of sacrifice, sometimes remote to the modern ear, yet shot through with ethical grandeur and at its fulcrum the two greatest moral imperatives of all – to love our neighbour as ourselves, and the far harder yet ultimately more important command to love the stranger, the other, the one not like ourselves. Numbers (*Bemidbar*) ushers in Shavuot, the festival of revelation, and does so with the story of the Israelites in the wilderness, a fraught tale of backslidings and rebellions, perhaps the most realistic narrative ever told of the birth of a nation. Summer is Deuteronomy (*Devarim*), that magnificent book of Moses's addresses in the last month of his life, his vision – never surpassed – of Jewish history and destiny as the people of the covenant, charged with living in faithfulness to God.

Jewish time is both cyclical and linear. We are part of nature and its rhythms – the cycle of the seasons and of a human life – as we move from birth through maturity to age and wisdom and sadness as we see the next generation, those who will carry on the story when we are no longer here. But we are also part of history – time as a non-repeating sequence of events, a journey in which no stage is exactly like any that has been or will be. Jewish time is like a fugue between these two themes, the eternal and the ephemeral, the timeless and the timely. That, I suspect, is what the Rebbe meant when he said we must live with the biblical portion of the week. It is that weekly encounter between the now and the then, the moment and eternity, which frames Jewish consciousness and gives us that unique sense of living out a narrative, the biblical story, to which we ourselves are writing the latest chapter.

That, at any rate, is how I have tried to live. Time and again, in the midst of troubled times or facing difficult decisions, I've found the words of the weekly *parasha* giving me guidance – or, conversely, the events themselves granting me deeper insight into the Torah text. For that is what "Torah" means: teaching, instruction, guidance. Torah is a commentary on life, and life is a commentary on Torah. Together they constitute a conversation, each shedding light on the other. Torah is a book not only to be read but to be lived. One of the things that gives us the courage and wisdom to chart our way through the wilderness of life is knowing that we are not alone, that God goes before us in a pillar of cloud and fire, signalling the way. The way He does so for us is through the words of the Torah, to which every Jewish life is a commentary, and each of us has our own annotation to write.

The following essays, each short and I hope simple, are records of how I have tried to live with the times through a dialogue with the Torah. Each is self-contained, yet taken together they constitute one person's encounter with the text that formed a people's identity and shaped its sense of destiny. Jews are, supremely, the people of the Book. They found God less in the mysteries of the cosmos or the secret recesses of the soul than in words, God's words to us, which ever since they were first spoken we have tried to decipher and apply to our lives. Wherever Jews were, they took the Torah with them. They carried it, and it carried them. Torah became, in Heinrich Heine's lovely phrase, the "portable homeland" of the Jew.

If there is one shared feature of these essays, it is that I have tried to set the biblical text in the wider context of ideas. Many traditional commentaries look at the Torah through a microscope: the detail, the fragment of text in isolation. I have tried to look at it through a telescope: the larger picture and its place in the constellation of concepts that make Judaism so compelling a picture of the universe and our place within it.

I have called these studies *Covenant and Conversation* because this, for me, is the essence of what Torah learning is – throughout the ages, and for us, now. The *text* of Torah is our covenant with God, our written constitution as a nation under His sovereignty. The *interpretation* of this text has been the subject of an ongoing conversation for as long as Jews have studied the divine word, a conversation that began at Sinai thirty-three centuries ago and has not ceased since. Every age has added its commentaries, and so must ours. Participating in that conversation is a major part of what it is to be a Jew. For we are the people who never stopped learning the Book of Life, our most precious gift from the God of life.

Genesis: An Introduction

Genesis, the book of *Bereshit*, is as its name suggests, about beginnings: the birth of the universe, the origins of humanity, and the first chapters in the story of the people that would be known as Israel or (after the Babylonian exile) the Jews. It tells of how this people began, first as an individual, Abraham, who heard a call to leave his land, birthplace and father's house and begin a journey, then as a family; it closes as the extended family stands on the threshold of becoming a nation. The journey turns out to be unexpectedly complicated and fraught with setbacks. In a sense, it continues till today. This is part of what makes Genesis so vivid. We can relate to its characters and their dilemmas. We are part of their world, as they are of ours. No other ancient literature has so contemporary a feel. This is our story; this is where we came from; this is our journey.

But this is not all Genesis is, and in reading it thus we risk missing its full significance. Maimonides makes the fundamental point that *Reshit* does not mean "beginning" in the sense of "first of a chronological sequence."[1] For that, biblical Hebrew has other words. *Reshit* implies the

---

1. Rambam, *Guide to the Perplexed*, (*Moreh Nevukhim*) book II, chapter 30. See also

most significant element, the part that stands for the whole, the foundation, the principle. Genesis is Judaism's foundational work, a philosophy of the human condition under the sovereignty of God.

This is a difficult point to understand, because there is no other book quite like it. It is not myth.[2] It is not history in the conventional sense, a mere recording of events.[3] Nor is it theology: Genesis is less about God than about human beings and their relationship with God. The theology is almost always implicit rather than explicit. What Genesis is, in fact, is *philosophy written in a deliberately non-philosophical way*. It deals with all the central questions of philosophy: what exists (ontology), what can we know (epistemology), are we free (philosophical psychology), and how we should behave (ethics). But it does so in a way quite unlike the philosophical classics from Plato to Wittgenstein. To put it at its simplest: philosophy is *truth as system*. Genesis is *truth as story*. It is a unique work, philosophy in the narrative mode.[4]

So we learn about what exists by way of a story about creation. We learn about knowledge through a tangled tale of the first man, the first woman, a serpent and a tree. We begin to understand human free-

Ramban, commentary to Genesis, Introduction, who says that the Torah begins with the stories of Genesis "because it teaches people the ways of faith."

2.   See Ernst Cassirer, *The Philosophy of Symbolic Forms*, vol. 2 (New Haven: Yale University Press, 1955), 119–20, 240, for the difference between mythic and historical consciousness. Myth deals primarily with the origins of the things that are timeless features of nature. It is a kind of primitive science. It does not deal, as does the Torah, with time as an arena of change. See also Mircea Eliade, *Cosmos and History* (New York: Harper and Row, 1959).

3.   "The concept that within the history of mankind itself a process was at work which would mould his future, and lead men to situations totally different from his past, seems to have found its first expression amongst the Jews... So, with the Jews, the past became more than a collection of tales, a projection of human experience, or a system of moral examples." J.H. Plumb, *The Death of the Past* (Harmondsworth: Penguin, 1973), 56–57. The idea of history as the unfolding of the relationship between God and humankind finds its classic expression not in Herodotus or Thucydides but in Tanakh.

4.   To be sure, other great literature deals with philosophical issues: on this, see the work of Martha Nussbaum and Stanley Cavell. On the difference between the two modes, system and story, see Jerome Bruner, *Actual Minds, Possible Worlds* (Cambridge, MA: Harvard University Press, 1986).

dom and its abuse through the story of Cain. We learn how to behave through the lives of Abraham and Sarah and their children. It is this that has helped to make Tanakh, the Hebrew Bible, the most widely read and influential book in the history of civilization. Only the gifted few can fully understand a philosophical classic, but everyone can relate to a story.

In Torah, form follows function. The fact that a piece of information is conveyed in a particular way is never accidental. The chosen genre, the literary medium, is there for a reason, and the reason is never merely aesthetic. Why then did the Torah adopt a story-telling mode for Genesis, its book of first principles?

Partly for the reason already stated: a story is universal. The Torah is a book written for all. One of the great themes of Tanakh is its consistent battle against elites, especially knowledge elites. The Torah defines Israel as "a kingdom of priests and a holy nation" (Exodus 19:6) – a kingdom whose members all aspire to be, at least metaphorically, priests; a nation all of whose members are holy. Every religion has its own elites: priests, bishops, gurus, saints, mystics, shamans, holy men and women who form a distinct class set aside from society as a whole. Judaism is about the democratization of holiness, the creation of a society in which everyone will have access to religious knowledge. Hence the importance of stories which everyone can understand.

Yet not understand at the same level: that is another feature of Genesis. Each of its stories has layer upon layer of meaning and significance, which we only grasp after repeated readings. Our understanding of the book grows as we grow. Each age adds insights, commentaries and interpretations of its own. The book's literary style allows it to be read afresh in each generation. That too tells us something significant about the Torah's view of human knowledge: The truths of the human condition are simply too deep to be understood at once and on the surface. Only stories have this depth, this ambiguity, this principled multiplicity of meanings.

Most importantly, only stories adequately reflect what it is to be human. Tell a story, even to young children, and they become instantly attentive. They want to know what happens next. In logical systems, there are no surprises as to what happens next: All men are mortal, Socrates is a man, therefore Socrates is mortal. The conclusion is already implicit in the premises. But in a story, as in life, we never know what will happen next, because human beings are free. Will Eve eat the forbidden fruit? Will Cain disregard God's warning? Will Esau kill Jacob when they meet after long separation? Will Joseph's dreams come true?

More than a narrative device, the element of suspense reflects a central theme of Genesis: God's gift of freedom to humanity. God created the universe; therefore God is free. By endowing human beings with His "image and likeness," He gave them freedom as well. We may be, like the first human, "dust of the earth," but there is within us the "breath of God." We are shaped by our environment, but we can also shape our environment as well. We are created, but also creative. To a degree shared by no other life form known to us, we can choose how to act and how to react. That is good news, but also bad, as we rapidly discover in the Torah's narrative. We can obey but also disobey; we can create harmony or discord. The freedom to do good comes hand-in-hand with the freedom to do evil. The result is the entire human drama as Judaism understands it.

Our fate does not lie in the stars, nor in the human genome, or in any other form of determinism. We become what we choose to be. Therefore, we don't know what will happen next. If some form of determinism were true, human fate could be summarised in a system, Marxist, Freudian, Darwinian or other. Determinism, we believe, is *not* true, and the best way of showing this is by way of stories, in all of which the outcome is in doubt. We don't know what will happen until it does. And, in Genesis, things never happen quite as we expect.

The story opens with the creation narrative. We discover the universe as a place of order and goodness, the result of a single creative will. Human beings are presented as the one exception to this rule. They can do evil and create chaos. At times – as in the generation of the Flood – they can endanger the entire future of life on earth. The Torah reveals this in a series of short, sharp vignettes. With Adam and Eve comes the first sin; with Cain the first murder. By the time of Noah, the world is "filled with violence." In the age of Babel, humanity becomes guilty of hubris. No sooner have they discovered how to make bricks and build on a monumental scale, than they attempt to "reach heaven," transgressing into God's domain.

As humanity develops, so does its capacity for evil. Having revealed the ever-expanding scope of corruption – from self, to other, to the world as a whole, and then to heaven itself – the narrative shifts its focus. From humanity as a whole we turn to one family: Abraham, Sarah and their descendants. God, as it were, no longer expects all humanity to reach the moral heights. Instead He charges one family with the task of leading exemplary lives from which others will learn.[5] From chapter 12 until the end, the book is a set of finely nuanced variations on the theme of relationships within the family: between husbands and wives, parents and children, brothers and sisters, across four generations.

Not by accident is Genesis a book about the family. The family is where we learn emotional and spiritual intelligence. There is nothing simple or idealized about the families of Abraham and Sarah, Isaac and Rebecca, Jacob, Leah and Rachel. There are tensions, rivalries, setbacks and unfulfilled hopes as well as love, kinship and loyalty. Only much later in Tanakh do we discover that the family will turn out to contain the most compelling metaphors for the relationship between human beings and God Himself. He is our father, we are His children. He is our husband, we are His betrothed. Something, however, becomes clear in one of the most haunting passages in Genesis, in which Jacob wrestles with an angel and receives the name that ever afterward his children will bear: Israel, one who "struggles with God and with man and prevails": The tensions within the patriarchal family are symptomatic of Israel's later, larger battles, with God, with humanity, and with itself.[6]

There is another significance to the focus of Genesis on the family. Unlike the god of the philosophers, the God of Abraham is a *personal* God. He is not an abstract concept: the first cause, the force of forces, the prime mover, pure Being. He is a God who relates to us as persons, sensing our suffering, hearing our prayers, a presence in our lives. And it is in personal relationships – first and foremost within the family –

---

5. Only in the book of Exodus do Abraham's children become a nation. Throughout Genesis, they remain, first a nuclear, then an extended family.

6. The sages recognized the principle 'What happened to the fathers was a portent of what would happen to the children.' See *Bereshit Raba* 40:6 for the parallels between the fate of Abraham and Sarah in Egypt (Genesis 12:10–20) and what would later happen to their descendants in the book of Exodus.

that He expects us to honour Him by honouring others, who bear His image no less than we do.

The protagonists of Genesis are astonishingly human. They are a world away from the heroes and heroines of myth. They are not mighty warriors or miracle workers. They are not rulers commanding armies and winning legendary victories. They are ordinary people made extraordinary by their willingness to follow God. We hear their hesitations and doubts, their fears and apprehensions. In the world of myth there is no clear boundary between the gods and human beings: the gods are all-too-human, and the humans are often portrayed as demigods. In the Torah, by contrast, it is as if the transcendence of God makes space for the humanity of humankind. By insisting on the absolute difference between heaven and earth – the distance the builders of Babel sought to abolish – the Torah allows us to see ourselves as we really are, infinitesimal, fallible and frail, yet touched by the wings of infinity.

By placing the stories of Genesis before the book of Exodus, with its story of the birth of the Israelites as a nation, the Torah is implicitly telling us of *the primacy of the personal over the political.* Exodus is about the big themes – slavery and freedom, miracles and deliverances, the rescue of an entire people from oppression and their wondrous journey through the sea and across the wilderness. It is about law and liberty and justice, and the nature of Israel as a nation under the sovereignty of God. But by focusing first on individuals and their relationships, Genesis reminds us of the complexity of the human heart, which no political order in and of itself can resolve: "How small, of all that human hearts endure / That part which laws or kings can cause or cure!" (Oliver Goldsmith). If we cannot create peace or justice or compassion within the family we will be unable to do so within the nation or the world. Not until Joseph forgives his brothers and is reconciled with them can the story move on to the larger canvas of history.

Framing the story of Abraham, Sarah and their descendants are three promises: children, a land, and an influence on humanity as a whole. Repeatedly Abraham is promised children – as many as the stars of the sky, the sand of the seashore, and the dust of the earth. Seven times he is promised the land. Five times in Genesis as a whole, with slight variations of terminology, the patriarchs are told that "through you all the families of the earth will be blessed."

Yet the more we read, the more we realise that these promises are not about to be fulfilled immediately. Three of the matriarchs, Sarah, Rebecca and Rachel, find it hard to have children. Ownership of the land remains a distant prospect. The relationship between Abraham's family and their neighbours is often fraught. There is no easy route from starting-point to destination. The way is long and hard. None of Genesis's stories ends with a simple, "and they all lived happily ever after." For these are not children's stories. They are profoundly adult. They tell us that the journey is worth making – none more so – but it did not begin with us, and it will not end with us. "It is not for you to complete the task, but neither are you free to stand aside from it."[7]

So, almost astonishingly, thousands of years later the three promises of Genesis remain the most pressing items on the Jewish agenda: children (Jewish continuity), the land (the State of Israel and its neighbours), and the relationship of Israel and the world (philo- and anti-Semitism). Genesis continues to be what it was at the outset, a book of first principles, the words in which, if we are truly open to them, we discover not only our ancestors but also ourselves.

Torah is God's book of humanity, and each of us is a chapter in its unfinished story. Its words form our covenant with heaven. And as we listen and respond, we add our voice to the unbroken conversation between the Jewish people and its destiny.

7. Mishna, *Avot* 2:16.

Bereshit
בראשית

The Book of books starts with the beginning of beginnings: the creation of the universe and life. The story is told from two different perspectives, first as cosmology (the origins of matter), then as anthropology (the birth of humanity).

The first narrative (1:1–2:3) emphasizes harmony and order. God creates the universe in six days and dedicates the seventh as a day of holiness and rest. The second (2:4–3:24) focuses on humanity, not as biological species but as persons-in-relation. God fashions man, sees that "It is not good for the man to be alone," and then fashions woman. The serpent tempts them; they sin and are banished from the Garden.

From then on, the human drama unfolds as tragedy. Cain murders his brother. By the end of the *parasha*, God sees "how great man's wickedness on the earth had become" and "regrets that He had made man on earth." God creates order, man creates chaos. Which will prevail?

In the four essays that follow, the first looks at divine and human freedom, the second at the three stages of creation. The third examines the origins of human violence, and the fourth uncovers a hidden story of love, born of the consciousness of our mortality.

The Book of Teaching

> *In the beginning, God created the heavens and the earth.... (1:1)*

I t is the most famous, majestic opening of any book in literature. It speaks of primal beginnings, creation, and ontology, and for many it stands as an emblem of Torah as a whole. But not for all. Consider the surpassingly strange way that Rashi – most beloved of all Jewish commentators – begins his commentary:

> Rabbi Isaac said: The Torah should have begun with the verse (Exodus 12:2): "This month shall be to you the first of the months," which was the first mitzva given to Israel. (Rashi, 1:1)

What are we to make of this? The question is not merely aesthetic. Does Rabbi Isaac, or for that matter Rashi, seriously suggest that the Book of books might have begun in the middle – a third of the way into Exodus? That it might have passed by in silence the creation of the universe – which is, after all, one of the fundamentals of Jewish faith?

Could we understand the history of Israel without its prehistory, the stories of Abraham and Sarah and their children? Could we have understood those narratives without knowing what preceded them: God's repeated disappointment with Adam and Eve, Cain, the generation of the Flood and the builders of the Tower of Babel?

The fifty chapters of Genesis together with the opening of Exodus are the source book of biblical faith. They are as near as we get to an exposition of the philosophy of Judaism. What then does Rabbi Isaac mean?

He means something profound, something which we often forget. To understand a book, one needs to know to which genre it belongs: Is it history or legend, chronicle or myth? To what question is it an answer? A history book answers the question: *what happened?*; a book of cosmology – be it science or myth – answers the question: *how did it happen?*

What Rabbi Isaac is succinctly saying in his enigmatic question is that if we seek to understand the Torah, we must read it as *Torah* – as law, instruction, teaching, guidance. Torah is an answer to the question: *how shall we live?* That is why he raises the question as to why it does not begin with the first mitzva given to Israel.

Torah is not a book of history, even though it includes history. It is not a book of science, even though the first chapter of Genesis – as the nineteenth-century sociologist Max Weber points out – is the necessary prelude to science: it represents the first time people saw the universe as the product of a single creative will, and therefore as intelligible rather than capricious and mysterious.[1]

Rather, it is, first and last, a book about how to live. Everything it contains – not only mitzvot but also narratives, including the narrative of creation itself – is there solely for the sake of ethical and spiritual instruction. For Jewish ethics is not confined to law. It includes virtues of character, general principles and role models. It is conveyed not only by commandments but also by stories, telling us how particular individuals responded to specific situations.

Torah moves from the minutest details to the most majestic visions of the universe and our place within it. But it never deviates from

1. Max Weber, *Ancient Judaism* (New York: Free Press, 1952); see also Peter Berger, *The Sacred Canopy* (New York: Doubleday, 1967), 105–25.

its intense focus on the questions: What should one do? How should one live? What kind of person should one strive to become? It opens, in Genesis 1, with the most fundamental question of all. As the Psalm (8:4) puts it: "What is man that You are mindful of him?"

The Essence of Man

P ico della Mirandola's fifteenth-century *Oration on Man* was one
of the turning points of Western civilization, the "manifesto" of the Ital-
ian Renaissance. In it he attributed the following declaration to God,
addressing the first man:

> We have given you, O Adam, no visage proper to yourself, nor
> endowment properly your own, in order that whatever place,
> whatever form, whatever gifts you may, with premeditation, select,
> these same you may have and possess through your own judge-
> ment and decision. The nature of all other creatures is defined
> and restricted within laws which We have laid down; you, by
> contrast, impeded by no such restrictions, may, by your own free
> will, to whose custody We have assigned you, trace for yourself
> the lineaments of your own nature. I have placed you at the very
> centre of the world, so that from that vantage point you may
> with greater ease glance round about you on all that the world
> contains. We have made you a creature neither of heaven nor of
> earth, neither mortal nor immortal, in order that you may, as the
> free and proud shaper of your own being, fashion yourself in the

form you may prefer. It will be in your power to descend to the lower, brutish forms of life; you will be able, through your own decision, to rise again to the superior orders whose life is divine.[1]

Homo sapiens, that unique synthesis of "dust of the earth" and breath of God, is unique among created beings in having no fixed essence: in being free to be what he or she chooses. Mirandola's *Oration* was a break with the two dominant traditions of the Middle Ages: the Christian doctrine that human beings are irretrievably corrupt, tainted by original sin, and the Platonic idea that humanity is bounded by fixed forms.

It is also a strikingly Jewish account – almost identical with the one given by Rabbi Joseph Soloveitchik in *Halakhic Man*: "The most fundamental principle of all is that man must create himself. It is this idea that Judaism introduced into the world."[2] It is therefore with a frisson of recognition that we discover that Mirandola had a Jewish teacher, Rabbi Elijah ben Moses Delmedigo (1460–1497), with whom he studied Tanakh in the original Hebrew, together with Talmud and Kabbala.[3]

The emphasis on choice, freedom and responsibility is one of the most distinctive features of Jewish thought. It is proclaimed in the first chapter of Genesis in the most subtle way. We are all familiar with its statement that God created man "in His image, after His likeness." Seldom do we pause to reflect on the paradox. If there is one thing emphasized time and again in the Torah, it is that God *has no image*. Hence the prohibition against making images of God. For God is beyond all representation, all categorization. "I will be what I will be," He says to Moses when Moses asks Him His name. All images, forms, concepts and

---

1. Pico della Mirandola, *On the Dignity of Man*, trans. Miller, Wallis and Carmichael (Hackett, 1998).
2. Joseph B. Soloveitchik, *Halakhic Man*, translated from the Hebrew by Lawrence Kaplan (Philadelphia: Jewish Publication Society, 1983), 109.
3. Born in Crete, Delmedigo was a Talmudic prodigy, appointed at a young age to be head of the yeshivah in Padua. At the same time, he studied philosophy, in particular the work of Aristotle, Maimonides and Averroes. At the age of twenty-three he was appointed professor of philosophy at the University of Padua. It was through this that he came to know Count Giovanni Pico della Mirandola, who became both his student and his patron.

categories are attempts to delimit and define. God cannot be delimited or defined; the attempt to do so is a form of idolatry.

"Image," then, must refer to something quite different than the possession of a specific form. The fundamental point of Genesis 1 is that God transcends nature. Therefore, He is free, unbounded by nature's laws. By creating human beings "in His image," God gave us a similar freedom, thus creating the one being capable itself of being creative. The unprecedented account of God in the Torah's opening chapter leads to an equally unprecedented view of the human person and the capacity for self-transformation. That is Mirandola's point. Everything else in creation is what it is, neither good nor evil, bound by nature and nature's laws. The human person alone has the possibility of self-transcendence. We may be a handful of dust but we have immortal longings.

Mirandola's late-fifteenth-century humanism was not secular but deeply religious. This period was one of the last times in European culture when religion, science and the arts walked hand in hand, giving rise to such figures as Brunelleschi, Michelangelo and da Vinci. It is fascinating to speculate what might have happened had the Renaissance continued along these lines. However, a series of corrupt rulers and popes, followed by the confrontation between the church and Galileo, led to a gradual break of this synthesis of religion and scientific humanism. The advent of the Reformation signalled the dominance of the quite different views of Luther and Calvin, while humanism swung in the opposite direction, becoming progressively more secular.

As it is, the great truth of Genesis 1 remains as the most powerful statement of a religiously-based humanism, based on the idea of the human person as God's image, the one creation that is also creative, the sole life-form capable of dialogue with the Author of life Himself. As the rabbis put it: "Why was man created last? In order to say, if he is worthy, all creation was made for you; but if he is unworthy, he is told, even a gnat preceded you."[4]

That is the simplest answer to Rabbi Isaac's question: Why did the Torah, a book of law, not begin with the first law? For law presupposes freedom. As Maimonides writes in his "Laws of Repentance," if

4. *Bereshit Raba* 8:1; *Sanhedrin* 38a.

we had no freedom, if all we did was determined by forces beyond our control, what would be the point of commanding people to do this, not that? Where would be the justice in rewarding obedience and punishing sin? Without freedom, the whole edifice of law and responsibility falls to the ground.[5]

The Torah is a sustained exploration of human freedom, the greatest gift God gave man, as well as the most fateful, for freedom can be used or abused. It can lead to the highest heights or the lowest depths: to love or hate, compassion or cruelty, graciousness or violence. The entire drama of Torah flows from this point of departure. Judaism remains God's supreme call to humankind to freedom and creativity on the one hand, and on the other, to responsibility and restraint – becoming God's partner in the work of creation.

---

5. Maimonides, *Mishneh Torah*, Hilkhot Teshuva, chapter 5.

Three Stages of Creation

"And God said, let there be… And there was…
and God saw that it was good."

T hus unfolds the most revolutionary as well as the most influential account of creation in the history of the human spirit.

In the previous chapter we noted that Rashi quotes Rabbi Isaac who questioned why the Torah should start with creation at all. Given that it is a book of law – the commandments that bind the children of Israel as a nation – it should have started with the first law given to the Israelites, which does not appear until the twelfth chapter of Exodus.

Rabbi Isaac's own answer was that the Torah opens with the birth of the universe to justify the gift of the Land of Israel to the People of Israel. The Creator of the world is *ipso facto* owner and ruler of the world. His gift confers title. The claim of the Jewish people to the land is unlike that of any other nation. It does not flow from arbitrary facts of settlement, historical association, conquest or international agreement (though in the case of the present state of Israel, all four apply). It follows from something more profound: the word of God Himself – the

God acknowledged, as it happens, by all three monotheisms: Judaism, Christianity and Islam. This is a political reading of the chapter. Let me suggest another (not incompatible, but additional) interpretation.

One of the most striking propositions of the Torah is that we are called on, as God's image, to imitate God. "Be holy, for I, the Lord your God, am holy" (Leviticus 19:2):

> The sages taught: "Just as God is called gracious, so you be gracious. Just as He is called merciful, so you be merciful. Just as He is called holy, so you be holy." So too the prophets described the Almighty by all the various attributes: long-suffering, abounding in kindness, righteous, upright, perfect, mighty and powerful and so on – to teach us that these qualities are good and right and that a human being should cultivate them, and thus imitate God as far as we can.[1]

Implicit in the first chapter of Genesis is thus a momentous challenge: Just as God is creative, so you be creative. In making man, God endowed one creature – the only one thus far known to science – with the capacity not merely to adapt to his environment, but to adapt his environment to him; to shape the world; to be active, not merely passive, in relation to the influences and circumstances that surround him:

> The brute's existence is an undignified one because it is a helpless existence. Human existence is a dignified one because it is a glorious, majestic, powerful existence...Man of old who could not fight disease and succumbed in multitudes to yellow fever or any other plague with degrading helplessness could not lay claim to dignity. Only the man who builds hospitals, discovers therapeutic techniques, and saves lives is blessed with dignity...Civilized man has gained limited control of nature and has become, in certain respects, her master, and with his mastery he has attained

---

1.   Maimonides, *Mishneh Torah*, Hilkhot De'ot 1:6.

dignity as well. His mastery has made it possible for him to act in accordance with his responsibility.[2]

The first chapter of Genesis therefore contains a teaching. It tells us how to be creative – namely in three stages. The first is the stage of saying "Let there be." The second is the stage of "and there was." The third is the stage of seeing "that it is good."

Even a cursory look at this model of creativity teaches us something profound and counter-intuitive: What is truly creative is not science or technology per se, but the word. That is what forms all being.

Indeed, what singles out Homo sapiens among other animals is the ability to speak. *Targum Onkelos* translates the last phrase of Genesis 2:7, "God formed man out of dust of the ground, and breathed into his nostrils the breath of life, and man became a living creature," as "and man became *ruah memallelah*, a *speaking* spirit." Because we can speak, we can think, and therefore imagine a world different from the one that currently exists. Creation begins with the creative word, the idea, the vision, the dream. Language – and with it the ability to remember a distant past and conceptualize a distant future – lies at the heart of our uniqueness as the image of God. Just as God makes the natural world by words ("And God said…and there was") so we make the human world by words, which is why Judaism takes words so seriously: "Life and death are in the power of the tongue," says the book of Proverbs (18:21). Already at the opening of the Torah, at the very beginning of creation, is foreshadowed the Jewish doctrine of revelation: that God reveals Himself to humanity not in the sun, the stars, the wind or the storm but in and through words – sacred words that make us co-partners with God in the work of redemption.

"And God said, let there be…and there was" – This, the second stage of creation, is for us the most difficult. It is one thing to conceive an idea, another to execute it. "Between the imagination and the act falls the shadow."[3] Between the intention and the fact, the dream and the

2. Joseph B. Soloveitchik, *The Lonely Man of Faith* (New York: Doubleday, 1992), 16–17.
3. T.S. Eliot, "The Hollow Men", in T.S. Eliot, *Collected Poems 1909–1962* (London: Faber and Faber, 1963), 92.

reality, lies struggle, opposition, and the fallibility of the human will. It is all too easy, having tried and failed, to conclude that nothing ultimately can be achieved, that the world is as it is, and that all human endeavour is destined to end in failure.

This, however, is a Greek idea, not a Jewish one: that hubris ends in nemesis, that fate is inexorable and we must resign ourselves to it. Judaism holds the opposite, that though creation is difficult, laborious and fraught with setbacks, we are summoned to it as our essential human vocation: "It is not for you to complete the work," said Rabbi Tarfon, "but neither are you free to desist from it."[4] There is a lovely rabbinic phrase: *maḥashva tova HaKadosh barukh Hu meztarfah lem'aaseh*.[5] This is usually translated as "God considers a good intention as if it were the deed." I translate it differently: "When a human being has a good intention, God joins in helping it become a deed," meaning – He gives us the strength, if not now, then eventually, to turn it into achievement.

If the first stage in creation is imagination, the second is will. The sanctity of the human will is one of the most distinctive features of the Torah. There have been many philosophies – the generic name for them is determinisms – that maintain that the human will is an illusion. We are determined by other factors – genetically encoded instinct, economic or social forces, conditioned reflexes – and the idea that we are what we choose to be is a myth. Judaism is a protest in the name of human freedom and responsibility against determinism. We are not pre-programmed machines; we are persons, endowed with will. Just as God is free, so we are free, and the entire Torah is a call to humanity to exercise responsible freedom in creating a social world which honours the freedom of others. Will is the bridge from "Let there be" to "and there was."

What, though, of the third stage: "And God saw that it was good"? This is the hardest of the three stages to understand. What does it mean to say that "God saw that it was good"? Surely, this is redundant. What does God make that is not good? Judaism is not Gnosticism, nor is it an Eastern mysticism. We do not believe that this created world of the senses is evil. To the contrary, we believe that it is the arena of bless-

4. Mishna, *Avot* 2:16.
5. Tosefta, *Pe'ah* 1:4.

ing and good. Perhaps this is what the phrase comes to teach us: that the religious life is not to be sought in retreat from the world and its conflicts into mystic rapture or nirvana. God wants us to be part of the world, fighting its battles, tasting its joy, celebrating its splendour. But there is more.

In the course of my work, I have visited prisons and centres for young offenders. Many of the people I met there were potentially good. They, like you and me, had dreams, hopes, ambitions, aspirations. They did not want to become criminals. Their tragedy was that often they came from dysfunctional families in difficult conditions. No one took the time to care for them, support them, teach them how to negotiate the world, how to achieve what they wanted through hard work and persuasion rather than violence and lawbreaking. They lacked a basic self-respect, a sense of their own worth. No one ever told them that they were good.

To see that someone is good and to say so is a creative act – one of the great creative acts. There may be some few individuals who are inescapably evil, but they are few. Within almost all of us is something positive and unique, but which is all too easily injured, and which only grows when exposed to the sunlight of someone else's recognition and praise. To see the good in others and let them see themselves in the mirror of our regard is to help someone grow to become the best they can be. "Greater," says the Talmud, "is one who causes others to do good than one who does good himself."[6] To help others become what they can be is to give birth to creativity in someone else's soul. This is done not by criticism or negativity but by searching out the good in others, and helping them see it, recognize it, own it, and live it.

"And God saw that it was good" – this too is part of the work of creation, the subtlest and most beautiful of all. When we recognise the goodness in someone, we do more than create it, we help it to become creative. This is what God does for us, and what He calls us to do for others.

6. *Bava Batra* 9a.

Violence in the Name of God

Religiously inspired violence has returned to haunt the world. Hostage-taking and hostage-killing, suicide bombings and massacres like the slaughter of schoolchildren in Beslan (in September 2004) have become the face of terror in our age. Much has been spoken about weapons of mass destruction. Yet Beslan was achieved by nothing more sophisticated than rifles and explosives. The atrocities of 9/11 were committed using box cutters and planes, not normally regarded as weapons at all. All along, we were looking in the wrong direction: at means instead of motives. The greatest weapon of mass destruction is the human heart.

The most eloquent words about our time are those at the end of the opening *parasha* of the Torah. Having created a universe of order, God sees human beings, his most precious creation, reduce it to chaos. The Torah then says: "God regretted that He had made man on earth and He was grieved to His very core (6:5–6). That is the ultimate refutation of those who claim that, in murdering the innocent, they are acting in the name of God.

The connection between religion and violence is set out at the beginning of the biblical story of mankind. The first two human children,

Cain and Abel, bring an offering. Abel's is accepted, Cain's is not. The first recorded act of worship leads to the first murder, the first fratricide. Religion, the Torah implies, is anything but safe. At its best it lifts human beings to become "little lower than the angels" (*Tehillim* 8:5). At its worst it leads them to become the most destructive form of life on earth.

What is the connection between religion and violence? There have been three major theories in the past hundred years. The first was Freud's. Freud believed that social pathology replicated the psychology of the individual, specifically the Oedipus complex. In ancient times, the children of the tribe, envious of the power of the tribal chief, murdered him. They were then haunted by guilt – what Freud calls "the return of the repressed." The ghost of the victim became, as it were, the voice of God, and religion was born through an act of violence.[1]

The second was Rene Girard's, which argues that religion was born in the attempt to deflect violence away from the group by turning it on an outsider. Social groups, especially those not ruled by law, are riven by vendettas. X kills Y. A member of Y's family kills X in revenge. X's family returns the violence. The feud continues, and the only way of ending it is to deflect it onto someone outside the group. Righteous anger is purged and order restored. For Girard, the primal religious act is human sacrifice. Its object is the scapegoat.[2]

Postmodernists go further. They argue that the very act of self-definition involves the creation of an "other." For there to be an "us" there must be a "them," the people not-like-us. Humanity is divided into friends and strangers, brothers and others. The people not-like-us become the screen onto which we project our fears.[3] They are seen as threatening, hostile, demonic. Identity involves exclusion which leads to violence, and religion, one of the foundation stones of identity, is by definition built of hostility.

The Torah's account is both simpler and more profound. Read-

1. See in particular, Sigmund Freud, *Totem and Taboo*, (London: Routledge Classics, 2001).
2. The key work is Rene Girard, *Violence and the Sacred*, (Johns Hopkins University Press, 1979).
3. See, for example, Vamik Volkan, *Killing in the Name of Identity*, (Pitchstone, 2006).

ing the story of Cain and Abel, we ask ourselves: Why did God accept Abel's offering but not Cain's? Was not that very act, that choice of one over the other, the cause of violence in the first place?

The reason God rejected Cain's offering becomes clear in the words stated immediately after: "Cain became very angry and depressed" (Genesis 4:5). Imagine the following: you offer someone a gift. Politely, they refuse it. How do you respond? There are two possibilities. You can ask yourself, "What did I do wrong?" or you can be angry with the intended recipient. If you respond in the first way, you were genuinely trying to please the other person. If the second, it becomes retrospectively clear that your concern was not with the other but with yourself. You were trying to assert your own dominance by putting the other in your debt: the so-called "gift relationship."[4] Even among primates, the alpha male exercises power by distributing food, giving gifts. When the refusal of a gift leads to anger, it shows that the initial act was not altruism but a form of egoism: I give, therefore I rule.

That is what sacrifices were in the pagan world: attempts to appease, placate, or bribe the gods, thereby coercing or manipulating them into doing one's will – whether sending rain, victory in battle, or restoring past imperial glories. This is the exact opposite of what the Torah views as true faith: humility in the face of God, respect for the integrity of creation, and reverence for human life – the only thing that bears the image of God.

There is no way of telling the difference externally. There can be two offerings – Cain's and Abel's – that look alike. They are both acts of worship, both superficially the same, yet between them there is all the difference in the world. One is an act of self-effacement in the presence of the Creator. The other is a Nietzschean will to power. How do you tell the difference? By the presence of anger when things don't turn out as one wished.

The story of Cain and Abel is the most profound commentary I know on the connection between religion and violence. Violence is the attempt to impose one's will by force. There are only two ways of living

---

4. Richard Titmuss, *The Gift Relationship*, (New York: Pantheon, 1971).

with the guilt this involves: either, like Nietzsche, by denying God, or, like Cain, by telling oneself that one is doing the will of God. Both end in tragedy. The only alternative – the Torah's alternative – is to see human life as sacred. This remains humanity's last and only hope.

Garments of Light

Adam named his wife Eve, because she would become the mother of all life. The Lord God made garments of skin for Adam and his wife and clothed them. (3:20–21)

The context is one of the best known stories of the Bible. Together in the Garden of Eden, surrounded by the rich panoply of creation, the first human couple have everything they could possibly want – except one thing: there is a tree from which they are forbidden to eat. Needless to say, that is the one thing they want. "Stolen waters taste sweet," says the book of Proverbs (9:17). They eat; their eyes are opened; they lose their innocence; for the first time they feel shame. When they hear "the voice of God" (Genesis 3:8) they try to hide, but discover that God is someone from whom one cannot hide. God asks them what they have done. Adam blames his wife. She blames the serpent. The result is paradise lost.

The episode is rich in its implications, but I want us to study one of its strangest features. The woman has been told that "with pain she will give birth to children" (3:16). Next, Adam is informed that he will face a life of painful toil. There then follows a sequence of three verses which seem to have no connection with one another. Indeed, they sound like a complete non sequitur. God says to Adam: "By the sweat of your brow you will eat your food until you return to the ground, since from it you were taken; for dust you are and to dust you will return." This is followed by: "And Adam named his wife Eve, because she would become the mother of all life. The Lord God made garments of skin for Adam and his wife and clothed them" (3:19–21).

The problems are obvious. Adam has just blamed his wife for leading him into sin. He has also been condemned to mortality. Why, at just this juncture, does he turn to her and give her a new name? And why, immediately afterward, as they are about to be exiled from Eden, does God perform an act of kindness to the couple – giving dignity to the very symbol of their sin, the clothes with which they hide their shame?

The mood seems to have undergone a mysterious change. The bitter acrimony of the previous verses suddenly dissolves, and instead there is a new tenderness – between Adam and his wife, and between God and the couple. Rashi is so perplexed by this sudden transformation that he is moved to suggest that the middle verse is out of chronological sequence. He argues that it comes to conclude not the story of the sin of the forbidden fruit, but rather the earlier scene in which Adam gave names to the animals and found "no suitable companion" (2:20).

More mysterious still is the interpretation given by the first century sage Rabbi Meir to the phrase "garments of skin," *bigdei 'or*. Rabbi Meir reads the *'ayin* of the second word as an *aleph*, *bigdei or* – and thus interprets the phrase as "garments of light."[1] This is an almost mystical suggestion and a deeply intriguing one. Why – not when they were in paradise, but as they were leaving it – were the couple bathed with divine radiance, clothed in garments of light?

Rabbi Elazar ben Azaryah said, "It is impossible for there to be a session in the house of study without some new interpretation."[2] In that spirit let us see whether we can find new meaning in this passage.

---

1. *Bereshit Raba*, 20:12.
2. *Ḥagiga* 3a.

The words, "dust you are and to dust you will return," awoke Adam, for the first time, to the consciousness of his mortality. There is no more profound self-knowledge than this – that the world will one day be without us, and we without the world. Much of civilization has turned on this single fact, that our lives are finite, a microsecond in the context of eternity; that however long we live, our time is limited and all too short.

The Torah is silent regarding Adam's thoughts in the wake of this discovery, but we can reconstruct them. Until that point, death had not entered his consciousness, but now he was brought face to face with it. What, if he was mortal, would live on? Was there a part of him that would continue, even though he himself would no longer be there? It was then that Adam remembered God's words to the woman. She would give birth to children – in pain, to be sure, but she would bring new life into the world.

Suddenly Adam knew that though we die, if we are privileged to have children, something of us will live on: our genes, our influence, our example, our ideals. That is our immortality. This was an idea that eventually shaped the character of the whole of Judaism in contradistinction to most other cultures in ancient and modern times. The Tower of Babel and the great buildings of Ramses II – the two most significant glimpses the Torah gives us of the empires of the ancient world – testify to the idea that one defeats mortality by building monuments that outlast the winds and sands of time. Judaism has a quite different idea, that we defeat mortality by engraving our ideals on the hearts of our children, and they on theirs, unto the end of time. Where the Mesopotamians and Egyptians thought of buildings, Abraham and his descendants thought of builders ("Call them not 'your children' but 'your builders'"[3]). Judaism became the most child-centred of faiths.

But there is one significant difference between personal immortality and the immortality we gain by those we bring to life and who live on after us. The latter cannot be achieved alone. Until he became aware of his mortality, Adam could think of his wife as a mere *ezer kenegdo*, usually translated as "a suitable helper" – as an assistant, not an equal.

3. *Berakhot*, 64a.

"She shall be called 'woman' [*ishah*] for she was taken from man [*ish*]" (2:23), he says. She was, in his eyes, an extension of himself.

Now he knew otherwise. Without her, he could not have children – and children were his share in eternity. With this awareness he ceased to think of her as an assistant. She was a person in her own right – more even than he was, for it was she, not he, who would actually give birth. In this respect she was more like God than he could be, for God is He-who-brings-new-life-into-being.

Once Adam experienced these thoughts, recrimination ended, for he saw that physical being, "nakedness," was not simply a source of shame. There is a spiritual dimension to the physical relationship between husband and wife. At one level it is the most animal of desires, but at another it is as close as we come to the principle of divine creativity itself, namely, that love creates life. That is when he turned to his wife and for the first time saw her as a person and gave her a personal name, Eve, meaning, "she who gives life."

The significance of this moment cannot be sufficiently emphasised. It was not that previously Adam had given his wife one name and now simply gave her another. It was that previously Adam had not given her a name at all. He called her *ishah*, "woman," a generic noun, not a proper name. He himself had not had a proper name until this point either. It is only after he confers a proper name on the woman that the man acquires one himself: Adam. Until then he was simply called *ha-adam*, "the man."

With the appearance of proper names, the concept of "person" is born. A noun designates a class, a group of things linked by common characteristics. Nouns speak of sameness and therefore substitutability. If we lose one watch we can buy another. If our car is stolen we can replace it. "Watch" and "car" are nouns, in both cases objects defined by their function.

A name is different. It refers not to a class or group of things but to an individual in his/her uniqueness. The primary bearer of a name is a human being. Only by extension do we give names to non-humans for which we have special affection – a pet, for example. The concepts of "name" and "person" are intimately linked. We cannot have one without the other. The single most important ethical truth about persons is that none is substitutable for any other. As persons, we are unique. "When a human being makes many coins in the same mint," say the sages, "they all come out alike. [By contrast,] God makes every human being in the same image, His image, and they are all different."[4]

This is what gives human life its dignity and preciousness. Without it, we would not know love – for love in its primary sense is always directed to a person: to this man, that woman, this child, in their uniqueness. One who truly loves does not love abstractly. The lovers in the *Song of Songs* never tire of describing each other – his hair, her cheeks, his eyes, her mouth – the things that make the loved one unique, and not someone-in-general. Love lives in particularity.

This is also what gives human love its pathos and vulnerability. We know that like us, our beloved will eventually grow old and die, and that he or she can never be replaced. If we knew we would never die, we would need no intimations of eternity. But because we know we will one day die, one of the greatest things we can experience is the moment beyond time (the one we know we will never forget) when two souls touch and between them form a bridge over the abyss of mortality. That is the meaning of the verse, "Love is as strong as death, its passion as unyielding as the grave" (*Song of Songs* 8:6), an idea Dylan Thomas would reiterate in the words, "Though lovers be lost, love shall not; / And death shall have no dominion."[5]

On another level, this is what gives human life its sanctity. "A single life," teach the sages, "is like a universe."[6] However lifelike robots may one day become, there will always be this fundamental difference between a machine and a person. Machines can be replaced. Persons cannot.

The moment when Adam turned to his wife and gave her a proper name, Eve, was a turning point in the history of humanity. It was then that God robed the couple in garments of light. For it is only when we relate to one another as persons possessed of non-negotiable dignity

---

4. Mishna, *Sanhedrin*, 4:5.
5. "And Death Shall Have No Dominion" in Dylan Thomas, *Collected Poems 1934–1952* (London: Dent, 1952), 68.
6. Mishna, *Sanhedrin*, 4:5.

that we respond to the "image of God" in the other. In a sense the whole of Judaism – or at least *mitzvot bein adam le-havero*, "the commands between us and our fellow human beings" – is an extended commentary to this idea. The rules of justice, mercy, charity, compassion, regard for the poor, love for the neighbour and the stranger, delicacy of speech and sensitivity to the easily-injured feelings of others, are all variants on the theme of respect for the human other as an image and likeness of the Divine Other.

The idea has even deeper implications. For there is an intimate connection between the way we relate to other people and the way we relate to God – and this too is expressed in the difference between a noun and a name.

Though God has many descriptions, two are primary: "*Elokim,*" and the four letter name we may not pronounce, known generally as *Hashem* – "the Name." The sages distinguished them by saying that Elokim refers to divine justice, *Hashem* to divine compassion. The eleventh-century poet and philosopher Judah HaLevi made a different distinction.[7] The word "el" was generally used by pagans to signify a god, by which they meant a force of nature (the sun, the storm, the earth, the sea, and the many other deities worshipped in ancient times). Monotheism was and is the insistence that none of these forces or powers represents ultimate reality. Each is only a segment of it. The One God is the totality of all powers. That is the idea represented by the word *Elokim*. It is a collective noun, meaning "the force of forces." *Elokim* is God as we encounter Him in nature, in the vastness and intricacy of creation.

Hashem, by contrast, is not a noun but a name. It refers to God not as a power, or even the totality of all powers, but as a person, a "Thou." *Hashem* is The One who speaks to us and to whom we speak, who loves us as a person loves, who hears our prayers, forgives our failures, gives us strength in times of crisis, and teaches us the path of life. In one of the most profound insights in the history of Jewish thought, HaLevi taught that the difference between *Elokim* and *Hashem* is the difference between the God of Aristotle and the God of Abraham. A philosopher can come to the realisation that the universe has an author, a creator, a

7. Judah HaLevi, *Kuzari*, book IV, para 1.

first cause, a "prime mover." But only a prophet (or a child of Abraham and the nation of prophets) can relate to God as a person. *Hashem* is God as we encounter Him not in creation, but revelation.

If we now turn back to the biblical text, we see a remarkable phenomenon. In Genesis 1, God is described as *Elokim*. In chapters 2 and 3, He is called *Hashem-Elokim*. In chapter 4, for the first time He is called *Hashem* alone. Something changes in the course of these chapters: not God, who does not change, but rather the human perception of God.

In the first chapter, which speaks about the birth of the universe and the slow emergence of order from chaos, man is part of nature. That is the (partial) truth in the discovery that we share much of our DNA with other life forms. This is why God is described here as *Elokim*, the Author of nature. In chapters 2 and 3, man begins to use language. He becomes, in the words of the Targum, "a speaking being" (Genesis 2:7). God brings the various forms of life to him "to see what he would name them, and whatever the man called each living thing, that was its name" (2:19). But thus far he only uses nouns, first for the animals, and then for his wife, whom he calls *ishah*, "woman." He has moved from nature to culture – of which language is the first step – but he has not yet understood the concept of a person. It is only after he gives his wife a proper name that the Torah uses the name *Hashem* on its own. It is only after he has become aware of his wife as a person that man is capable of understanding God as a "person."

Judaism was much more than the discovery of monotheism, the discovery of a single unified God. That idea is contained in the word *Elokim*. It was also the discovery that God is a "person" – that the fact that we are persons, with loves, fears, hopes and dreams, is not an accidental by-product of evolution (as some neo-Darwinians claim), but rather an echo of the ultimate reality of the cosmos. We are not gene-producing machines but individuals, each of us unique, irreplaceable, here because God wants us to be here. That is the world-transforming concept of *Hashem* – and it was only when Adam responded to Eve as a person that he could see himself as a person, and so respond to God as such. That is why the mitzvot regulating the relationship between us and God are inseparable from the mitzvot defining the relationship between us and our fellow human beings.

Now we understand that extraordinary sequence of three verses. Discovering his mortality, Adam knew that he could only live on through his children, born through an act of love. That was when he realised that immortality cannot be achieved by one alone, but only by the union of two. For the first time he looked on his wife as a person in her own right, and expressed this by giving her a proper name. Having done this, he was able to experience God through His proper name, *Hashem*. At that moment humanity ceased to be a mere biological species and became *Homo religiosus*, man-in-search-of-God who meets *Hashem*, God-in-search-of-man. That is the profound message of the first three chapters of Genesis, a story about language, relationships and what it is to be a person. Judaism is the story of how the love we feel for another person leads to the love of God, and robes us in garments of light.

Noaḥ
נח

Man's wickedness leads God to bring a Flood. Noah alone is found righteous. He is commanded to bring his family, and animals, into an ark. Alone, they survive the Flood. After the waters subside, Noah emerges and offers a sacrifice to God. God then makes a covenant, through Noah, with all humanity, laying down basic commands and vowing never again to destroy the world by flood. Noah plants a vineyard, makes wine, and becomes drunk. A new generation of humans aspires to build a city whose tower will reach heaven. God frustrates their plan by confusing their language. The *parasha* ends with a genealogy tracing the ten generations between Noah's son Shem and Abraham.

The first of the following essays looks at the limits of Noah as a religious personality. The second asks what the sin of the builders of Babel was. The third examines the moral basis of the covenant with Noah in the light of recent scientific discoveries. The fourth explores the inner connection between the different stories leading up to the call of Abraham.

Beyond Obedience

Noah is one of the most tantalising figures in the Torah, and nowhere is this more evident than in the first and last glimpses we catch of him in the *parasha* that bears his name. The opening is full of expectation:

> Noah was a righteous man, faultless in his generation. Noah walked with God. (6:9)

No one else in the Torah receives such accolades: not Abraham, Isaac or Jacob, not Joseph or Moses or Joshua. Yet the last scene of his life is full of pathos:

> Noah began to be a man of the soil, and he planted a vineyard. When he drank some of its wine, he became drunk and lay uncovered in his tent. Ham, the father of Canaan, saw his father's nakedness and told his two brothers outside. But Shem and Yefeth took a garment and laid it across their shoulders; then they walked in backwards and covered their father's nakedness. Their faces were turned the other way so that they would not see their father's nakedness. (9:20–23)

The decorousness of Shem and Yefeth's behaviour cannot hide from us the embarrassment they felt at knowing that their father – the sole human being worthy of rescue during the Flood – had become debased. How had a man so great fallen so low?

That is the question to which the sages of the midrash sought an answer, and since midrash plays a major role in these essays, it is worth explaining here. Midrash is the name given generally to early rabbinic interpretations of Torah. Some, called *midrash halakha*, have to do with Jewish law and the way it is derived from the biblical text. Others, known generically as *midrash aggada*, flesh out the biblical narrative, adding details not specified in the text, or offering insight into its deeper meaning. Through midrash, the sages made a bridge across time, from ancient text to contemporary application. The tacit question to which midrash is the answer, is "What do these words mean, not when they were first spoken or written down, but to us, here, now?" Midrash takes with absolute seriousness the idea that the Torah, as the word of God who is beyond time, has a message for every time and each generation. That is why midrash is rarely simple or literal; it is often daring and radical, because much had changed in the centuries between Moses and the days of the sages. Midrash involves hearing, in God's word for *all* time, His word for *this* time.

There are many midrashic comments on Noah and his place in the history of faith, but one is unrivalled in its sharpness:

> Once the waters had abated, Noah should have left the ark. However, Noah said to himself, "I entered with God's permission, as it says, 'Go into the ark' (7:1). Shall I now leave without permission?" The Holy One, blessed be He, said to him, "Is it permission, then, that you are seeking? Very well, then, here is permission," as it is said [Then God said to Noah,] "Come out of the ark" (8:17).
>
> Rabbi Yehudah bar Ilai said: If I had been there I would have broken down the ark and taken myself out.[1]

---

1. Solomon Buber, comp., *Tanhuma*, Noah, 13–14 (Vilna, 1885). I am indebted for the idea of this essay to my teacher, Rabbi Dr. Nachum Rabinovitch.

To understand this midrash one must read the story of the Flood carefully, with an ear to the pace of the narrative. The story begins rapidly. God announces the imminent destruction of life on earth. He orders Noah to build an ark, specifying its precise measurements. Details follow as to what Noah must take with him – his family, two (or in the case of pure animals, seven) of all the species of life, and provisions. The rain comes; the earth is flooded; Noah and those with him are the sole survivors. The rain ceases and the water abates.

We expect to read next that Noah emerges. Instead the narrative slows down and for fourteen verses almost nothing happens. The water recedes. The ark comes to rest. Noah opens a window and sends out a raven. Then he sends out a dove. He waits seven days and sends it out again. It returns with an olive leaf. Another seven days pass. He sends the dove a third time. This time it does not return, but Noah still does not step out onto dry land. Eventually God Himself says, "Come out of the ark." Only then does Noah do so. The midrash is unmistakable in its note of exasperation. When it comes to rebuilding a shattered world, you do not wait for permission.

What does Noah say to God when the decree is issued that the world is about to perish? What does he say when he is told to make an ark to save himself and his family? What does he say as the rain begins to fall? The answer is: nothing. During the whole sequence of events, Noah is not reported as saying a single word. Instead we read, four times, of his silent obedience: "Noah did everything just as God had commanded him" (6:22); "And Noah did all that the Lord had commanded him" (7:5); He brought pairs of animals into the ark "as God had commanded Noah" (7:9, 16). Noah is the paradigm of biblical obedience. He does as he is commanded. What his story tells us is that *obedience is not enough.*

This is an extraordinary phenomenon. It is reasonable to assume that in the life of faith, obedience is the highest virtue. In Judaism it is not. One of the strangest features of biblical Hebrew is that – despite the fact that the Torah contains 613 commands – there is no word for "obey." Instead the verb the Torah uses is *shema / lishmoa*, "to listen, hear, attend, understand, internalise, respond." So distinctive is this word that, in effect, the King James Bible had to invent an English equivalent, the word "hearken." Nowadays the word has gone out of circulation, and there is no precise translation. Equally, modern Hebrew had to invent a word to mean pure, unquestioning obedience. It chose *letzayet* (from the root *tz-u-t²*) – not *lishmoa* which means something else, reflective response.

In Judaism, God does not command blind obedience: *Ein haKadosh Barukh Hu ba biturnya im beriyotav*; "God does not deal despotically with His creatures."[3] If He sought no more than mindless submission to the divine will, He would have created robots, machines, or genetically programmed people who responded automatically to commands as dogs to Pavlov's bell. God wants us to be mature, deliberative, to do His will because we understand or because we trust Him when we do not understand. He seeks from us something other and greater than obedience, namely *responsibility*.

Intuitively, the sages understood that the hero of faith was not Noah but Abraham – Abraham who fought a war to rescue his nephew, who prayed for the people of the plain even though he knew they were wicked; Abraham who challenged heaven itself in words unrivalled in the history of the human encounter with God: "Shall the Judge of all the earth not do justice?" (18:25).

What might an Abraham not have said when confronted with the possibility of a flood. "What if there are fifty righteous people? What if there are ten? Far be it from You to do such a thing – to kill the righteous with the wicked, treating the righteous and the wicked alike" (18:24–25). Abraham might have saved the world. Noah saved only himself and his family. Abraham might have failed, but Noah – at least on the evidence of the text – did not even try (to be sure, there are midrashic traditions that he did try, but most prefer to accept that he did not). Noah's end – drunk, dishevelled, an embarrassment to his children – eloquently tells us that if you save yourself while doing nothing to save the world, you do not even save yourself. Noah, so the narrative seems to suggest, could not live with the guilt of survival.

The difference between Noah and Abraham is eloquently summarised by the midrashic comment of Rabbi Yehudah:

2. See, for example, *Targum Yerushalmi* to *Devarim* 32:1.
3. *Avoda Zara* 3a.

"Noah walked with God" – The meaning of this phrase can be understood by a parable. A king had two sons, one grown up, the other a child. To the child, he said: Walk with me. But to the adult son he said: Walk before me.

So it was that to Abraham, God said: "Because you are wholehearted, walk before Me" (17:1). But of Noah, the Torah says that he "walked with God." (6:9)[4]

It takes courage to rebuild a shattered world. That was the courage shown by those who built and fought for the State of Israel in the years after the Holocaust. It was the same kind of courage that led the handful of survivors from the East European yeshivot and Hassidic groups to reconstruct their devastated worlds of learning and piety in Israel, the United States and elsewhere. They were different kinds of people but they shared that intuitive knowledge that Noah lacked: That when it comes to rebuilding the ruins of catastrophe, you do not wait for permission. You take the risk and walk ahead. Faith is more than obedience. It is the courage to create.

4. *Bereshit Raba* 30:10.

Babel: A Story of Heaven and Earth

Set between the pre-history of humanity as a whole and the particular covenant with Abraham, the story of the Tower of Babel is one of the turning points of the biblical narrative, central to its vision of what can go wrong in civilizations and societies.

The story itself – told in a mere nine verses – is a compact masterpiece of literary and philosophical virtuosity. The first thing to note is that its historical background is exceptionally precise. The tower or ziggurat was the great symbol of the ancient Mesopotamian city states of the lower Tigris-Euphrates valley, the cradle of civilization. It was there that human beings first settled, established agriculture, and built cities.

As the Torah makes clear with unusual attention to what seems like a peripheral fact, one of the great discoveries of Mesopotamia (along with the wheel, the arch and the calendar) was the ability to manufacture building materials, especially bricks made by pouring clay into moulds, drying it in the sun, and eventually firing it in kilns: "And they said one to another: 'Come, let us make brick, and burn them thoroughly.' And they had brick for stone, and slime had they for mortar" (11:3). This made possible the construction of buildings on a larger scale and reaching greater heights than hitherto. From this grew the ziggurat, a stepped building of many storeys, which came to have profound religious significance.

Essentially these towers – of which the remains of at least thirty have been discovered – were man-made "holy mountains," the mountain being the place where heaven and earth most visibly meet. Inscriptions on several of these buildings, decoded by archaeologists, refer, as does the Torah, to the idea that their top "reaches heaven": "And they said: 'Come, let us build us a city, and a tower, with its top in heaven,'" (11:4). The largest – the great ziggurat of Babylon to which the Torah refers – was a structure of seven stories, three hundred feet high, on a base of roughly the same dimensions.[1]

Not only is the story of Babel historically precise, it is also shot through with literary devices: inversions, word plays, ironies and puns. One of the most masterly is that the two key words, *l-v-n*, "brick," and *n-v-l*, "confuse," are precise inversions of one another. As so often in the Torah, literary technique is closely related to the moral or spiritual message being conveyed. In this case the word play draws attention to the phenomenon of inversion itself. The results of human behaviour are often the opposite of what was intended. The builders wanted to concentrate humanity in one place: "Let us build a city...and not be scattered over the face of the whole earth" (11:4). The result was that they were dispersed: "from there the Lord scattered them over the face of the whole earth" (11:8). They wanted to "make a name" (11:4) for themselves, and they did, but the name they made – Babel – became an eternal symbol of confusion.

Their pride lay in their newfound technological ability to construct buildings of unprecedented grandeur. They did not realise that the greatest creative power is language – a message signalled in the opening verses of the Torah with the grand simplicity of the repeated formula "And God said...and there was." What is holy for the Torah is not power, but the use to which we put it, and this is intrinsically linked to language – the medium in which we frame our ideals, construct imaginative possibilities, and call others to join us in realising them. The word is prior

---

1. Further details can be found in Nahum M. Sarna, *Understanding Genesis: The World of the Bible in the Light of History*. (New York: Schocken, 1970).

to the work. With great poetic justice, it was not a technical problem that caused the builders to abandon the project, but rather the loss of the ability to communicate.

What, though, was the builders' sin? The narrative signals this by a series of verbal cues. The first is the phrase with which the episode both begins and ends, *kol ha-aretz*, "the whole earth." It opens, "And the whole earth was of one language" (11:1) and closes, "from there the Lord scattered them over the face of the whole earth" (11:9). A framing device of this kind is highly significant. Indeed, the phrase *kol ha-aretz* appears five times in the nine verses – and all three-, five- and especially seven-fold repetitions in a biblical passage signal the presence of a key theme.

The second cue is the repeating phoneme (a basic unit of sound) *sh-m*, either as *sham*, "there," or *shem*, "name." This appears seven times in the passage. It is clearly linked to the word *shamayim*, "heaven" – the place the builders were attempting to reach in building the tower. The thematic elements of the narrative are thus clear. This is a story about heaven and earth – returning us to the opening scene of Genesis and its description of the creation of *shamayim* and *aretz*.

One of the most well-marked words in that account is *tov*, "good," which appears seven times. God says, "Let there be," there is, and God sees "that it is good." Creation in Genesis 1 is not primarily about the power of God but about the goodness of God and the universe He made. In historical context, this is an extraordinary statement. For the most part, the ancients saw the world as a perilous and threatening place, full of dangers, disasters, famines and floods. There was no overarching meaning to any of it. It was the result of clashing powers, personified as conflicts between the gods. Religion was either an attempt to assert human power over the elements through magic and myth, or a mysti-cal escape from the world into a private nirvana of the soul. Against this, Judaism made the astonishing assertion that the world is good. It is intelligible. It is the result not of blind collisions and random muta-tions but of a single creative will. This alone is enough to set Judaism apart as the most hopeful of the world's faiths.

There is however another key word in the creation narrative, the root *b-d-l*, "to separate, distinguish, divide," which appears five times in Genesis 1: The goodness of the universe is itself a matter of order, boundaries and distinctions. God separates the different domains (day 1, light and dark; day 2, upper and lower waters; day 3, land and sea) and fills each with its appropriate objects or life-forms (day 4, sun and moon; day 5, birds and fish; day 6, land animals and mankind). So important was this idea to Judaism that we have a special ceremony, *havdalah* (differentiation, from *b-d-l*), to mark the end of Shabbat and the beginning of each cycle of "the six days of creation." Like God, we begin creation by *havdalah*: making, noting and consecrating distinctions.

This too is fundamental to the Judaic world view. Goodness is order; evil is disorder, an act or person or entity in the wrong place. The word *het*, sin, comes from a verb meaning "to miss the target." The word *avera*, like its English equivalent "transgression," means to stray across a border, to enter forbidden territory. Many of the *hukkim* or "statutes"of Judaism are about inculcating respect for the inherent orderliness of the universe – and thus not mixing milk (life) and meat (death), wool (an animal product) and linen (a vegetable product) or sowing a field with "mixed kinds" of seed.

Creation itself is seen as the slow emergence of order from chaos. This, as the physicist Gerald Schroeder points out, is implicit in the Hebrew words *erev* and *boker*, "And it was evening (*erev*) and it was morning (*boker*)" (1:5, 8, 13, 19, 23, 31): *Erev* in Hebrew means an undifferentiated mixture of elements; *Boker* comes from a root meaning "to reflect, contemplate, seek clarity."[2] Much recent work in physics, biology and cosmology has converged on the discovery that the birth of stars, planets and life itself is a matter of the slow emergence of ever more complex systems of order swimming, as it were, against the tide of entropy.

An ordered universe is a peaceable universe in which every form of being, inanimate, animate and human, has its proper place. Violence, injustice and conflict are forms of disorder – a failure to respect the integrity of each life-form or (in the case of humanity, where "every life is like a universe"[3]) each person. That was the state of the universe before the Flood, when "all flesh had corrupted its way on earth" (6:12).

2. Gerald L. Schroeder, Genesis *and the Big Bang: The Discovery of Harmony between Modern Science and the Bible.* (New York: Bantam, 1991), 97.
3. Mishna, *Sanhedrin*, 4:5.

This is not an abstract idea. The world of myth, against which Judaism is a sustained protest, is one in which boundaries are not observed. There are human beings who are like gods, and gods who are like human beings. There are strange mythological hybrids – like the sphinx, half human, half animal. Religious ecstasy is often accompanied by a ceremonial breaking of boundaries in various ways. To the Judaic mind this is paganism, and it is never morally neutral. God creates order; man creates chaos—and the result is inevitably destructive.

The most fundamental boundary is the one created first: the differentiation between "heaven" and "earth." Never before or since, except among religions or cultures influenced by Judaism, has God been conceived in so radically transcendent a way. God is not to be identified with anything on earth. "The heavens are the heavens of the Lord," says the Psalmist, "but the earth He has given to man" (Psalms 115:16). This ontological divide is fundamental. God is God; humanity is humanity. There can be no blurring of the boundaries.

That was the sin of the builders of the tower. Their aspiration to "reach heaven" (11:4) was laughable, and indeed the Torah makes a joke of it. They think that their construction – three hundred feet high – has reached heaven, whereas God has to "come down" to look at it (in general, the one thing that makes God laugh in the Torah is the pretensions of human beings when they think themselves divine).

However, it was worse than laughable. The Netziv (R. Naftali Zvi Yehudah Berlin, 1817–1893), writing in Czarist Russia and prophetically foreseeing the worst excesses of communism, sees Babel as the world's first totalitarianism, in which to preserve the masses as a single entity, all freedom of expression is suppressed (that, for him, is the meaning of "the whole world had one language and a unified speech"). Intoxicated by their technological prowess, the builders of Babel believed they had become like gods and could now construct their own cosmopolis, their man-made miniature universe.[4] Not content with earth, they wanted to build an abode in heaven. It is a mistake many civilizations have made, and the result is catastrophe.

In modern times, the reenactment of Babel is most clearly

---

4. Netziv, *Ha'amek Davar* to *Bereshit*, 11:1–9.

associated with the name of Nietzsche (1844–1890). For the last ten years of his life, he was clinically insane, but shortly before his final breakdown he had a nightmare vision which has become justly famous:

> Have you not heard of that madman who lit a lantern in the bright morning hours, ran to the market place, and cried incessantly, "I seek God! I seek God!"…"Whither is God?" he cried. "I shall tell you. We have killed him – you and I. All of us are his murderers… God is dead. God remains dead. And we have killed him. How shall we, the murderers of all murderers, comfort ourselves? What was holiest and most powerful of all that the world has yet owned has bled to death under our knives. Who will wipe this blood off us?…Is not the greatness of this deed too great for us? Must we not ourselves become Gods simply to seem worthy of it?"[5]

As George Steiner pointed out, there was less than three-quarters of a century between Nietzsche and the Holocaust, between his vision of the murder of God and the deliberate, systematic attempt to murder the "people of God" (Hitler called conscience "a Jewish invention").[6]

When human beings try to become more than human, they quickly become less than human. As Lord Acton pointed out, even the great city-state of Athens which produced Socrates, Plato and Aristotle, self-destructed when "the possession of unlimited power, which corrodes the conscience, hardens the heart, and confounds the understanding of monarchs, exercised its demoralising influence." What went wrong in Athens, he writes, was the belief that "there is no law superior to that of the State – the lawgiver is above the law." [7]

Only when God is God can man be man. That means keeping heaven and earth distinct, organising the latter only under the conscious sovereignty of the former. Without this there is little to prevent

---

5. Friedrich Nietzsche, *The Gay Science* (1882, 1887) para. 125; Walter Kaufmann ed. (New York: Vintage, 1974), 181–82.
6. George Steiner, *In Bluebeard's Castle: Some Notes Towards the Redefinition of Culture* (New Haven, CA: Yale University Press, 1971).
7. Lord Acton, *Essays in the History of Liberty* (Indianapolis: Liberty Classics, 1986), 13.

human beings from sacrificing the many for the sake of the few, or the few for the sake of the many. Only a respect for the integrity of creation stops human beings destroying themselves. Humility in the presence of divine order is our last, best safeguard against mankind arrogating to itself power without restraint, might without right. Babel was the first civilization, but sadly not the last, to begin with a dream of utopia and end in a nightmare of hell. A world of *tov*, good, is a world of *havdalah*, boundaries and limits. Those who cross those boundaries and transgress these limits make a name for themselves, but the name they make is Babel, meaning chaos, confusion and the loss of that order which is a precondition of both nature – the world God creates – and culture – the world we create.

The Objectivity of Morality

For some time, in secular circles, the idea of an objective basis for morality has seemed absurd. Morality is what we choose it to be. We are free to do what we like so long as we don't harm others. Moral judgments are not truths but choices. There is no way of getting from "is" to "ought," from *de*scription to *pre*scription, from facts to values, from science to ethics. This was the received wisdom in philosophy for a century after Nietzsche had argued for the abandonment of morality – which he saw as the product of Judaism – in favour of the "will to power."[1]

Recently, however, an entirely new scientific basis has been given to morality from two surprising directions: neo-Darwinism on the one hand, and the branch of mathematics known as Game Theory on the other. As we will see, the discovery is intimately related to the story of Noah and the covenant made between God and humanity after the Flood.

Game theory was invented by one of the most brilliant minds of the twentieth century, John von Neumann (1903–1957). He realised that the mathematical models used in economics were unrealistic and did

---

1. Nietzsche argues this in his books *The Gay Science, Thus Spoke Zarathustra*, and *Beyond Good and Evil*.

not mirror the way decisions are made in the real world. Rational choice is not simply a matter of weighing alternatives and deciding between them. The reason is that the outcome of our decision often depends on how other people react to it, and usually we cannot know this in advance. Game theory, which Von Neumann invented in 1944, was an attempt to produce a mathematical representation of choice under conditions of uncertainty. Six years later, it yielded its most famous paradox, known as the Prisoner's Dilemma.

Imagine two people, arrested by the police under suspicion of committing a crime. There is insufficient evidence to convict them on a serious charge; there is only enough to convict them of a lesser offence. The police decide to encourage each to inform against the other. They separate them and make each the following proposal: If you testify against the other suspect, you will go free, and he will be imprisoned for ten years. If he testifies against you, and you stay silent, you will be sentenced to ten years in prison, and he will go free. If you both testify against one another, you will each receive a five-year sentence. If both of you stay silent, you will each be convicted of the lesser charge and face a one-year sentence.

It doesn't take long to work out that the optimal strategy for each is to inform against the other. The result is that each will be imprisoned for five years. The paradox is that the best outcome would be for both to remain silent. They would then only face one year in prison each. The reason that neither will opt for this strategy is that it depends on collaboration. However, since each is unable to know what the other is doing – there is no communication between them – they cannot take the risk of staying silent. The Prisoner's Dilemma is remarkable because it shows that two people, both acting rationally, will produce a result that is bad for both of them.

There is, however, another possibility: The reason for the paradox is that the two prisoners find themselves in this situation only once. If the prisoners knew that they would be in this situation again, they could eventually work out a cooperative outcome.

In the meantime, biologists were wrestling with a phenomenon that puzzled Darwin. The theory of natural selection – popularly known as the survival of the fittest – suggests that the most ruthless individuals in any population will survive and hand their genes on to the next generation. Yet almost every society ever observed values individuals who are altruistic, who sacrifice their own advantage to help others. There seems to be a direct contradiction between these two facts.

The prisoner's dilemma suggested an answer. Individual self-interest often produces bad results. Any group which learns to cooperate, instead of compete, will be at an advantage relative to others. But, as the prisoner's dilemma demonstrates, repeated encounters are needed for such cooperation to develop – the so-called "Iterated (= repeated) Prisoner's Dilemma."

In the late 1970s, a competition was announced to find the computer program that did best at playing the iterated prisoner's dilemma against itself and other opponents. The winning programme was devised by a Canadian, Anatol Rapoport, and was called Tit-for-Tat. It was dazzlingly simple: it began by cooperating, and then repeated the last move of its opponent, working on the rule of "What you did to me, I will do to you," or "measure for measure." This was the first time scientific proof had been given for any moral principle.

What is fascinating about this chain of discoveries is that it precisely mirrors the central principle of the covenant God made with Noah:

> Whoever sheds the blood of man, by man shall his blood be shed; for in the image of God has God made man. (9:6)

This is measure for measure (in Hebrew, *middah keneged middah*), or retributive justice: as you do, so shall you be done to. Indeed, the Torah uses a subtle poetic device to emphasize the point. The six words in which the principle is stated are a mirror image of one another: [1] Who sheds [2] the blood [3] of man, [3a] by man [2a] shall his blood [1a] be shed. This is a perfect example of style reflecting substance: what is done to us is a mirror image of what we do. The extraordinary fact is that *the first moral principle set out in the Torah is also the first moral principle ever to be scientifically demonstrated.* Tit-for-Tat is the computer equivalent of (retributive) justice: Whoever sheds the blood of man, by man shall his blood be shed.

The story has a sequel. In 1989, the Polish mathematician Martin

Nowak produced a programme that beats Tit-for-Tat. He called it Generous. It overcame one weakness of Tit-for-Tat, namely that when you meet a particularly nasty opponent, you get drawn into a potentially endless and destructive cycle of retaliation, which is bad for both sides. Generous avoided this possibility by randomly but periodically forgetting the last move of its opponent, thus allowing the relationship to begin again. What Nowak had produced, in fact, was a computer simulation of *forgiveness*.

Once again, the connection with the story of Noah and the Flood is direct. After the Flood, God vowed: "I will never again curse the ground for man's sake, although the imagination of man's heart is evil from his youth; nor will I again destroy every living thing as I have done" (8:21). This is the principle of divine forgiveness.

Thus the two great principles of the Noahide covenant are also the first two principles to have been established by computer simulation. There is an objective basis for morality after all. It rests on two key ideas: justice and forgiveness, or what the sages called *middat haDin* and *middat rahamim*. Without these, no group can survive in the long run.

In one of the first great works of Jewish philosophy – *Sefer Emunot veDeot* (*The Book of Beliefs and Opinions*) – R. Saadia Gaon (882–942) explained that the truths of the Torah could be established by reason. Why then was revelation necessary? Because it takes humanity time to arrive at truth, and there are many slips and pitfalls along the way. It took more than a thousand years after R. Saadia Gaon for humanity to demonstrate the fundamental moral truths that lie at the basis of God's covenant with humankind: that cooperation is as necessary as competition, that cooperation depends on trust, that trust requires justice, and that justice itself is incomplete without forgiveness. Morality is not simply what we choose it to be. It is part of the basic fabric of the universe, revealed to us by the universe's Creator, long ago.

Drama in Four Acts

The *parasha* of *Noaḥ* brings to a close the eleven chapters that precede the call to Abraham and the beginning of the special relationship between him and his descendants, and God. During these eleven chapters, the Torah gives prominence to four stories: Adam and Eve, Cain and Abel, Noah and the generation of the Flood, and the Tower of Babel. Each of these stories involves an interaction between God and humanity. Each represents another step in the maturation of humanity. If we trace the course of these stories, we can discover a connection that goes deeper than chronology, a developmental line in the narrative of the evolution of humanity.

The first story is about Adam and Eve and the forbidden fruit. Once they have eaten, and discovered shame, God asks them what they have done:

> And He said, "Who told you that you were naked? Have you eaten from the tree that I commanded you not to eat from?"
> The man said, "The woman you put here with me – she gave me some fruit from the tree, and I ate it."

>Then the Lord God said to the woman, "What is this you have done?"

>The woman said, "The serpent deceived me, and I ate." (3:11–13)

Faced with primal failure, the man blames the woman, the woman blames the serpent. Both deny *personal* responsibility: it wasn't me; it wasn't my fault. This is the birth of what today is called the victim culture.

The second drama is about Cain and Abel. Both bring offerings. Abel's is accepted, Cain's is not – why this is so is not relevant here.[1] In his anger, Cain kills Abel. Again there is an exchange between a human being and God:

>Then the Lord said to Cain, "Where is your brother Abel?"

>"I don't know," he replied. "Am I my brother's keeper?"

>The Lord said, "What have you done? Listen! Your brother's blood cries out to me from the ground (4:9–10).

Once again the theme is responsibility, but in a different sense. Cain does not deny *personal* responsibility. He does not say, "It wasn't me." He denies *moral* responsibility. "I am not my brother's keeper." I am not responsible for his safety. Yes, I did it because I felt like it. Cain has not yet learned the difference between "I can" and "I may."

The third is the story of Noah. Noah is introduced with great expectations: "He will comfort us" (5:29), says his father Lamech, giving him his name. This is the one to redeem man's failure, to offer comfort for "the earth which God cursed." Yet though Noah is a righteous man, he is not a hero. Noah does not save humanity. He saves only himself, his family and the animals he takes with him in the ark. The *Zohar* contrasts him unfavourably with Moses: Moses prayed for his generation, Noah did not. In the end, his failure to take responsibility for others diminishes him as well: in the last scene we see him drunk and exposed in his tent. In the words of the Midrash, "he profaned himself and became

---

1. For more on Cain and Abel, see the essay "Violence in the Name of God," p. 29

profaned."[2] One cannot be a sole survivor and still survive. *Sauve-qui-peut* ("let everyone who can, save himself") is not a principle of Judaism. We have to do what we can to save others, not just ourselves. Noah failed the test of *collective* responsibility.

The fourth is the enigmatic story of the Tower of Babel. The sin of its builders is unclear, but is indicated by two key words in the text. The story is framed, beginning and end, with the phrase *kol ha'aretz*, "the whole earth" (11:1, 8). In between, there is a series of similar sounding words: *sham* (there), *shem* (name), and *shamayim* (heaven). The story of Babel is a drama about the two key words of the first sentence of the Torah: "In the beginning God created *heaven* (*shamayim*) and *earth* (*aretz*)" (1:1). Heaven is the domain of God; earth is the domain of man. By attempting to build a tower that would "reach heaven," the builders of Babel were men trying to be like gods.

This story seems to have little to do with responsibility, and to be focusing on a different issue than do the first three. However, not accidentally does the word responsibility suggest *response*-ability. The Hebrew equivalent, *aḥrayut*, comes from the word *aḥer*, meaning "an other." Responsibility is always a *response* to something or someone. In Judaism, it means response to the command of God. By attempting to reach heaven, the builders of Babel were in effect saying: we are going to take the place of God. We are not going to respond to His law or respect His boundaries, not going to accept His Otherness. We are going to create an environment where we rule, not Him, where the Other is replaced by Self. Babel is the failure of *ontological* responsibility – the idea that something beyond us makes a call on us.

What we see in Genesis 1–11 is an exceptionally tightly constructed four-act drama on the theme of responsibility and moral development, presenting the maturation of humanity, as echoing the maturation of the individual. The first thing we learn as children is that our acts are under our control (personal responsibility). The next is that not everything we *can* do, we *may* do (moral responsibility). The next stage is the realization that we have a duty not just to ourselves but to those on whom we have an influence (collective responsibility). Ultimately

2. *Bereshit Raba* 36:3.

we learn that morality is not a mere human convention, but is written into the structure of existence. There is an Author of being, therefore there is an Authority beyond mankind to whom, when acting morally, we respond (ontological responsibility).

This is developmental psychology as we have come to know it through the work of Jean Piaget, Eric Erikson, Lawrence Kohlberg and Abraham Maslow. The subtlety and depth of the Torah is remarkable. It was the first, and is still the greatest, text on the human condition and our psychological growth from instinct to conscience, from "dust of the earth" to the morally responsible agent the Torah calls "the image of God."

Lekh Lekha
לֶךְ-לְךָ

In response to the call of God, Abraham and Sarah begin their journey to a new land and a new kind of faith, that will become the context of the entire Jewish drama thereafter. There are initial setbacks. There is a famine and they have to leave. There is a quarrel between Abraham and his nephew Lot, and they part. Lot is captured in a local war, and Abraham has to fight a battle to free him. God makes a covenant with Abraham, who remains childless. He has a son by Sarah's handmaid Hagar, but God tells him this is not the heir to the covenant. The sign of the covenant is circumcision.

The first of the following essays is about the new path Abraham charts by way of responsibility: the human response to the divine call. The second looks at the dimensions of the journey and the multiple meanings of the phrase *Lekh Lekha*. The third is about fathers and sons and the paradox of continuity and change. The last is about the long delay Abraham and Sarah must endure before they have a child, and what this implies for our understanding of faith.

The Long Walk to Freedom

We have arrived at the watershed of the book of Genesis. Prior to Abraham, all four dramas of Genesis dealt with the evasion and abdication of responsibility. Adam denies personal responsibility. Cain denies moral responsibility. Noah fails the test of collective responsibility. Babel was a rejection of ontological responsibility – the idea that the ethical imperative comes from a source beyond the self.[1] Abraham represents the turning point, offering a counterpoint to the previous failures.

Unlike Adam, Abraham accepts *personal* responsibility, heeding the word of God and setting out on a journey in obedience to the divine call. Adam is exiled from Eden against his will. Abraham undergoes a kind of voluntary exile, bidding farewell to the familiar in search of the unknown, guided only by the voice of God.

Unlike Cain, he accepts *moral* responsibility, rescuing his nephew Lot from war. He is his brother's – more precisely, his brother's son's – keeper, the very principle Cain denied. Abraham knows that we have duties not only to ourselves but to others. This is the moral sense.

---

1. See the previous chapter.

In contrast to Noah he accepts *collective* responsibility. He prays for the inhabitants of Sodom, even though he knows they are sinful, on the grounds that there may be innocent, righteous people among them. They are not his brothers, not his kin, not part of his specific covenant with God, but they are human beings, and Abraham feels the imperative of praying, even arguing with God, on their behalf.

In contrast to the builders of Babel, he understands *ontological* responsibility, the duty of human beings to respond to the otherness, and the command, of God. This is the basis of the greatest of his trials, his willingness to sacrifice even his son if God so commands it. Abraham knows that we are but "dust and ashes" (18:27) in the face of the Infinite. He does not try to build a tower to heaven; his task is to obey the will of heaven on earth.

Abraham is a new human type: the person whose life is a response to the call of God. Until now, with the exception of Noah, we have encountered human beings for whom God's command is a constraint from which they try to break free, by violence in the case of Cain and the generation of the Flood, by hubris in the case of the builders of Babel. Abraham is different. For him, the command is life itself. God speaks; Abraham listens and acts, without resistance on the one hand, and with pride on the other. His life is an answer to God's question; his existence is lived in the conscious presence of the divine will.

With Abraham a new faith is born: the faith of responsibility, in which the divine command and the human act meet and give birth to a new and blessed order, built on the principles of righteousness and justice. Judaism is supremely a religion of freedom – not freedom in the modern sense, the ability to do what we *like*, but in the ethical sense of the ability to choose to do what we *should*, to become co-architects with God of a just and gracious social order. The former leads to a culture of rights, the latter to a culture of responsibilities: *freedom as responsibility*.

The advent of Abraham was not a small turning point. For almost as long as we have documentary evidence, human beings have attributed their misfortunes to factors other than the human will and the "responsible self."[2] In large part, they still do today. In the past, men blamed

---

2.   The phrase comes from Reinhold Niebuhr, *The Responsible Self* (New York: Harper

the stars, the fates, the furies, the gods. Today they blame their parents, their environment, their genes, the educational system, the media, the politicians, and when all else fails – the Jews.

There is a Jewish joke that exposes the desire to escape responsibility better than any philosophical treatise: For a year, Rabbi Cohen has laboured to teach his unruly class the book of Joshua. No one has paid much attention, so he makes the end-of-year exam as easy as possible. He asks Marvin, at the back of the room, "Who destroyed the walls of Jericho?" Marvin replies: "Please sir, it wasn't me." Scandalised, he reports this to Marvin's parents. Instead of apologising, they indignantly reply, "If Marvin says it wasn't him, then it wasn't him." In despair he goes to the president of the congregation and tells him the story. The president listens, opens his drawer, gets out his chequebook, writes in it and says: "Here's a thousand dollars. Get the walls repaired, and stop complaining."

Ours is an age of "Please sir, it wasn't me." In one famous American court case, the attorney defending two young men who murdered their parents, claimed that they were innocent on the grounds that their parents had been psychologically abusive. In another, the lawyer argued that his client was not to blame for his violence. What he ate made him excitable. This became known as the "junk food defence."[3] We live in what is called *the victim culture.*

Nowadays, to win sympathy for your cause, you have to establish your credentials as a victim. This has overwhelming advantages. People empathise with your situation, give you support, and avoid criticising your actions. It has, however, three drawbacks: it is false, it is corrupting, and it is a denial of humanity. A victim is an object, not a subject; a done-to, not a doer. He or she systematically denies responsibility, and those who wish to help only prolong the denial. They become what is known in addiction therapy as co-dependents. By locating the cause of someone's plight in factors external to the person, the victim culture

---

& Row, 1963). See also Jonathan Sacks, *To Heal a Fractured World: The Ethics of Responsibility* (London: Continuum, 2005); New York: Schocken, 2005.

3. On this, see James Q. Wilson, *Moral Judgment: Does the Abuse Excuse Threaten our Legal System?* (New York: Basic Books, 1997).

perpetuates the condition of victimhood. Instead of helping the prisoner out of prison, it locks him in and throws away the key.

The call of God to Abraham – "Leave your land, your birthplace and your father's house" (11:2) – was a summons to chart a new and different path, the most fateful and at the same time the most hopeful in the history of mankind. The best description of it is the title of Nelson Mandela's autobiography: *The Long Walk to Freedom*.

Fundamental to the Torah are two freedoms: the freedom of God and the freedom of human beings. God is not, in Judaism, an impersonal force. He acts, whether in creation, revelation or redemption, not on the basis of necessity but of choice. In choosing to make mankind in His own image, He endowed us too, with choice. There is no such thing as fate or predestination. "I call heaven and earth to witness," said Moses, "that I have set before you life and death, blessing and curse. Therefore choose life" (Deuteronomy 30:19).

Alasdair MacIntyre once pointed out that there are two kinds of atheist: one who does not believe in God, and one for whom atheism itself is a kind of religion.[4] Of the latter, some of the greatest examples were lapsed, converted, or non-believing Jews – most famously, Spinoza, Marx and Freud. Instead of merely denying the truths of Judaism, they set out to provide systematic alternatives. Each sought to show that we are not free. Man is a predictable animal. Our nature and character are subject to quasi-scientific laws. There is a science of human behaviour as there is a science of atoms. History, personal or collective, is a form of inevitability. We are what we are because we could not be otherwise.

Unwittingly these three provide the best commentary on the opening verse of *Parashat Lekh Lekha*. At the heart of God's threefold call is a summons to a life of radical freedom, which is Judaism's living protest to these approaches.

Marx said that man is a product of social forces, themselves shaped by the interests of the ruling class, the owners of property of which the most significant is land. Therefore God said to Abraham, *Leave your land*.

---

4. Alasdair MacIntyre, "God and the Theologians," in *Against the Self-Images of the Age: Essays on Ideology and Philosophy*, (University of Notre Dame Press, 1978), 12–26.

Spinoza said that man is made by innate instincts and biological drives given by birth, positing a genetic determinism. Therefore God said to Abraham, *Leave the circumstances of your birth.*

Freud said that we are the way we are because of the traumas of childhood, the influence of our early years, our relationships and rivalries with our parents, especially our father. Therefore God said to Abraham, *Leave your father's house.*

Freedom is not a given of the human situation. Like the other distinctive achievements of the spirit – art, literature, music, poetry – it needs training, discipline, apprenticeship, the most demanding routines and the most painstaking attention to detail. No one composed a great novel or symphony without years of preparation. That is why most theories of human behaviour are simply false. They claim that we are either free or not; either we have choice or our behaviour is causally determined. Freedom is not an either/or. It is a process. It begins with dependence and only slowly, gradually, does it become liberty, the ability to stand back from the pressures and influences upon us and act in response to educated conscience, judgment, wisdom, moral literacy. It is, in short, a journey: Abraham's journey.

That is the deep meaning of the words *Lekh Lekha.* Normally they are translated as, "Go, leave, travel." What they really mean is: journey (*lekh*) to yourself (*lekha*). Leave behind all external influences that turn you into a victim of circumstances beyond your control, and travel inward to the self. It is there – only there – that freedom is born, practised and sustained.

A New Kind of Hero

> *God said to Abram: "Leave your land, your birthplace and your father's house and go to the land I will show you." (12:1)*

These words are among the most consequential in the history of mankind. With them a new faith was born that has lasted for two-thirds of the course of civilisation and remains young and vigorous today. Not only did Abraham give rise to what is now known as Judaism, he was also the inspiration of two other religions. Christianity and Islam both trace their descent, biological or spiritual, to him, and now number more than half the six billion people on the face of the earth among their adherents.

There has never been anyone like Abraham, yet the Torah is exceptionally understated in its account of him. As children we may have learned that he was the first iconoclast, the person who, while still young, broke the idols in his father's house. But this is a midrash, a tradition inferred from hints in the biblical text rather than from explicit statement. The Torah's actual presentation of Abraham does not fit any conventional image of the religious hero. He is not, like Noah, the survivor of a world hastening to its destruction and the progenitor of a new human order. He is not, like Moses, a law-giver and liberator. He is not, like the later prophets, a man who spends his life confronting kings, wrestling with his contemporaries and "speaking truth to power."

To be sure, he is a man of exemplary virtue. He welcomes strangers and gives them food. He fights a battle on behalf of the cities of the plain in order to rescue his nephew Lot. He prays for Sodom in one of the greatest dialogues in religious literature. He patiently waits for a child and then, when the command comes, is willing to offer him as a sacrifice, only to discover that the God of truth does not want us to sacrifice our children but to cherish them. But if we were asked to characterise him with adjectives, the words that spring to mind – gentle, kind, gracious – are not those usually associated with the founder of a new faith. They are the kind of attributes to which any of us could aspire. None of us can be an Abraham, but all of us can take him as a role model. Perhaps that is the deepest lesson of all.

In *Sincerity and Authenticity*, Lionel Trilling made the following comment:

> Not all cultures develop the idea of the heroic. I once had occasion to observe in connection with Wordsworth that in the rabbinical literature there is no touch of the heroic idea. The rabbis, in speaking of virtue, never mention the virtue of courage, which Aristotle regarded as basic to the heroic character. The indifference of the rabbis to the idea of courage is the more remarkable in that they knew that many of their number would die for their faith. What is especially to our point is that, as ethical beings, the rabbis never see themselves – it is as if the commandment which forbade the making of images extended to their way of conceiving the personal moral existence as well.[1]

Trilling is not quite accurate. The rabbis did speak of courage, *gevura*. But he is right to say that Judaism did not have heroes in the sense that

---

1. Lionel Trilling, *Sincerity and Authenticity* (Cambridge, MA: Harvard University Press, 1972), 85.

the Greeks and other cultures did. A hero is one convinced of his or her own importance. He is conscious of playing a part on the world stage – under the admiring gaze of his contemporaries. The rabbis, said Trilling, "would have been quite ready to understand the definition of the hero as an actor and to say that, as such, he was undeserving of the attention of serious men." Abraham is the paradigm of an unheroic hero, one who (in Maimonides' lovely phrase) "does what is right because it is right"[2] and not for the sake of popularity or fame.

Interestingly, Trilling's point is underscored by a striking feature of biblical Hebrew. It contains no word that is a precise equivalent of the English word "person." It has many words with similar meaning: *adam* (human), *ben adam* (mortal, literally "son of man"), *ish* (male as opposed to female; an individual), and *enosh* (man, humanity), but none with the exact resonances of *person*. The reason is that the word derives from the Latin *persona*, which meant "a mask" worn by an actor on the stage, and hence a character or role within a theatrical drama. It belongs to a culture in which, in Shakespeare's words, "All the world's a stage, And all the men and women merely players."[3] In such cultures we are what we seem to others. We are judged by appearances. In Judaism, we are known directly by God for what we are, not how we seem: "Man looks at the outward appearance, but the Lord looks at the heart" (I Samuel 16:7).

As the founder of Judaism, Abraham gives us a vision of what it is to live directly and immediately in the presence of God, who knows our thoughts, our hopes, our fears, our dreams. This involves a radically new kind of heroism: the heroism of ordinary life, of decency and goodness, integrity and faithfulness, the humble, unostentatious heroism of being willing to live by one's convictions though all the world thinks otherwise, being true to the call of eternity, not the noise of now.

---

2. Maimonides, *Mishneh Torah,* Hilkhot Teshuva, 10:2.
3. Shakespeare, *As You Like It,* act II, scene 7.

Four Dimensions of the Journey

Within the first words that God addresses to the bearer of a new covenant, there are already hints as to the nature of the heroism he would come to embody. The multilayered command "*Lekh lekha* – go forth" contains the seeds of Abraham's ultimate vocation.

Rashi, following an ancient exegetic tradition, translates the phrase as "Journey for yourself."[1] According to him, God is saying "Travel for your own benefit and good. There I will make you into a great nation; here you will not have the merit of having children." Sometimes we have to give up our past in order to acquire a future. In his first words to Abraham, God was already intimating that what seems like a sacrifice is, in the long run, not so. Abraham was about to say goodbye to the things that mean most to us – land, birthplace and parental home, the places where we belong. He was about to make a journey from the familiar to the unfamiliar, a leap into the unknown. To be able to make that leap involves trust – in Abraham's case, trust not in visible power but in the voice of the invisible God. At the end of it, however, Abraham would discover that he had achieved something he could not have

---

1. Rashi, 12:1.

done otherwise. He would give birth to a new nation whose greatness consisted precisely in the ability to live by that voice and create something new in the history of mankind. "Go for yourself" – believe in what you can become.

Another interpretation, more midrashic, takes the phrase to mean "Go *with* yourself" – meaning, by travelling from place to place you will extend your influence not over one land but many:

> When the Holy One said to Abraham, "Leave your land, your birthplace and your father's house..." what did Abraham resemble? A jar of scent with a tight fitting lid put away in a corner so that its fragrance could not go forth. As soon as it was moved from that place and opened, its fragrance began to spread. So the Holy One said to Abraham, "Abraham, many good deeds are in you. Travel about from place to place, so that the greatness of your name will go forth in My world."[2]

Abraham was commanded to leave his place in order to testify to the existence of a God not bounded by place – Creator and Sovereign of the entire universe. Abraham and Sarah were to be like perfume, leaving a trace of their presence wherever they went. Implicit in this midrash is the idea that the fate of the first Jews already prefigured that of their descendants[3] who would be scattered throughout the world in order to spread knowledge of God throughout the world. Unusually, exile is seen here not as punishment but as a necessary corollary of a faith that sees God everywhere. *Lekh lekha* means "Go with yourself" – your beliefs, your way of life, your faith.

A third interpretation, this time more mystical, takes the phrase to mean, "Go *to* yourself." The Jewish journey, said R. David of Lelov, is a journey to the root of the soul.[4] In the words of R. Zushya of Hanipol,

2. *Bereshit Raba* 39:2.
3. On the principle, "What happened to the fathers is a portent of what would happen to the children," see for example, Nahmanides, commentary to Genesis 12:6. On Nahmanides' use of this principle throughout his commentary, see Ezra-Tzion Melamed, *Mefarshei Hamikra* (Jerusalem: Magnes Press, 1975), vol. 2, 950–53.
4. R. David of Lelov, *Pninei Ha-Hassidut* (Jerusalem, 1987), vol. 1, 88.

"When I get to heaven, they will not ask me, why were you not Moses? They will ask me, Zushya, why were you not Zushya?"[5] Abraham was being asked to leave behind all the things that make us someone else – for it is only by taking a long and lonely journey that we discover who we truly are. "Go to yourself."

There is, however, a fourth interpretation: "Go by yourself." Only a person willing to stand alone, singular and unique, can worship the God who is alone, singular and unique. Only one able to leave behind the natural sources of identity – home, family, culture and society – can encounter God who stands above and beyond nature. A journey into the unknown is one of the greatest possible expressions of freedom. God wanted Abraham and his children to be a living example of what it is to serve the God of freedom, in freedom, for the sake of freedom.

Lekh Lekha means: Leave behind you all that makes human beings predictable, unfree, delimited. Leave behind the social forces, the familial pressures, the circumstances of your birth. Abraham's children were summoned to be the people that defied the laws of nature because they refused to define themselves as the products of nature. That is not to say that economic or biological or psychological forces have no part to play in human behaviour. They do. But with sufficient imagination, determination, discipline and courage we can rise above them. Abraham did. So, at most times, did his children.

Those who live within the laws of history are subject to the laws of history. Whatever is natural, said Maimonides, is subject to disintegration and decline. That is what has happened to virtually every civilisation that has appeared on the world's stage. Abraham, however, was to become the father of an *am olam*, an eternal people, that would neither decay nor decline, a people willing to stand outside the laws of nature. What for other nations are innate – land, home, family – in Judaism are subjects of religious command. They have to be striven for. They involve a journey. They are not given at the outset, nor can they be taken for granted. Abraham was to leave behind the things that make most people and peoples what they are, and lay the foundations for a land, a Jewish

5. R. Ephraim Lundschitz, *Kli Yakar* to *Bereshit*, 12:1.

home and a family structure, responsive not to economic forces, biological drives and psychological conflicts but to the word and will of God.

Lekh Lekha in this sense means being prepared to take an often lonely journey: "Go by yourself." To be a child of Abraham is to have the courage to be different, to challenge the idols of the age, whatever the idols and whichever the age. In an era of polytheism, it meant seeing the universe as the product of a single creative will – and therefore not meaningless but coherent and meaningful. In an era of slavery it meant refusing to accept the status quo in the name of God, but instead challenging it in the name of God. When power was worshipped, it meant constructing a society that cared for the powerless, the widow, orphan and stranger. During centuries in which the mass of mankind was sunk in ignorance, it meant honouring education as the key to human dignity and creating schools to provide universal literacy. When war was the test of manhood, it meant striving for peace. In ages of radical individualism like today, it means knowing that we are not what we own but what we share; not what we buy but what we give; that there is something higher than appetite and desire – namely the call that comes to us, as it came to Abraham, from outside ourselves, summoning us to make a contribution to the world.

"Jews," wrote Andrew Marr, "really have been different; they have enriched the world and challenged it."[6] It is that courage to travel alone if necessary, to be different, to swim against the tide, to speak in an age of relativism of the absolutes of human dignity under the sovereignty of God, that was born in the words *Lekh Lekha*. To be a Jew is to be willing to hear the still, small voice of eternity urging us to travel, move, go on ahead, continuing Abraham's journey toward that unknown destination at the far horizon of hope.

6. Andrew Marr, *The Observer*, 14 May 2000.

Fathers and Sons

The call to Abraham, with which *Lekh Lekha* begins, seems to come from nowhere:

> Leave your land, your birthplace, and your father's house, and go to a land which I will show you (12:1).

Nothing has prepared us for this radical departure. We have not had a description of Abraham as we had in the case of Noah: "Noah was a righteous man, perfect in his generations; Noah walked with God" (6:9). Nor have we been given a series of glimpses into his childhood, as we will in the case of Moses. It is as if Abraham's call is a sudden break with all that went before. There seems to be no prelude, no context, no background.

Added to this is a sudden, unexpected verse in the last speech delivered by Moses's successor Joshua:

> And Joshua said to all the people, "Thus says the Lord, the God of Israel, 'Long ago, your fathers lived beyond the river [Euphrates], Terah, the father of Abraham and of Nahor; and they served other gods (Joshua 24:2).

The implication seems to be that Abraham's father was an idolater. Hence the famous midrashic tradition that as a child, Abraham broke his father's idols. When Terah asked him who had done the damage, he replied, "The largest of the idols took a stick and broke the rest."

"Why are you deceiving me?" Terah asked, "Do idols have understanding?"

"Let your ears hear what your mouth is saying," replied the child.[1]

On this reading, Abraham was a breaker of images, one who rebelled against his father's faith – an iconoclast who burst out of his context, his culture and all that came before.

According to Maimonides' powerful philosophical rendition, originally human beings believed in one God. Later, they began to offer sacrifices to the sun, the planets and stars, and other forces of nature, as creations or servants of the one God. Later still, they began to worship them as entities – gods – in their own right. It took Abraham, using logic alone, to realize the incoherence of polytheism:

> After he was weaned, while still an infant, his mind began to reflect. Day and night, he thought and wondered, how is it possible that this celestial sphere should be continuously guiding the world, without something to guide it and cause it to revolve? For it cannot move of its own accord. He had no teacher or mentor, because he was immersed in Ur of the Chaldees among foolish idolaters. His father and mother and the entire population worshipped idols, and he worshipped with them. He continued to speculate and reflect until he achieved the way of truth, understanding what was right through his own efforts. It was then that he knew that there is one God who guides the heavenly bodies, who created everything, and besides whom there is no other god.[2]

According to this reading, Abraham's rejection of the past was intellectual rather than physical. He broke no idols, merely the thoughts that gave rise to them. But whether the iconoclasm was literal or metaphoric, what

---

1. *Bereshit Raba*, 38:8; Tanḥuma, *Bereshit*, 3.
2. *Mishneh Torah*, Hilkhot Avoda Zara, 1:3.

is common to Maimonides and the midrash is discontinuity. Abraham represents a radical break with all that preceded him.

Remarkably however, the previous chapter gives us a quite different perspective:

> These are the generations of Terah. Terah fathered Abram, Nahor, and Haran; and Haran fathered Lot...Terah took Abram, his son, and Lot the son of Haran, his grandson, and Sarai his daughter-in-law, his son Abram's wife, and they went forth together from Ur of the Chaldees to go into the land of Canaan, but when they came to Haran, they settled there. The days of Terah were two hundred and five years, and Terah died in Haran (11:31).

The implication of this verse seems to be that far from breaking with his father, Abraham was continuing a journey Terah had already begun.

The two passages seem contradictory. Many commentators explain this away by assuming that they are not in chronological sequence: The call to Abraham (in Genesis 12) came first. Abraham heard the divine summons, and communicated it to his father. The family set out together, but Terah stopped halfway, in Haran. The passage recording Terah's death is actually chronologically out of place, and is noted *before* Abraham's call, in order to guard him from the accusation that he failed to honour his father by leaving Terah in his old age.[3]

Yet there is another obvious possibility. Abraham's spiritual insight did not come from nowhere. Terah had already made the first tentative move toward monotheism. Children complete what their parents begin.

Significantly, both the Bible and rabbinic tradition understood divine parenthood in this way: God signals the way, then challenges His children to walk on ahead, to complete the path on their own. The Midrash contrasts the description of Noah ("Noah walked with God," 6:9) and that of Abraham ("The God before whom I have walked,"

---

3.   Rashi to Genesis 11:32; *Bereshit Raba* 39:7.

24:40).[4] The ultimate challenge, in God's words to Abraham, is to "Walk ahead of Me and be perfect" (17:1).

In one of the most famous of all Talmudic passages, the sages disagreed with Rabbi Eliezer's opinion and outvoted him, despite the fact that his view was supported by a heavenly voice. Afterwards, Rabbi Natan encountered the prophet Elijah:

> Rabbi Natan asked Elijah: "What did the Holy One, blessed be He, do in that hour?" Elijah replied: "He laughed [with joy], saying, 'My sons have defeated Me, My sons have defeated Me!'"[5]

To be a parent in Judaism is to make space within which a child can grow. Astonishingly, this applies even when the parent is God *Avinu*, "our Father," Himself. In the words of Rabbi Joseph Soloveitchik, "The Creator of the world diminished the image and stature of creation in order to leave something for man, the work of His hands, to do, in order to adorn man with the crown of creator and maker."[6]

This idea finds expression in halakha, Jewish law. Despite the emphasis in the Torah on honouring and revering parents, Maimonides rules:

> Although children are commanded to go to great lengths [in honouring parents], a father is forbidden to impose too heavy a yoke on them, or to be too exacting with them in matters relating to his honour, lest he cause them to stumble. He should forgive them and close his eyes, for a father has the right to forgo the honour due to him.[7]

There must be a balance between what a child owes its parents – the

4. *Bereshit Raba* 30:10.
5. *Bava Metzia*, 59b.
6. Joseph B. Soloveitchik, *Halakhic Man*, translated from the Hebrew by Lawrence Kaplan (Philadelphia: Jewish Publication Society of America, 1983), 107.
7. *Mishneh Torah*, Hilkhot Mamrim 6:8.

honour due to them – and the space within which the child can grow. God, like the parent, forgoes, "diminishes" His own creation.

The story of Abraham can be read in two ways, depending on how we reconcile the end of chapter 11 with the beginning of chapter 12. One reading emphasizes discontinuity. Abraham broke with all that went before. The other emphasizes continuity. Terah, his father, had already begun to wrestle with idolatry. He had set out on the long walk to the land which would eventually become holy, but stopped halfway. Abraham completed the journey his father began.

Perhaps childhood itself has the same ambiguity. There are times, especially in adolescence, when we tell ourselves that we are breaking with our parents, charting a path that is completely new. Only in retrospect, many years later, do we realize how much we owe our parents – how, even at those moments when we felt most strongly that we were setting out on a journey uniquely our own, we were, in fact, living out the ideals and aspirations that we learned from them. And it began with God Himself, who left, and continues to leave, space for us, His children, to walk on ahead.

Promise and Fulfillment

An extraordinary drama begins to unfold in these early chapters of Abraham's journey, all the more powerful for being understated and unexplained. One of the aspects of God's promise to Abraham, whom He has asked to leave his family, is that he would have a family of his own. Time and again, the note is sounded, the promised repeated, the assurance given. It is there in the opening call of God to Abraham: "I will make you into a great nation and I will bless you" (12:2). This is no accidental blessing. We have already been told at the end of the previous chapter that "Sarah was barren, she had no children" (11:30). Rashi comments that the blessing is connected to the journey, as if to say that in the new land, Abraham and Sarah will be able to have children.[1] According to the sages, a change of place is one of the things that brings about a change in fortune.[2] The promise is repeated and expanded in the next chapter:

I will make your offspring like the dust of the earth, so that

1. Rashi to *Bereshit* 12:1.
2. *Rosh HaShana* 16b.

> if anyone could count the dust, then your offspring could be counted. (13:16)

Two chapters later, we hear it a third time, now with a new and dramatic image:

> He took him outside and said, "Look up at the heavens and count the stars – if indeed you can count them." Then He said to him, "So shall your offspring be." (15:5)

The sages, cited by Rashi, gave a pointed interpretation to the phrase "He took him outside." Abraham had apparently said to God, "I see in my stars that I am not destined to have children." God said to him: "Leave behind [i.e. "stand outside"] your astronomical calculations. The stars will have no influence on your people's destiny [*ein mazal beYisrael*]."[3]

The promise is stated for a fourth time, when God makes a covenant with Abraham. Now we are told that he will not be the father of a single nation, but of many. To signal the seriousness of this promise, God changes Abraham's name:

> "As for Me, this is My covenant with you: You will be the father of many nations. No longer will you be called Abram; your name will be Abraham, for I have made you a father of many nations. I will make you very fruitful; I will make nations of you, and kings will come from you." (17:4–6)

Abraham will be a parent. He will have not the normal number of children, but a vast panoply of offspring. They will become a great nation. His children will be as many as the dust of the earth and the stars of the sky. He will give rise not to one but to many nations. The promise could not be more explicit. Indeed, it is already implicit in Abraham's name. *Av* means father; *Abram* is "mighty father;" *Abraham* means "father of many nations." Yet even at this early stage, we discover that the course of events will be anything but simple and straightforward. *Lekh Lekha*

---

3. Rashi to *Bereshit* 15:5; *Bereshit Raba* ad loc.

contains three stories, each of which has to do with Abraham's succession and his failure to have a child.

The first concerns his nephew Lot. Surprisingly, when Abraham sets out on his journey, Lot, son of Abraham's brother Nahor, goes with him. A reasonable assumption would be that Abraham, without children and with a barren wife, has decided to adopt Lot or at least make him his heir and successor.

If that was the plan, it failed. After their sojourn in Egypt, Abraham and Lot have extensive flocks and herds, so many that they are unable to pasture together. There is a quarrel between their respective herdsmen. Abraham realises that they will have to separate:

> Abram said to Lot, "There should be no arguing between you and me, or between your herdsmen and mine, because we are brothers. We should separate. The whole land is there in front of you. If you go to the left, I will go to the right. If you go to the right, I will go to the left." (13:8–9)

"We are brothers" – implying, not adoptive father and adopted son. It is what happens next that convinces us that there is something deeper at stake in the separation:

> Lot looked all around and saw the whole Jordan Valley and that there was much water there. It was like the Lord's garden, like the land of Egypt in the direction of Zoar. (This was before the Lord destroyed Sodom and Gomorrah.) So Lot chose to move east and live in the Jordan Valley. In this way Abram and Lot separated. Abram lived in the land of Canaan, but Lot lived among the cities in the Jordan Valley, very near to Sodom. Now the people of Sodom were very evil and were always sinning against the Lord. (13:10–13)

Lot chooses the good land with evil inhabitants. Evidently, he puts the material before the moral and spiritual. This alone is sufficient to tell us that, as far as the covenant is concerned, he is not a child of Abraham. The text goes out of its way to emphasize this, using a prolepsis –

telling us in advance things we would not otherwise discover until later. There is the comparison with Egypt, whose full significance we will not realize until the book of Exodus. We are told that in the future, Sodom and Gomorrah will be destroyed. Twice the text stresses the wickedness of their inhabitants. The people are "very evil" and "always sinning."

None of this would have been apparent to Lot at the time. We imagine him standing on a hilltop surveying the panorama. He has no way of knowing the character of the people in the towns he sees, nor of what would be their ultimate fate. Evidently Lot's character failure lies in the fact that "he looked around and saw." Like Eve when she saw that the fruit of the tree of knowledge was "pleasant to the eyes" (3:6), Lot judged by appearances. The children of the covenant follow sound, not sight, the voice of God in the depths of the soul, not the seductive surfaces of the visible. So Abraham loses his first potential heir.

If not Lot, then whom? This creates a crisis for Abraham. These are his first recorded words to God:

> After these things happened, the Lord spoke His word to Abram in a vision: "Abram, don't be afraid. I will defend You, and I will give you a great reward."
>
> But Abram said, "Lord God, what can You give me? I have no son, so my slave Eliezer from Damascus will get everything I own after I die." Abram said, "Look, You have given me no son, so a slave born in my house will inherit everything I have." (15:2–3)

Abraham's patience breaks. The first Jew feared that he would be the last. The reference to Eliezer has taken on a new intelligibility in the light of ancient documents from the Nuzi archives, which show that it was a well established practice in Abraham's day for childless individuals to adopt someone, even a slave, as a son. He would then have all the attendant duties and rights of a natural son and heir.[4] Whether or not Abraham had adopted his slave Eliezer, it is clear that with the departure of Lot, there was no one else he could look to. God reassures Abram: "He [Eliezer] will not be the one to inherit what you have. You will have

---

4. See Nahum M. Sarna, *Understanding Genesis* (New York: Schocken, 1970), 122–23.

a son of your own [literally, 'one that goes out of your own body'] who will inherit what you have" (15:4). There then follows the promise of as many children as the stars.

The third drama is the most poignant. Sarai, recognising her own infertility, suggests to Abram that he take her handmaid Hagar as a wife. She may bear him a child. Abram listens and agrees:

> So Abram had sexual relations with Hagar, and she became pregnant. But when Hagar knew she was pregnant, she began to treat her mistress, Sarai, with contempt. Then Sarai said to Abram, "This is all your fault! I put my servant into your arms, but now that she's pregnant she treats me with contempt. The Lord will show who's wrong – you or me!"
>
> Abram replied, "Look, she is your servant, so deal with her as you see fit." Then Sarai treated Hagar so harshly that she finally ran away. (16:4–6)

This is a strange passage that portrays all three protagonists in a less-than-good light. Hagar is disrespectful, Sarai querulous, and Abram seemingly indifferent. For once, Nahmanides, reluctant as were all the classic Jewish commentators to criticize the behavior of the patriarchs and matriarchs, delivers a negative judgment:

> Our mother [Sarah] transgressed by this affliction [of Hagar], and Abraham also by permitting her to do so. And so God heard her [Hagar's] affliction and gave her a son who would be a wild ass of a man to afflict the seed of Abraham and Sarah with all kinds of affliction.[5]

Whichever way we interpret the passage, the tensions show. Abraham and Sarah are acting out of character. Their nerves are frayed by the long-delayed and disappointed hope. Eventually God makes it clear: Ishmael, Hagar's child by Abraham, will not be the promised son, bearer of the covenant, continuer of the faith. Despite all the evidence to the

---

5. Nahmanides to *Bereshit* 16:6.

contrary – Sarai's age and infertility – she will give birth to a son. For once, Abraham gives voice to disbelief, followed closely by his paternal feelings toward Ishmael:

> God also said to Abraham, "As for Sarai your wife, you are no longer to call her Sarai; her name will be Sarah. I will bless her and will surely give you a son by her. I will bless her so that she will be the mother of nations; kings of peoples will come from her."
> Abraham fell face down; he laughed and said to himself, "Will a son be born to a man a hundred years old? Will Sarah bear a child at the age of ninety?" And Abraham said to God, "If only Ishmael might live under Your blessing!" (17:15–18)

So, by the time the *parasha* ends, we have heard four promises of children and seen three prospective heirs, Lot, Eliezer and Ishmael, fail to fit the specification. Lot makes his home among evildoers. Eliezer is not part of the patriarchal family. Ishmael will become "a wild ass of a man: his hand will be against everyone, and everyone's hand against him" (16:12).

What are we to make of all this? Undoubtedly, one theme is miraculous birth. Sarah, like Rebecca and Rachel after her, is infertile, so that the children born to them are seen, in some way, to be marked out as divine gifts: in a strong sense, God's children. Similarly, Moses, the tongue-tied stammerer, will be one whose words palpably come from God, not from his own mouth.

But there is also a counter-theme, moving in the opposite direction. The patriarchs and prophets move in the real world, not a world of magic and myth and larger-than-life legend. Abraham begins a journey, but it is beset by obstacles. He receives a promise, but its fulfillment is long-delayed and fraught with diversions and false turns.

Whatever the divine promise, it is not fulfilled immediately. Abraham's journey, like that of Moses and the Israelites in a later generation, takes longer than they or we expect. There is no sudden transition from here to the promised land, from starting point to destination. Taking Genesis literally, the universe might be made in seven days, but anything in the human world that involves profound change, takes time. The biblical drama is set in the arena of time. *Faith is the ability to live with delay without losing trust in the promise; to experience disappointment without losing hope, to know that the road between the real and the ideal is long and yet be willing to undertake the journey.* That was Abraham's and Sarah's faith, and that of Moses and the prophets and those who came after them.

And surely it must be ours. God delivers all He promises, but not always when we expect. Jews are often restless and impatient: in the Talmud they are described (by a Sadducee) as an *ama peziza*, a "rash people."[6] Yet none has waited longer – for freedom and equality, for the return to the land, and for the Messiah. To wait without despair, to hope and keep on hoping: that is the faith of Abraham and Sarah's children, the faith that they themselves lived. And though it was shot through with disappointments, and though they themselves sometimes gave expression to their doubts and fears, it did not prove in vain. Jews kept faith alive. Faith kept the Jewish people alive.

6. *Shabbat* 88a.

Vayera
וירא

God appears to Abraham. Three strangers pass by. Abraham offers them hospitality. One of them tells Abraham that Sarah will have a child. Sarah, overhearing, laughs in disbelief.

God then tells Abraham of the judgment He is about to visit on the people of Sodom. Abraham engages in a momentous dialogue with God about justice. God agrees that if there are ten innocent men in the city He will spare it.

Two of the visitors, by now identified as angels, go to Abraham's nephew, Lot, in Sodom and rescue him, his wife and two of their daughters from the destruction.

Eventually, the promised child, Isaac, is born to Sarah. The *parasha* ends with the great test of the "binding of Isaac."

The first of the following essays looks at the significance of the way the Torah describes Abraham's hospitality to the strangers. The second reflects on Abraham's dialogue with God and its implications for the nature of justice. The third is about Lot's reluctance to leave Sodom despite the fact that he knew it was about to be destroyed. The fourth offers an interpretation of the delays and trials involved in the birth and binding of Isaac.

God and Strangers

> *God appeared to Abraham by the oaks of Mamre,*
> *as he sat at the entrance to his tent in the heat of*
> *the day. He lifted up his eyes and looked, and, lo,*
> *three men were standing over against him; and*
> *when he saw them, he ran to meet them from*
> *the tent entrance, and bowed down to the earth…*
> *(18:1–2)*

T hus *Parashat Vayera* opens with one of the most famous scenes in the Bible: Abraham's meeting with the three enigmatic strangers. The text calls them men. We later discover that they were in fact angels, each with a specific mission.

The chapter at first glance seems simple, almost fable-like. It is, however, complex and ambiguous. It consists of three sections:

Verse 1:   God appears to Abraham.
Verses 2–16:   Abraham meets the men/angels.

Verses 17–33: The dialogue between God and Abraham about the fate of Sodom.

The relationship between these sections is far from clear. Do they represent one scene, two or three?

The most obvious possibility is three. Each of the above sections is a separate event. First, God appears to Abraham, as Rashi explains, "to visit the sick"[1] after Abraham's circumcision. Then the visitors arrive with the news that Sarah will have a child. Then takes place the great dialogue about justice and the imminent punishment of the people of Sodom.

Maimonides suggests that there are only two scenes: The visit of the angels, and the dialogue with God. The first verse does not describe an event at all; it is, rather, a *chapter heading.*[2] It tells us that the events that follow are all part of a prophetic revelation, a divine-human encounter.

The third possibility is that we have a single continuous scene. God appears to Abraham, but before He can speak, Abraham sees the passers-by and asks God to wait while he serves them food. Only when they have departed – in verse 17 – does he turn to God, and the conversation begins.

The interpretation of the chapter affects – and hinges upon – the way we translate the word *Adonai* in Abraham's appeal: "Please *Adonai,* if now I have found favour in your sight, do not pass by, I pray you, from your servant" (18:3). *Adonai* can be a reference to one of the names of God. It can also be read as "my lords" or "sirs." In the first case, Abraham would be addressing God. In the second, he would be speaking to the passers-by.

The same linguistic ambiguity appears in the next chapter (19:2), when two of Abraham's visitors – now described as angels – visit Lot in Sodom:

And the two angels came to Sodom in the evening, and Lot sat

1. Rashi to *Bereshit* 18:1; *Sotah* 14a.
2. *Moreh Nevuhim* II:42.

by the city gates. When he saw them, he rose to meet them and bowing low, he said, "I pray you now, *adonai,* turn aside to your servant's house and tarry all night and bathe your feet and you shall rise up early and go on your way." (19:1–2)

As there is no contextual element to suggest that Lot might be speaking to God, it seems clear, in this case, that *adonai* refers to the visitors.

The simplest reading then of both texts – the one concerning Abraham, the other, Lot – would be to read the word consistently as "sirs." Several English translations indeed take this approach. Here, for example, is the New English Bible's:

> The Lord appeared to Abraham...He looked up, and saw three men standing in front of him. When he saw them, he ran from the opening of his tent to meet them and bowed low to the ground. "Sirs," he said, "if I have deserved your favour, do not pass by my humble self without a visit."

Jewish tradition, however, does not.

Normally, differences of interpretation of biblical narrative have no halakhic implications. They are matters of legitimate disagreement. This case of Abraham's addressee is unusual, however, because if we translate *Adonai* as "God," it is a holy name, and both the writing of the word by a scribe, and the way we treat a parchment or document containing it, have special stringencies in Jewish law. If, by contrast, we translate it as "my lords" or "sirs," it has no special sanctity. Jewish law rules that in the scene with Lot, *adonai* is read as "sirs," but in the case of Abraham it is read as "God."

This is an extraordinary fact, because it suggests that *Abraham actually interrupted God as He was about to speak, asking Him to wait while he attended to the visitors.* According to tradition, the passage should be read thus:

> The Lord appeared to Abraham...He looked up and saw three men standing over against him. On seeing them, he hurried from his tent door to meet them, and bowed down. [Turning to God]

he said: "My God, if I have found favour in Your eyes, do not leave Your servant [i.e. Please wait until I have given hospitality to these men]." [He then turned to the men and said:] "Let me send for some water so that you may bathe your feet and rest under this tree…"[3]

This daring interpretation became the basis for a principle in Judaism: "Greater is hospitality than receiving the Divine Presence."[4] Faced with a choice between listening to God, and offering hospitality to what seemed to be human beings, Abraham chose the latter. God acceded to his request, and waited while Abraham brought the visitors food and drink, before engaging him in dialogue about the fate of Sodom.

How can this be so? It seems disrespectful at best, heretical at worst, to put the needs of human beings before attending on the presence of God.

What the passage is telling us, though, is something of immense profundity. The idolaters of Abraham's time worshipped the sun, the stars, and the forces of nature as gods. They worshipped power and the powerful. Abraham knew, however, that God is not *in* nature but *beyond* nature. There is only one thing in the universe on which He has set His image: the human person, *every* person, powerful and powerless alike.

The forces of nature are impersonal, which is why those who worship them eventually lose their humanity. As the book of Psalms puts it:

Their idols are silver and gold, the work of men's hands.
They have mouths, but cannot speak,
eyes, but cannot see;
they have ears, but cannot hear,
nostrils but cannot smell…
They that make them become like them,
and so do all who put their trust in them. (Psalms 115:4–8)

One cannot worship impersonal forces and remain a person; compas-

3. See *Shabbat* 127a.
4. Ibid. See also *Shavuot* 35b.

sionate, humane, generous, forgiving. Precisely because we believe that God is personal, someone to whom we can say "You," we honour human dignity as sacrosanct.

Abraham, father of monotheism, knew the paradoxical truth that to live the life of faith is to see the trace of God in the face of the stranger. It is easy to receive the Divine Presence when God appears as God. What is difficult is to sense the Divine Presence when it comes disguised as three anonymous passers-by. That was Abraham's greatness. He knew that serving God and offering hospitality to strangers were not two things but one.

In one of the most beautiful comments on this episode, Rabbi Shalom of Belz notes that in verse 2, the visitors are spoken of as standing above Abraham (*nitzavim alav*), while in verse 8, Abraham is described as standing above them (*omed aleihem*). At first, the visitors were higher than Abraham because they were angels and he a mere human being. But when he gave them food and drink and shelter, he stood even higher than the angels.[5]

By choosing the most radical of the three possible interpretations of Genesis 18, the sages allowed us to hear one of the most fundamental principles of the life of faith: We honour God by honouring His image, humankind.

5.   Dover Shalom ad loc.; cited in *Peninei Ḥassidut* (Jerusalem, 1987) to *Bereshit* 18:2.

Challenging God

The great argument between Abraham and God in Genesis 18 is a turning point in the history of the spirit. For the first time, a human being challenges God Himself on a matter of justice. Hearing about the impending destruction of Sodom and the cities of the plain, Abraham says:

> Will You indeed sweep away the righteous with the wicked? What if there are fifty righteous people in the city? Will You indeed sweep it away and not spare the place for the sake of the fifty righteous people in it? Far be it from You to do such a thing – to slay the righteous with the wicked, so that the righteous should be like the wicked. Far be it from You! Shall not the Judge of all the earth do justly? (18:23–25)

There was nothing like this before, nor is there, to my knowledge, anything like it in any other religious literature. Yet it is no isolated phenomenon. It is the birth of one of the great Jewish traditions: the argument with Heaven, for the sake of Heaven, the covenantal dialogue between God and man in the name of justice.

We hear it again in the words of Moses, when his initial intervention on behalf of the Israelites in Egypt only seems to make matters worse:

> Moses returned to the Lord and said, "O Lord, why have You brought trouble upon this people? Is this why You sent me?" (Exodus 5:22)

We hear it again when, during the Koraḥ rebellion, God's anger threatens to destroy the Israelites as a whole:

> But they fell on their faces and said, "O God, God of the spirits of all flesh, when one man sins, will You be angry with the entire congregation?" (Numbers 16:22)

Jeremiah questions the justice of history:

> You are always righteous, O Lord,
> when I bring a case before You.
> Yet I would speak with You about Your justice:
> Why does the way of the wicked prosper?
> Why do all the faithless live at ease? (Jeremiah 12:1)

So too does Habakkuk:

> How long, O Lord, must I call for help, but You do not listen? Or cry out to You, "Violence!" but You do not save? Why do You make me look at injustice? Why do You tolerate wrong? Destruction and violence are before me; there is strife, and conflict abounds. (Habakkuk 1:2–3)

Nor does the argument end with the Hebrew Bible. It continues into the rabbinic tradition. Far from softening the contours of these sharp exchanges, the sages accentuated them, speaking of *ḥutzpa kelapei shemaya*, "audacity towards Heaven."[1]

---

1. *Sanhedrin* 105a.

Yet how can this be? How can finite, fallible human beings challenge God Himself, and this, not in opposition to faith, but as part of the life of faith itself? For it is notable that it is not heretics, skeptics or atheists who raise these questions, but heroes of the spirit. How, in our *parasha*, can Abraham, who describes himself as mere "dust and ashes," confront "the Judge of all the earth," challenging God's verdict on the people of Sodom?

The answer is given by the Torah itself. Immediately prior to Abraham's intervention, we read these words:

> Then the Lord said, "Shall I hide from Abraham what I am about to do? Abraham will surely become a great and powerful nation, and all nations on earth will be blessed through him. For I have chosen him, so that he will direct his children and his household after him to keep the way of the Lord by doing what is right and just, so that the Lord will bring about for Abraham what He has promised him." (18:17–19)

It is clear that this speech of God is an invitation to Abraham to speak. What else can be the meaning of "Shall I hide from Abraham what I am about to do?" Not only does God invite Abraham to speak; he even signals in advance the words he wants Abraham to use – "right" (*tzedek/tzedaka*) and "just" (*mishpat*). These constitute "the way of the Lord" that God wants Abraham to teach his children.

Abraham responds by using precisely these words in his challenge. He uses the root *tz-d-k* seven times. He uses the root *sh-p-t* twice, at the beginning and end of the key sentence: "Shall the Judge [*hashophet*] of all the earth not do justly [*mishpat*]?"

Yet the answer only serves to intensify the question. God wants Abraham to challenge His verdict. But why? Does Abraham know something that God does not? Or is his sense of justice stronger than that of God Himself? Both suggestions are absurd. God knows more than any human being ever can or will. And God's justice is, we believe, complete:

> He is the Rock, His works are perfect, and all His ways are just. A faithful God who does no wrong, upright and just is He. (Deuteronomy 32:4)

How could it be otherwise? The fundamental principle of the Torah is that God rules by right, not might. That in itself was enough to separate Judaism from every other faith in the ancient world. God is not merely powerful but ethical, and it is precisely the pursuit of the ethical that brings God and humanity together in a covenant based on righteousness and justice.

So what did God want of Abraham? Why did He invite him to join in a conversation about the fate of the people of Sodom? It cannot be that the verdict of heaven was questionable. The Torah itself rules out this possibility twice, once before and once after Abraham's dialogue. Several chapters beforehand it tells us:

> Now the men of Sodom were wicked and were sinning greatly against the Lord. (13:13)

Note the threefold emphasis in this sentence: the people were (1) wicked, (2) sinning and (3) greatly.

In the chapter following Abraham's dialogue, two of the men, now identified as "angels," visit Lot in Sodom. That night, the following scene takes place:

> Before they had gone to bed, all the men from every part of the city of Sodom – both young and old – surrounded the house. They called to Lot, "Where are the men who came to you tonight? Bring them out to us so that we can know them." (19:4–5)

The sin – attempted homosexual rape – is itself a multiple offence, involving (1) forbidden sex, (2) violence and (3) a breach of the strict code of hospitality in the ancient Near East (it is significant that Lot, when he confronts the crowd, speaks only of this, the most minor of the offences: "Don't do anything to these men, for they have come under the protection of my roof"). Again there is a threefold emphasis in the way the text speaks about those involved. They were: (1) all the men, (2) from every part of the city, (3) both young and old. The Torah is telling us that there were not "fifty" or "ten" innocent people in the town – the numbers cited by Abraham and agreed to by God. There was not even one.

So again we ask: why did God invite Abraham's challenge?

The answer, I believe, is that the Torah is intimating a profound truth, not about a human challenge to God, but the opposite: God's challenge to humanity.

God wants Abraham and his descendants to be agents of justice. *For justice to be done and seen to be done, both sides must be heard.* There must be not only an advocate for the prosecution but also for the defence.

So deep does this principle go in Jewish law, that it contains the extraordinary proviso that if, in a capital case, the judges are unanimous in finding the plaintiff guilty, *the case is dismissed.*[2] Since no argument has been heard in defence or mitigation of the accused, the presumption is that justice has not been seen to be done.[3]

That is what God wants of Abraham: to be the defence attorney for the people of Sodom; to argue their case; to be the voice of the other side. And that is precisely what Abraham does. If God invites His own verdict to be challenged in this way, how much more so does He expect the verdict of a human court to be challenged.

Justice is a process, not just a product. It is not enough for the court to be right. It must hear both sides of the argument. Ultimately, this is what the book of Job is about. Job does not insist on being found innocent. But he does insist on being heard.

Justice, as the philosopher Stuart Hampshire has argued, always involves conflict.[4] There is always more than one point of view. That is why a court case is called a "hearing." It must adhere to the rule of *audi alteram partem* ("Hear the other side"). Justice involves conversation, dialogue, argument. It requires the ability to see things from more than one perspective. Justice, even divine justice, can only be seen to be done if there is a counsel for the defence. That is what God empowers Abraham and subsequent prophets to be.

If this is so, then the implication is truly extraordinary. God needs humanity to become His partner in the administration of justice. He needs to hear a dissenting voice. No judge, however omniscient and

2. *Sanhedrin* 17a; Maimonides, Hilkhot Sanhedrin 9:1.
3. See the comments of Maharatz Chajes to *Sanhedrin* 17a.
4. Stuart Hampshire, *Justice is Conflict* (London: Duckworth, 1999).

infallible, can execute justice in the absence of counterargument. That is why Judaism – the religion for which justice is central – is a religion of argument and debate, for the sake of heaven, even if it involves argument with heaven itself. And it began with Abraham, the man empowered by God to argue with God so that justice might be seen to be done.

The Ambivalent Jew

The Torah does not have a word for ambivalence – the nearest is Elijah's question to the Baal-worshipping Israelites: "How long will you waver between two opinions?" (1 Kings 18:21). It does, however, have a tune for it. This is the rare note known as the *shalshelet*.

The *shalshelet* is an unusual note, going up and down, up and down, as if unable to move forward to the next note. The sixteenth-century commentator Rabbi Joseph ibn Caspi[1] best defined what it was meant to convey: namely, a psychological state of uncertainty and indecision. The graphic notation of the *shalshelet* itself looks like a streak of lightning, a "zigzag movement" (*tenua me'uvetet*), a mark that goes repeatedly backwards and forwards. It conveys frozen motion – what Hamlet called "the native hue of resolution sicklied o'er by the pale cast of thought"[2] – in which the agent is torn by inner conflict. The *shalshelet* is the music of ambivalence.

The rare notation appears three times in Genesis, in each case

---

1. In his commentary to *Bereshit* 19:16.
2. Shakespeare, *Hamlet*, act III, Sc. 1

signifying an existential crisis.[3] The individual concerned is called upon to make a choice, one on which his whole future will depend – but finds that he cannot. He is torn between two alternatives, both of which exercise a powerful sway. He must resolve the dilemma one way or another, but either choice will involve letting go of intensely felt temptations or deeply held aspirations. These are moments of high psychological drama.

One instance occurs in Genesis 24:12. Abraham has sent his servant (not identified in the text, but taken by the commentators to be Eliezer) to find a wife for his son Isaac in the city of Haran. Arriving at the town's well, Eliezer proposes a test: the woman who comes to draw water, offers some to the traveller, and in addition gives water to his camels, will be the one chosen by God for his master's son. Over the "and he said" introducing his request of God that this test should succeed, the masoretic tradition has placed a *shalshelet*.

The commentators identify multiple sources of ambivalence at this point. First are doubts about the permissibility of the test – Jewish law forbids relying on "omens," and Eliezer may have felt that his test was dangerously close to pagan practice[4] (the Ran to *Hullin* 95b, however, states that Eliezer's conduct was legitimate; he sought not an omen but a sign of the woman's character). Ibn Caspi suggests that Eliezer was unsure as to whether a single test like this was sufficient grounds on which to base so fateful a decision as the choice of a marriage partner for Isaac. The Midrash, however, offers the most insightful explanation: Eliezer had mixed feelings not about the test, but about the mission itself. Until that point, says the Midrash, he had been "sitting and weighing whether his own daughter was suitable for Isaac."[5] He had hoped, in other words, that one way or another, Abraham's estate would pass to him.

There are two cues that led the Midrash to this hypothesis. The first is that when Abraham first spoke to God about his childlessness, he said: "O Sovereign Lord, what can You give me since I remain childless

3. It appears a fourth time in Leviticus 8:23, where its significance is less apparent, and beyond the scope of this essay.
4. *Devarim* 18:10, *Ḥullin* 95b.
5. *Bereshit Raba* 59:9.

and the one who will inherit my estate is Eliezer of Damascus" (15:2). Eliezer, at that time, was Abraham's putative heir.

The second is that when Abraham charges his servant with the mission to find a wife for his son, Eliezer replies, "Perhaps [*ulai*] the woman will not be willing to come back with me to this land" (24:5). As Ibn Ezra notes, the word *ulai* is not neutral.[6] It signifies an emotional involvement in the outcome: one wishes for the eventuality to either come to pass or not come to pass. Eliezer's "perhaps" may have been an unconscious expression of the fact that, with half his mind, he wanted the mission to fail. This would have once again placed him or his daughter in a position to be Abraham's heir. It was therefore with profoundly mixed feelings that he prayed for the woman who would be God's choice of Isaac's wife to appear.

More dramatic still is the case of Joseph. Child of a shepherd, Jacob, an almost youngest son, hated by his brothers and sold by them into slavery, he finds himself in Egypt as head of household to one of its prominent citizens, Potiphar. Left alone with his master's wife, he finds himself propositioned by her: "Now Joseph was beautiful of form and fair to look upon. And it came to pass that his master's wife cast her eyes upon Joseph and she said: 'Lie with me'" (39:6–7). The text continues: "But he refused..." (39:8). Over this verb, tradition has placed a *shalshelet*.

We can imagine the conflict in Joseph's mind at that moment. On the one hand, his entire moral sense said No. It would be a betrayal of everything his family stood for: their ethic of sexual propriety and their strong sense of identity as children of the covenant. It would also be, as Joseph himself says, a betrayal of Potiphar himself:

> With me in charge, my master does not concern himself with anything in the house; he has entrusted everything he has to my care. No one is greater in this house than I. My master has withheld nothing from me but you, because you are his wife. How then could I do such a wicked thing and sin against God? (39:8–9)

And yet, the temptation must have been intense. He was in an urban

6. Commentary to *Tehillim* 116:16.

civilisation of a kind he had not seen before. It was his first experience of "bright lights, big city." He was far from home. No one could see him. After all the hostility he had suffered in his childhood, being propositioned by Potiphar's wife must have been flattering as well as seductive. It was a decisive moment. A slave, with no realistic hope of rescue – was he to become an Egyptian, with all the sexual laissez faire that implied? Or would he remain faithful to his past, his conscience, his identity?

The Talmud gives a graphic description of his inner torment:

> The image of his father appeared to him in the window and said, "Joseph, your brothers' names are destined to be inscribed on the stones of the [high priest's] breastplate, and you will be among them. Do you want your name to be erased? Do you want to be called an adulterer?"[7]

The *shalshelet* is an elegant commentary to Joseph's *crise de conscience*. In the end, Joseph refuses, but not without deep inner struggle.

Which brings us to *Parashat Vayera*, the first appearance of the *shalshelet* in the Torah. Here the conflict is explicit. Two of the angels who had visited Abraham now come to Lot in Sodom. They warn him that the city and its inhabitants are about to be destroyed. He and his family must leave immediately. But Lot delays:

> The two men said to Lot, "Do you have anyone else here – sons-in-law, sons or daughters, or anyone else in the city who belongs to you? Get them out of here, for we are going to destroy this place. The outcry to the Lord against its people is so great that God has sent us to destroy it."
>
> So Lot went out and spoke to his sons-in-law, who married his daughters. He said, "Hurry and get out of this place, because the Lord is about to destroy the city!"
>
> But his sons-in-law thought he was joking. With the coming of dawn, the angels urged Lot, saying, "Hurry! Take your wife and your two daughters who are here, or you will be swept away

7. *Sotah* 36b.

when the city is punished." When he hesitated, the men grasped his hand and the hands of his wife and of his two daughters and led them safely out of the city, for the Lord was merciful to them. (19:12–16)

Over "he hesitated" is a *shalshelet*.

Lot's hesitation goes to the core of his identity. Earlier, when he and Abraham had agreed to separate to end the quarrel between their herdsmen, "Lot looked up and saw that the whole plain of the Jordan was well watered, like the garden of the Lord, like the land of Egypt, toward Zoar…So Lot chose for himself the whole plain of the Jordan and set out toward the east" (13:10–11). He chose to make his home in Sodom, despite the fact that, as the Torah notes at that point, its inhabitants "were wicked and were sinning greatly against the Lord" (13:13).

Having chosen to put down roots in the Jordan valley and the cities of the plain, Lot no longer sees himself, as did Abraham, as "a stranger and temporary resident" (23:4). On the contrary, Lot and his family become profoundly assimilated. His daughters marry local men; Lot rises to public position. The sages interpret the phrase at the beginning of the chapter, "Lot was sitting in the gateway of the city" (19:1), as meaning "he had just been appointed as a judge" – the gate of the city being the place where, in Abrahamic times, the judges and elders sat to resolve disputes.[8] Sodom is where Lot sees himself as belonging – so much so that the visitors have to drag him away physically.

Lot's sense of belonging, however, is either naiveté or self-deception. The text makes this clear at three points. The first is the attempted sexual assault on Lot's visitors (19:4–5). Evidently the people of Sodom do not take kindly to strangers. This is the first hint that perhaps Lot is also, in their eyes, a stranger. In fact, he is. The Torah, in its second indication, is brutally explicit:

"Get out of our way," they replied [to Lot, when he begged them to respect his visitors]. Then they said, "This fellow came here

8. Rashi to *Bereshit* 19: 1; *Bereshit Raba* 50: 3.

as an alien, and now he wants to play the judge! We'll treat you worse than them." (19:7–9)

The third comes when he tells his daughters' husbands that they must escape because the city is about to be destroyed, and "his sons-in-law thought he was joking." Lot's elaborate new identity is about to come crashing down about him – not only because of the impending destruction but because he has discovered in successive blows that he has not been accepted in this place. Sodom hates strangers, they still consider Lot "an alien" and his sons-in-law regard him as a fool.

Yet despite this, he hesitates. He has invested too much of himself into the project of making his home among the people of the plain. He is a prime example of what Leon Festinger called cognitive dissonance.[9] According to Festinger, the need to avoid dissonance and the unbearable tension it creates, is fundamental to human beings. It is this tension that Lot cannot resolve – and which is signalled by the *shalshelet* over "he hesitated." This was a moment when he faced the ultimate existential question: "Who am I?" Having tried so hard to become one of them, he finds it almost impossible to tear himself away.

Festinger's theory also explains the behaviour of Lot's wife who "looked back [against the explicit instruction of the angels] and was turned into a pillar of salt" (19:36). Festinger called this syndrome "post-decision dissonance." He predicted that the more important the issue, the longer the person delays a decision and the harder it is to reverse, the more he or she will agonize over whether they have made the right choice. They have second thoughts; they need reassurance; they "look back."

The *shalshelet* over Lot's hesitation is no mere detail of the biblical text. It is, in a real sense, the story of the modern Jew. Entering mainstream society for the first time, and yet still encountering overt or covert anti-Semitism, many nineteenth-century European Jews became ambivalent about their identity. They tried to hide it and to assimilate. They became secular Marranos. It did not work. The more they strove

---

9. Leon Festinger, Henry W. Riecken and Stanley Schachter, *When Prophecy Fails* (New York: Harper & Row, 1956); Leon Festinger, *A Theory of Cognitive Dissonance*, Evanston, IL., Row, Peterson, 1957).

to be like everyone else, the more conspicuous they were, and the stronger anti-Semitism grew. They themselves lost much in the process – not only their Jewish heritage itself, but also the simple capacity to know and take pride in who they were. Tragically, the confusion and emotional investment was so deep that many repeated the hesitancy of Lot: many Jews in Germany and Austria in the 1930s refused to leave because they would not or could not believe the evidence around them that Hitler was serious in his threats to destroy the Jews.

The lives of Lot and Abraham exemplify for all time the contrast between ambivalence and the security that comes from knowing who one is and why. Lot, who tried to become someone else, found himself regarded by his neighbours as an alien, an arriviste, an interloper, a parvenu. To his own sons-in-law he was a "joker." Abraham lived a different kind of life. He fought a war on behalf of his neighbours. He prayed for them. But he lived apart, true to his faith, his mission and his covenant with God. Yet even as he called himself a "stranger and sojourner" (23:4), the Hittites saw him as "a prince of God in our midst" (23:6). That equation has not changed. Non-Jews respect Jews who respect Judaism. They are embarrassed by Jews who are embarrassed by Judaism. Never be ambivalent about who and what you are.

The Miracle of a Child

There is a mystery at the heart of Jewish existence, engraved into the first syllables of our recorded time. The opening words of God to Abraham were: "Go out from your land, your birthplace, and your father's house... And I will make you a great nation..." (12:1–2). In the next chapter there is another promise: "I will make your children like the dust of the earth, so that if anyone could count the dust of the earth, so shall your offspring be counted" (13:14–16). And then, two chapters later, comes a third: "God took him outside and said, 'Look at the heavens and count the stars – if indeed you can count them.' Then He said to him, 'So shall your children be'" (15:5). Finally, the fourth: "Your name will be Abraham, for I have made you a father of many nations" (17:15). Four escalating promises: Abraham would be the father of a great nation, as many as the dust of the earth and the stars of the sky. He would be the father not of one nation but of many.

The reality, though, was different. Early in the story, Abraham became "very wealthy in livestock and in silver and gold" (13:2). He had all he could desire except one thing – a child. Then God appeared to Abraham and said, "Your reward will be very great."

Until that point, Abraham had been silent. Now, something

within him breaks, and he asks: "O Lord God, what will You give me if I remain childless?" (15:2). The first recorded words of Abraham to God are a plea for there to be future generations. The first Jew feared he would be the last.

Then a child is born. Sarah gives Abraham her handmaid Hagar, hoping that she will give him a child. She gives birth to a son whose name is Ishmael, meaning "God has heard." Abraham's prayer has been answered, or so we think. But in the next chapter, that hope is destroyed. Yes, says God, Ishmael will be blessed. He will be the father of twelve princes and a great nation. But he is not the child of Jewish destiny, and one day Abraham will have to part from him.

This pains Abraham deeply. He pleads: "If only Ishmael might live under Your blessing"(17:18). Later, when Sarah drives Ishmael away, we read that "This distressed Abraham greatly on account of his son" (21:11). Nonetheless, the decree remains. The promised child must be Sarah's child.

Finally, the birth of this child is announced. Both Abraham and Sarah laugh. How can it be? They are old. Sarah is postmenopausal. Yet against possibility, the son is born. His name is Isaac, meaning "laughter":

> Sarah said, "God has brought me laughter, and everyone who hears about this will laugh with me." And she added, "Who would have said to Abraham that Sarah would nurse children? Yet I have borne him a son in his old age." (20:6–7)

The story seems to reach a happy ending. After all the promises and prayers, Abraham and Sarah at last have a child. Then come the words which, in all the intervening centuries, have not lost their power to shock:

> After these things, God tested Abraham. He said to him, "Abraham!"
>
> "Here I am," he replied.
>
> Then God said, "Take your son, your only son, Isaac, whom you love, and go to the land of Moriah. Sacrifice him there as a burnt offering on one of the mountains that I will show you." (22:1–2)

Abraham takes his son, travels for three days, climbs the mountain, prepares the wood, ties his son, takes the knife and raises his hand. Then a voice is heard from heaven: "Do not lay a hand on the boy" (22:12). The trial is over. Isaac lives.

Why all the promises and disappointments? Why the hope so often raised, so often unfulfilled? Why delay? Why Ishmael? Why the binding? Why put Abraham and Sarah through the agony of thinking that the son for whom they have waited for so long is about to die?

Many answers have been offered over the generations, but one transcends all others: We cherish what we wait for and what we most risk losing. Life is full of wonders. The birth of a child is a miracle. Yet, precisely because these things are natural, we take them for granted, forgetting that nature has an architect, and history an author.

Judaism is a sustained discipline in not taking life for granted. We were the people born in slavery so that we would value freedom. We were the nation always small, so that we would know that strength does not lie in numbers but in the faith that begets courage. Our ancestors walked through the valley of the shadow of death, so that we could never forget the sanctity of life.

Throughout history, Jews were called on to treasure children. Our entire value system is built on it. Our citadels are schools, our passion, education, and our greatest heroes, teachers. The *seder* service on Passover opens with questions asked by a child. On the first day of the New Year, we read not about the creation of the universe but about the birth of a child – Isaac to Sarah, Samuel to Hannah. Ours is a supremely child-centred faith.

That is why, at the dawn of Jewish time, God put Abraham and Sarah through these trials – the long wait, the unmet hope, the binding itself – so that neither they nor their descendants would ever take children for granted. Every child is a miracle. Being a parent is the closest we get to God – bringing life into being through an act of love.

Even today, when too many children live in poverty and illiteracy, dying for lack of medical attention because those who rule nations prefer weapons to welfare, hostage-taking to hospital-building, fighting the battles of the past rather than shaping a safe future, it is a lesson the world has not yet learned. For the sake of humanity it must, for the tragedy is vast and the hour is late.

Ḥayei Sara
חיי-שרה

Ḥayei Sara contains three narratives: the death of Sarah and Abraham's purchase of a burial plot for her, the first part of the Holy Land to be owned by the people of the covenant; the search for a wife for Isaac, the first Jewish child; and the last period of Abraham's life, and his death.

In the first of the following essays we explore the continuing significance of the first two of these stories to the Jewish present. In the second we look at Isaac's evening meditation, which the sages took as the model for *minḥa*, the afternoon prayer. In the third we analyze the halakhic implications of the way a wife was chosen for Isaac, by Abraham and his servant. Surprisingly, this was taken by the rabbis to be an exception rather than a general rule. In the fourth we look at a remarkable series of midrashim about Abraham's second marriage, after the death of Sarah, and their implications for relations between Judaism and Islam.

Land and Children

Parashat Ḥayei Sara focuses on two episodes, both narrated at length and in intricate detail. The first deals with Abraham's purchase of a field with a cave as a burial place for Sarah; the second with the mission to find a wife for his son Isaac. The juxtaposition of these two events goes beyond happenstance. The Torah does not narrate them at length simply because they happened. Torah means "teaching." It tells us what happened only when events that occurred *then* have a bearing on what we need to know *now*. The focus on these two issues thus requires closer attention.

Abraham, the first bearer of the covenant, receives two promises – both stated five times. The first is of a land. Time and again he is told, by God, that the land to which he has travelled – Canaan – will one day be his:

> Then the Lord appeared to Abram and said, "To your offspring I will give this land." So he built an altar there to the Lord who had appeared to him. (12:7)

> The Lord said to Abram after Lot had parted from him, "Lift up

your eyes from where you are and look north, south, east and west. All the land that you see, I will give you and your offspring for ever…Go, walk through the length and breadth of the land, for I am giving it to you." (13:14–17)

Then He said to him, "I am the Lord, who brought you out of Ur of the Chaldees to give you this land to take possession of it." (15:7)

On that day the Lord made a covenant with Abram and said, "To your descendants I give this land, from the river of Egypt to the great river, the Euphrates – the land of the Kenites, Kenizzites, Kadmonites, Hittites, Perizzites, Rephaites, Amorites, Canaanites, Girgashites and Jebusites." (15:18–21)

I will establish My covenant as an everlasting covenant between Me and you and your descendants after you for the generations to come, to be your God and the God of your descendants after you. The whole land of Canaan, where you are now an alien, I will give you as an everlasting possession to you and to your descendants after you; and I will be their God. (17:7–8)

The second was the promise of children, also stated five times:

I will make you into a great nation and I will bless you; I will make your name great and you will be a blessing. (12:2)

I will make your offspring like the dust of the earth, so that if anyone could count the dust, then your offspring could be counted. (13:16)

He took him outside and said, "Look up at the heavens and count the stars – if indeed you can count them." Then He said to him, "So shall your offspring be." (15: 5)

As for Me, this is My covenant with you: You will be the father of many nations. No longer will you be called Abram; your name will be Abraham, for I have made you a father of many nations. (17:4–5)

I will surely bless you and make your descendants as numerous as the stars of the sky and as the sand on the seashore. (22:17)

These are remarkable promises. The land in its length and breadth will be Abraham's and his children's as "an everlasting possession." Abraham will have as many children as the dust of the earth, the stars of the sky, and the sand on the seashore. He will be the father, not of one nation, but of many. What, though, is the reality at the time Sarah dies? Abraham owns no land and has only one son (he had another, Ishmael, but was told that he would not be the bearer of the covenant).

Within this context, the significance of the two central episodes of Ḥayei Sara become clear. First, Abraham undergoes a lengthy bargaining process with the Hittites to buy a field with a cave in which to bury Sarah. It is a tense, even humiliating, encounter. The Hittites say one thing and mean another. As a group they say, "Sir, listen to us. You are a prince of God in our midst. Bury your dead in the choicest of our tombs" (23:6). Ephron, the owner of the field Abraham wants to buy, says: "Listen to me, I give you the field, and I give you the cave that is in it. I give it to you in the presence of my people. Bury your dead" (23:11).

As the narrative makes clear, this elaborate generosity is a façade for some extremely hard bargaining. Abraham knows he is "an alien and sojourner amongst you" (23:4), meaning, among other things, that he has no right to own land. That is the force of their reply which, stripped of its overlay of courtesy, means: "Use one of our burial sites. You may not acquire your own."

Abraham is not deterred. He insists that he wants to buy his own. Ephron's reply – "It is yours. I give it to you" – is in fact the prelude to a demand for a highly inflated price: four hundred silver shekels. Finally, however, Abraham fulfils his wish. The transfer of ownership is recorded in precise legal prose (23:17–20) to signal that, at last, Abraham owns part of the land. It is a small part: one field and a cave. A burial place, bought at great expense. That is as much of the divine promise of the land as Abraham will see in his lifetime.

The next section tells of Abraham's concern that Isaac should have a wife. He is – we must assume – at least thirty-seven years old (his age at Sarah's death) and still unmarried. Abraham has a child but no grandchild – no posterity. As with the purchase of the cave, so here: acquiring a daughter-in-law will take much money and hard negotiation.

The servant, on arriving in the vicinity of Abraham's family, prays for God's help to find the right girl. In answer, he immediately encounters Rebecca. Securing her release from her family is, however, another matter. The servant brings out gold, silver, and clothing for the girl. He gives her brother and mother costly gifts. The family have a celebratory meal. But when the servant wants to leave, brother and mother say, "Let the girl stay with us for another year or ten [months]" (24:55). Laban, Rebecca's brother, plays a role not unlike that of Ephron: the show of generosity conceals a tough, even exploitative, determination to make a profitable deal. Eventually patience pays off. Rebecca leaves. Isaac marries her. The covenant will continue.

These are, then, no minor episodes. They tell a difficult story. Yes, Abraham will have a land. He will have countless children. But these things will not happen soon, or suddenly, or easily. Nor will they occur without human effort. To the contrary, only the most focused willpower and determination will bring them about. The divine promise is not what it first seemed: a statement that God will act. It is in fact a request, an invitation from God to Abraham and his children that *they* should act. God will help them. The outcome will be what God said it would be. But not without total commitment from Abraham's family against what will sometimes seem to be insuperable obstacles.

A land: Israel. And children: Jewish continuity. The astonishing fact is that today, four thousand years later, they remain the dominant concerns of Jews throughout the world – the safety and security of Israel as the Jewish home, and the future of the Jewish people. Abraham's hopes and fears are ours.

Now as then, the divine promise does not mean that we can leave the future to God. That idea has no place in the imaginative world of the first book of the Torah. On the contrary: the covenant is God's challenge to us, not ours to God. The meaning of the events of *Ḥayei Sara* is that Abraham realised that God was depending on him. Faith does not mean passivity. It means the courage to act and never to be deterred. The future will happen, but it is we – inspired, empowered, given strength by the promise – who must bring it about.

Prayer and Conversation

The first meeting between Isaac and his future wife is captured for us by the Torah in a fascinating scene. Abraham has sent his servant to find a wife for Isaac. He does so, and brings back Rebecca. As they arrive from Haran, Isaac is coming towards them, for he had "gone out into the field towards evening to meditate" (24:63). The Talmud identifies this moment as having historic and halakhic implications: Isaac's "meditation" was a prayer; "Towards evening" means afternoon. If Isaac's behaviour had normative implications, it meant that he instituted *minḥa*, the afternoon prayer.

This identification is part of a wide-ranging dispute recorded in the Talmud, regarding the origin of the three daily prayers. Some sages held that they were a substitute for the sacrifices that had taken place in the Temple. Others hold that their sources go further back into Israel's past, to the biblical patriarchs and matriarchs:

> It has been stated: R. Yose son of R. Hanina said: the prayers were instituted by the patriarchs. R. Joshua son of Levi said: the prayers were instituted to replace the daily sacrifices.
>
> It has been taught in accordance with R. Yose son of

R. Hanina, and it has been taught in accordance with R. Joshua son of Levi. It has been taught in accordance with R. Yose son of R. Hanina: Abraham instituted the morning prayer, as it says: *And Abraham got up early in the morning to the place where he had stood* (19:27), and "standing" means prayer, as it says then *Pinchas stood up and prayed* (Psalms, 106:30).

Isaac instituted the afternoon prayer, as it says, and *Isaac went out to meditate in the field towards evening* (24:63), and "meditation" means prayer, as it says: *A prayer of the afflicted when he faints and pours out his meditation before the Lord* (Psalms 102:1).

Jacob instituted the evening prayer, as its says: *And he encountered (vayifga) a place* (28:11), and *pegia* means prayer, as it says: *Therefore do not pray for this people nor lift up prayer or cry for them, nor make intercession (tifga) to Me* (Jeremiah 7:16).

It has been taught in accordance with R. Yehoshua son of Levi: why did they say that the morning prayer could be said until midday? Because the regular morning sacrifice could be brought until midday. R. Yehuda, however, says that it may be said up to the fourth hour because the regular morning sacrifice may be brought until the fourth hour.

And why did they say that the afternoon prayer can be said until the evening? Because the regular afternoon offering could be brought until the evening. R. Yehuda, however, says that it can be said only up to the middle of the afternoon, because the afternoon offering could only be brought up to the middle of the afternoon.

And why did they say that for the evening prayer there is no limit? Because the limbs and fat that were not consumed on the altar by the evening could be brought during the whole of the night. (*Berakhot* 26b)

More is at stake in this disagreement than halakha and history. At issue is the very nature of prayer itself.

There were two distinct spiritual traditions in biblical Judaism. On the one hand were the patriarchs and prophets. They were, if one can put it this way, ordinary people with extraordinary gifts – above all,

the gift of being able to speak and listen to the voice of God. The patriarchs were shepherds. So too was Moses. They wore no robes of office.
They lived far from the cities of their time. Alone – away from the noise
of urban civilization – they heard and heeded God's word. They prayed
as the situation demanded. No two prayers were the same. They spoke
from the depths of their being to the One who is the depth of all Being.
That is patriarchal and prophetic prayer.

There was another type of religious personality: the priest. He *did*
have special robes of office. He was a "holy man," set apart from others
(this is the root meaning of *kadosh*, "holy," in Judaism). For him, *avoda*,
divine "service," primarily meant the offerings. Everything about the sacrifices was subject to detailed prescriptive rules. The *temidim*, or regular
sacrifices, had their own time (morning and afternoon), their own place
(the Sanctuary, later the Temple), and their own precisely defined ritual,
never varying, always the same. Spontaneity, essential to the prophet, is
disastrous for the priest. Aaron's two sons, Nadav and Avihu, seized by
the mood of the moment, made their own offering at the inauguration
of the sanctuary, and died as a result (Leviticus 10:1–2).

If the prophet represents the "now," the immediate responsiveness
of religious life, the priest represents eternity. They speak to different
aspects of the soul, and different needs of society. Without spontaneity, the spirit withers; without structure, it lapses into chaos. Without
prophets, the faith of Israel would have grown old; without priests, it
would never have been able to become the code of a nation.

The question debated between Rabbi Yose son of Rabbi Hanina
and Rabbi Yehoshua son of Levi was therefore: to which of these traditions does prayer belong? To the patriarchs or the priests? To supplica-
tion or to sacrifice? Is Jewish prayer the personal dialogue of the soul
or the collective worship of the nation?

In practice, it is both. One of the most remarkable and little
noted facts about Judaism is that to this day we maintain both aspects,
saying the *Amida* (standing prayer) twice: once privately and silently
as individuals, and then a second time publicly and collectively as a
community (the "reader's repetition"). The silent prayer belongs to the
world of Abraham, Isaac and Jacob, Rachel and Hannah – it is private,
personal and can include individualized requests. The reader's repetition

follows the logic of the sacrifices – it is public, collective and includes no personal requests. That is also why there is no repetition in the case of *ma'ariv*, the evening service: for there was no night-time sacrifice in the Temple. We thus preserve both the patriarchal and priestly traditions.

Linking the prayers to the patriarchs not only deepens their history and highlights the individual responsiveness that lies at their core, but also points to the differences between the three daily prayers. The divergent personalities and histories of the patriarchs give a unique character to each of the prayers.

My predecessor as Chief Rabbi, the late Lord Jacobovits of blessed memory, used to point out that the position of the sun at the various stages of the day mirrored that of the patriarchs themselves. In the morning, the sun is in the east – and Abraham began his life in the east, in Ur of the Chaldees, namely Mesopotamia. In the early afternoon, the sun is overhead in the middle of the sky – reminding us of Isaac who spent his entire life within the land of Canaan, later to become Israel. In the evening the sun is in the west, as was Jacob who ended his life in the west, in exile in Egypt.

The verbs associated with each of the patriarch's prayers are also different. Abraham "rises early in the morning" and "stands." When it comes to prayer, he is the initiator. Acknowledging that he is "but dust and ashes" (18:27), he nonetheless utters the most audacious prayer of all time: "Shall the Judge of all the earth not do justice?" (18:25). That is prayer as *Amida*, as standing up in the presence of God.

Jacob, by contrast, "encounters." It is not he who seeks God on his flight from home, but God who seeks him.[1] The phrase the Torah uses just before Jacob has his vision of the angelic ladder is *vayifga baMakom*, which in rabbinic Hebrew can be read as "He bumped into God." There are spiritual experiences we have when we are least expecting them – when we are alone, afraid, thinking of something else altogether. That was Jacob's vision of prayer. Not everything in the life of the spirit is under our control. The great transformative experiences – love, a sudden sense of beauty, an upsurge of happiness – happen unpredictably, leaving us, in Wordsworth's famous phrase, "surprised by joy." The glory

---

1.   See also "Encountering God" and "The Ladder of Prayer," pp. 179–189.

of Jacob's epiphany is that it happened at night, in the midst of fear and flight. That is prayer as *pegia*.

There is a third kind of prayer. Isaac is "meditating" in the field – but the word *siha* means not only meditation but also, and primarily, conversation. When the Talmud says, in the context of Isaac, *ein siha ela tefilla*, we could translate this phrase as "conversation is a form of prayer" – and in a profound sense, it is so.

Prayer is a conversation between heaven and earth. But conversation is also a prayer – for in true conversation, I open myself up to the reality of another person. I enter his or her world. I begin to see things from a perspective not my own. In the touch of two selves, both are changed.

How appropriate, therefore, is the fact that Isaac is seen praying immediately prior to his first encounter with the woman who was to become his wife. Abraham and Jacob are alone when they pray. Isaac is just about to meet the woman with whom he will share his life. For him, prayer is the prelude to a human relationship. Our openness to God shapes and is shaped by our openness to other people. Love of God is, or should be, interwoven with our love for human beings. That surely is the meaning of the book known as *Shir HaShirim*, "The Song of Songs," a poem of love for God cast in the metaphor of a dialogue between two human lovers.

A genuine human conversation is a preparation for, and a microcosmic version of, the act of prayer. For in prayer I attend to the presence of God, listening as well as speaking, opening myself up to a reality other and infinitely vaster than my own, and I become a different person as a result. Prayer is not monologue but dialogue.

Before every *Amida* we say, "O God open my lips, and my mouth shall declare Your praise." In a real sense, in prayer we do not simply speak; we are also spoken. God, and the traditions of Jewish faith, speak through us. The very words we use are not our own, but those of thousands of years of our people's history, distilling the response to innumerable encounters with God. Prayer is like a Bluetooth connection and while it lasts we become a channel through which flows the energy of the universe and Jewish history – the force of creation and the drive towards redemption. While it lasts, we make those energies our own. That is prayer as *siha*.

Thus there are three modes of spirituality and we experience each in the course of a single day. There is the human quest (Abraham, morning prayer), the divine encounter (Jacob, evening prayer), and the dialogue (Isaac, afternoon prayer). That is how three events in the life of the patriarchs – Abraham's early morning rise, Isaac's afternoon meditation in a field, and Jacob's vision at night – became not isolated events in the past but permanent possibilities for those who follow in their footsteps, guided by their precedent, lifted by their example, enlarged by their spirit, summoned to their heights.

Parental Authority and the Choice of a
Marriage Partner

Genesis 24 presents us with the Torah's first detailed description of a marriage arrangement. Abraham instructs his servant to travel back to Aram-Naharaim, his family's home, and to return with a wife for Isaac. It is a striking passage. Isaac takes no part in the process. There is no indication that his father consulted him, that he gave his consent to the arrangement, or that his views were taken into account in any way. Only after Rebecca arrives do we hear of his reaction in a few brief words:

> Isaac conducted her into the tent and took her as his wife. So she became his wife, and he loved her and was consoled for the death of his mother. (24:67)

This is consistent with the general impression we have of Isaac as a figure in the shadow of Abraham, who does what his father does rather than strike out in any new direction of his own.

The Torah's next presentation of marriage is different. Esau and

Jacob each choose their own wives. Yet once again there is an emphasis on parental wishes. Of Esau we are told:

> When Esau was forty years old, he married Judith daughter of Be'eri the Hittite and Bosemat daughter of Elon the Hittite. This was a source of bitter grief to Isaac and Rebecca. (26:34–35)

Jacob, by contrast, "obeyed his father and mother" by going to Padan-Aram to find a wife from his mother's family (28:7).

These episodes – especially that of Isaac – raise the question of the role of parental authority in marriage. To what extent is Abraham's initiative in choosing, or getting his servant to choose, a wife for his son, normative? Does it constitute a precedent? Does a parent have a right, in Judaism, to determine who their child will marry? May a child choose a marriage partner against the wishes of a parent? In the case of conflict, whose view do we follow?

These issues were much debated in the Middle Ages, an era in which parental authority, as well as respect for age and tradition, were far stronger than they are now. Normally it was expected that a child would act in accordance with the will of his or her parents. Indeed, as late as 1680, Sir Robert Filmer, in his *Patriarcha*, argued for the divine right of kings on the basis of the absolute authority – even the power of life and death – of parents over children, and did so on the basis of biblical texts. Shakespeare presents the prevailing view succinctly in *A Midsummer Night's Dream*, when Egeus tries to force his daughter to marry the man of his choice: "As she is mine, I may dispose of her: / Which shall be either to this gentleman / Or to her death, according to our law" (act 1, scene 1).

Strikingly, though, the halakhists did not follow this line. Writing in the thirteenth century, Rabbi Solomon ibn Adret (Rashba, 1235–1310) argued that getting married is a positive commandment. As the wishes of God take precedence over those of human beings, parental wishes cannot override the desire of a child to marry and fulfil the mitzva. Since the child wants to do God's will, he is not bound to do his parent's will. What is more, he points out that the Talmud declares that "Forty days before a child is formed, a heavenly voice declares: the daughter of X to the son of Y."[1] In other words, marriages are made in heaven, and presumably the child is in a better position than his parents to recognise his soulmate.

The case of Isaac, Rashba argues, was unique. Isaac was a "perfect offering," a child of special sanctity; having been offered at the altar he was not allowed to leave the Land of Israel – in contrast to Abraham and Jacob, both of whom travelled to Egypt. Had this not been so, says Rashba, he would certainly have undertaken the journey himself to choose a wife.[2]

Rabbi Joseph Kolon (Maharik, 1420–1480), considering the same issue, refers to a responsum of Rabbenu Asher in which the author rules that a son is not bound to obey his father if he tells him not to speak to X, with whom the father is in dispute. The command to love your neighbour overrides the command to obey your parents. Since the love of husband and wife is a supreme example of love-of-neighbour, it too takes priority over a parent's wishes.[3]

There is a further consideration. Children are bound to revere and honour their parents and to do them service, specifically in matters that concern their welfare. The command to "honour your father and mother" does not, however, extend open-endedly to deferring to their wishes in matters that do not directly concern their welfare. The choice of a child's marriage partner directly involves the child's welfare and only indirectly that of the child's parents. So, says Kolon, it does not fall within the scope of "honour your father and mother."

Elaborating on this position, Rabbi Elijah Capsali gave the following ruling in a case where a father forbad his son to marry the woman whom "his soul desired":

> Though the command of filial honour and reverence is inexpressibly great…nonetheless it appears in my humble opinion that if the girl about whom you ask is a proper wife for the aforementioned Reuven – that is, there is in her or in her family no

---

1. *Moed Katan* 18b.
2. Rashba, *Teshuvot HaMeyuḥasot LehaRamban* (Warsaw, 1883), 272.
3. R. Joseph Kolon, Responsa (Warsaw: name of publisher, 1884), 164:3.

blemish – then the command of filial honour and reverence is irrelevant, and the son is not to abandon her so as to fulfil his father's command.

For it is nearly certain that this father virtually commands his son to violate the Torah... for we see in the Talmud that a man ought not to marry a woman who does not please him. So that when the father commands his son not to marry this woman, it is as though he commands him to violate the Torah; and it is well known that the son is not to obey his father in such cases...

Now, if we were to decide that the son is obliged to obey his parents and marry, though his heart is not in the match, we would cause the growth of hatred and strife in the home, which is not the way of our holy Torah – most certainly in this case, where he loves another. Indeed, we can cite in this situation: "Many waters cannot quench love, neither can the floods drown it" (Song of Songs 8:7). Were he to marry another whom he does not desire, his entire life would be painful and bitter.

Moreover we may also argue that the Torah obliges the son to filial honour and reverence only in matters that affect the parents' physical well-being and support... but in matters that do not affect the parent in these areas, we may say that the Torah does not oblige us to be obedient. Therefore, the son is not obliged by the rules of reverence and honour to accept his father's command in the matter of marriage. [4]

On the basis of these responsa, Rabbi Moses Isserles (Rema, 1520–1572) rules in *Yoreh Deah* 240:25 that "If the father objects to his son's marriage to the woman of his choice, the son is not obliged to listen to his father."

What we see from all these sources is that despite its immense emphasis on honouring parents, Jewish law also insists that parents make space for their children to make their own decisions in matters affecting their personal happiness. The rabbis extended to parents nothing like the absolute authority attributed to them by figures like Sir Robert Filmer.

4. Adapted from Gerald Blidstein, *Honour thy Father and Mother* (New York, Ktav), pp 85–94).

Abraham did not command his servant to find a wife for Isaac because he believed he had the right to make the choice, but because he knew that Isaac was not allowed to leave the land and make the journey himself.

There is great wisdom in this approach. The Jewish family is not authoritarian. It is based, rather, on mutual respect – the children's respect for those who have brought them into the world, and the parents' respect for the right of adult children to make their choices free of excessive parental interference.

In this respect, as in so many others, Jewish law is a reflex of Jewish theology, a set of rules that act out Judaism's deepest ideals. For what we find in the Torah is a profound sense of empowerment of human beings by God. "Walk before Me," says God to Abraham (17:1). God, in Judaism, does not represent what Theodor Adorno called "the authoritarian personality."[5] If he were, he would not have given humans freedom, and with it, responsibility.

God is seen, in the Torah, as a father, a parent. He speaks of "My child, My firstborn, Israel" (Exodus 4:22). But He is a parent who wants His children to experience freedom, to make their own choices, to be responsible, to grow. It is this fundamental idea that led the great halakhists, R. Solomon ibn Adret, R. Joseph Kolon and R. Elijah Capsali, to interpret the case of Isaac as an exception rather than the rule.

Nowadays we take the rights of children for granted, but it was not always so; indeed, outside Judaism it is a very recent phenomenon indeed. It is perhaps no coincidence that it was a great Jewish doctor in Poland before the Second World War, Janusz Korczak, who became the pioneer of what he called "the child's right to respect."

Korczak, famous throughout Poland because of his radio broadcasts and bestselling children's books, established a Jewish orphanage in Warsaw. It used revolutionary methods. Korczak empowered the children to develop their own newspaper, the first of its kind in Poland. He gave them responsibility for the conduct of the orphanage itself, getting them to form their own court, to which he himself could be summoned. So successful was it that Polish Catholics asked him to create a similar institution for their orphans, which he did.

5. T. W. Adorno, *The Authoritarian Personality* (New York: Harper, 1950).

Korczak was one of the first people to call for a charter of rights for children. He travelled to Palestine to share his ideas and methods with the Jewish community there. During the war, he and the orphanages were confined to the Warsaw ghetto. He was offered several chances to escape, but he declined them all, refusing to be parted from the children. Eventually he and they were taken to Treblinka in 1942, where they were all killed.[6] Only belatedly is his work receiving the attention it deserves, for he was an original and inspirational figure whose ideas were far ahead of their time.

Yet they belong to an ancient Jewish tradition, one of whose aspects we have explored in this essay. To be a Jewish parent is to make space for your child, as God makes space for us, His children.

6. On Korczak, see Betty Jean Lifton, *The King of Children: a Biography of Janusz Korczak* (New York: Farrar, Straus and Giroux, 1988); Mark Bernheim, *Father of the Orphans: The Story of Janusz Korczak* (New York: Dutton, 1989); Sandra Joseph (ed.), *Loving Every Child: Wisdom for Parents: The Words of Janusz Korczak* (Chapel Hill, NC: Algonquin Books, 2007).

On Judaism and Islam

The language of the Torah is, in Erich Auerbach's famous phrase, "fraught with background." Behind the events that are openly told are shadowy stories left for us to decipher. Hidden beneath the surface of *Parashat Ḥayei Sara*, for example, is another story, alluded to only in a series of hints. There are three clues in the text.

The first occurs when Abraham's servant is returning with the woman who is to become Isaac's wife. As Rebecca sees Isaac in the distance, we are told that he is "coming from the way of Be'er-laḥai-ro'i" (24:62) to meditate in the field. The placement is surprising. Thus far we have situated the patriarchal family at Beersheva, to which Abraham returns after the binding of Isaac, and Hebron, where Sarah dies and is buried. What is this third location, Be'er-laḥai-ro'i, and what is its significance?

The second is the extraordinary final stage of Abraham's life. For chapter after chapter we read of the love and faithfulness Abraham and Sarah had for one another. Together they embarked on a long journey to an unknown destination. Together, they stood against the idolatry of their time. Twice, Sarah saved Abraham's life by pretending to be his sister. They hoped and prayed for a child and endured the long years of childlessness until Isaac was born. Then Sarah's life draws to a close. She dies. Abraham mourns and weeps for her and buys a cave in which she is buried, and he is to be buried beside her. We then expect to read that Abraham lived out the rest of his years alone before being placed beside "Sarah his wife" (25:10) in the "Cave of Makhpelah" (25:9).

Unexpectedly, however, once Isaac is married, Abraham marries a woman named Keturah and has six children by her. We are told nothing else about this woman, and the significance of the episode is unclear. The Torah does not include mere incidental details. We have no idea, for example, what Abraham looked like. We do not even know the name of the servant he sent to find a wife for Isaac. Tradition tells us that it was Eliezer, but the Torah itself does not. What then is the significance of Abraham's second marriage and how is it related to the rest of the narrative?

The third clue to the hidden story is revealed in the Torah's description of Abraham's death:

> And Abraham expired, and died in a good old age, an old man, and full of years, and was gathered to his people. Isaac and Ishmael his sons buried him in the Cave of Makhpelah, in the field of Ephron the son of Zohar the Hittite, which is before Mamre, the field which Abraham purchased of the children of Het. There was Abraham buried, and Sarah his wife. (25:8–10)

Ishmael's presence at the funeral is surprising. After all, he had been sent away into the desert years before, when Isaac was young. Until now, we have assumed that the two half-brothers have lived in total isolation from one another. Yet the Torah places them together at the funeral without a word of explanation.

The sages pieced together these three puzzling details to form an enthralling story.

First, they point out that Be'er-laḥai-ro'i, the place from which Isaac was coming when Rebecca saw him, is mentioned once before in Genesis (16:14): It is the spot where Hagar, pregnant and fleeing from Sarah, encountered an angel who told her to return. It is indeed she who gives the place its name, meaning "the well of the Living One who sees me" (16:14). The midrash thus says that Isaac went to Be'er-laḥai-ro'i in search of Hagar. When Isaac heard that his father was seeking a wife for him, he said, "Shall I be married while my father lives alone? I will go and return Hagar to him."[1]

Hence the sages' answer to the second question: who was Keturah? She was, they said, none other than Hagar herself. It is not unusual for people in the Torah to have more than one name: Jethro, Moses's father-in-law, had seven. Hagar was called Keturah because "her acts gave forth fragrance like incense (*ketoret*)."[2] This indeed integrates Abraham's second marriage as an essential component of the narrative. Hagar did not end her days as an outcast. She returned, at Isaac's prompting and with Abraham's consent, to become the wife of her former master.

This also changes the painful story of the banishment of Ishmael. We know that Abraham did not want to send him away – Sarah's demand was "very grievous in Abraham's sight on account of his son" (21:11). Nonetheless, God told Abraham to listen to his wife. There is, however, an extraordinary midrash, in *Pirkei deRabbi Eliezer*, which tells of how Abraham twice visited his son. On the first occasion, Ishmael was not at home. His wife, not knowing Abraham's identity, refused the stranger bread and water. Ishmael, continues the midrash, divorced her and married a woman named Fatimah. This time, when Abraham visited, again not disclosing his identity, the woman gave him food and drink. The midrash then says "Abraham stood and prayed before the Holy One, blessed be He, and Ishmael's house became filled with all good things. When Ishmael returned, his wife told him about it, and Ishmael knew that his father still loved him."[3] Father and son were reconciled.

The name of Ishmael's second wife, Fatimah, is highly significant. In the Koran, Fatimah is the daughter of Mohammad. *Pirkei deRabbi Eliezer* is an eighth-century work, and it is here making an explicit, and positive, reference to Islam.

The hidden story of Ḥayei Sara has immense consequence for our time. Jews and Muslims both trace their descent from Abraham – Jews

1. *Bereshit Raba* 60:14.
2. *Bereshit Raba* 51:4.
3. *Pirkei deRabbi Eliezer* 30.

through Isaac, Muslims through Ishmael. The fact that both sons stood together at their father's funeral tells us that they too were reunited.

Beneath the surface of the narrative in *Ḥayei Sara*, the sages read the clues and pieced together a moving story of reconciliation between Abraham and Hagar on the one hand, Isaac and Ishmael on the other. Yes, there was conflict and separation; but that was the beginning, not the end. Between Judaism and Islam there can be friendship and mutual respect. Abraham loved both his sons, and was laid to rest by both. There is hope for the future in this story of the past.

Toledot
תולדות

Toledot tells the story of Isaac and Rebecca's twin sons, Jacob and Esau, who struggle in the womb and seem destined to clash throughout their lives and those of their descendants. It contains two great passages: the birth and childhood of the boys, and the scene in which Jacob, at Rebecca's behest, dresses in Esau's clothes and takes his blessing from their father Isaac, now blind. Between them is a narrative about Isaac and Rebecca going to Gerar because of famine, very similar to that told about Abraham and Sarah in Genesis 20.

The first of the following essays is about the close similarity between Isaac and Abraham in appearance and in other ways, which has a message about a contemporary question in medical ethics: the desirability or otherwise of eugenic cloning. The second is about the precise meaning of the revelation given to Rebecca about the twins and their destiny, before they are born. The third is about Isaac in the land of the Philistines, one of the first intimations of what would later be called anti-Semitism. The fourth is about the surprisingly sympathetic portrayal of Esau in the scene in which Jacob takes his blessing.

On Clones and Identity

Around the gaps, silences and seeming repetitions of the biblical text, midrash weaves its interpretations, enriching the written word with oral elaboration, giving the text new resonances of meaning. Often, to the untutored ear, midrash sounds fanciful, far removed from the plain sense of the verse. But once we have learned the language and sensibility of midrash, we begin to realise how deep are its spiritual and moral insights.

One example was prompted by the opening verse of *Parashat Toledot*:

> And these are the generations of Isaac, son of Abraham: Abraham begat Isaac. (25:19)

The problem is obvious. The first half of the sentence tells us that Isaac was the son of Abraham. Why then does the text repeat, "Abraham begat Isaac"? Looking at the apparent redundancy of the text in the context of the Abraham-Isaac narrative as a whole, the sages offered the following interpretation:

The cynics of the time were saying, "Sarah became pregnant through Avimelekh. See how many years she lived with Abraham without being able to have a child by him." What did the Holy One blessed be He do? He made Isaac's facial features exactly resemble those of Abraham, so that everyone had to admit that Abraham begat Isaac. This is what is meant by the words "Abraham begat Isaac" – there was clear evidence that Abraham was Isaac's father.[1]

This is an ingenious reading, taken in the context of the narrative as a whole. The opening of Genesis 21 speaks of the birth of Isaac to Sarah. Immediately prior to this, in Genesis 20, we are told that Sarah was taken into the harem of Avimelekh, king of Gerar. Hence the speculation of the sages that gossips were suggesting that Abraham was infertile; that Avimelekh was Isaac's father and that the conception took place during the time Sarah was in Avimelekh's harem. Hence the double emphasis of the verse: not only was Abraham Isaac's father *in fact*, but also everyone could see this because father and son looked exactly alike.

But there is a deeper point at stake. To understand it we need to turn to another midrash, this time on the opening verse of Genesis 24:

> And Abraham was old, well advanced in years: and the Lord had blessed Abraham in all things. (24:1)

Again there is a problem of an apparently superfluous phrase. If Abraham was old, why does the verse need to add that he was "well advanced in years"? The rabbis noticed something else as well: Abraham and Sarah are the first people in the Torah described as being old, despite the fact that many previously mentioned biblical characters lived to a much greater age. Putting these two facts together with the tradition that Abraham and Isaac looked identical, they arrived at the following interpretation:

> Until Abraham, people did not grow old. However [because

---

1.   Rashi to Bereshit 25:19, on the basis of *Bava Metzia* 87a.

Abraham and Isaac looked alike] people who saw Abraham said, "That is Isaac," and people who saw Isaac said, "That is Abraham." Abraham then prayed to grow old, and this is the meaning [of the phrase] "And Abraham was old." (*Sanhedrin* 103b)

The close physical resemblance between Abraham and Isaac refuted the charge of those who said that Abraham was not the real father, but it gave rise to an unexpected difficulty. Both father and son, identical in appearance, suffered a loss of individuality. Nor is this pure speculation – it is pointing to a subtle but important aspect of the story. Examine Genesis carefully, and we see that Isaac is the least individuated of the patriarchs. His life reads like a replay of his father's. Like Abraham, he is forced by famine to go to the land of the Philistines.[2] He too encounters Avimelekh. He too feels impelled to say that his wife is his sister. He re-digs the wells his father dug. Isaac seems to do little that is distinctively his own.

Sensitive to this, the rabbis told a profound psychological story. Parents are not their children. Children are not replicas of their parents. We are each unique and have a unique purpose. That is why Abraham prayed to God that there be some clear and recognizable difference between father and son.

There is, I believe, contemporary relevance to this midrash, especially in relation to a new medical technology: eugenic or reproductive cloning. Cloning – the method of nuclear cell transfer pioneered by Dr Ian Wilmut in the experiment that created Dolly the sheep in 1997 – raises profound issues of medical ethics, especially in relation to humans.

Cloning is not just another technology. It raises issues not posed by other forms of assisted reproduction such as artificial insemination or in vitro fertilisation. Nuclear cell transfer is a form of asexual reproduction. We do not know why it is that large, long-living creatures reproduce sexually. From an evolutionary point of view, asexual reproduction would have been much simpler. Yet none of the higher mammals

---

2. The land of the Philistines was part of what would later become the land of Israel. Unlike Abraham or Jacob, Isaac was not allowed to go to Egypt (see 26:2–3).

reproduce asexually.[3] Some biologists argue that this is because only by the unpredictable combination of genetic endowments of parents and grandparents, can a species generate the variety it needs to survive. The history of the human presence on earth is marked by a destruction of biodiversity on a massive scale. To take risks with our own genetic future would be irresponsible in the extreme.

There is another objection to cloning, namely the threat to the integrity of children so conceived. To be sure, genetically identical persons already exist in the case of identical twins. It is one thing, though, for this to happen, quite another to bring it about deliberately. Cloning represents an ethical danger in a way that naturally occurring phenomena do not. Identical twins cannot be brought into being so that one may serve as a substitute or replacement for the other. Cloning, however, can bring us to treat persons as means rather than as ends in themselves. It risks the commoditisation of human life.[4] It cannot but transform some of the most basic features of our humanity.

Every child born of the genetic mix between two parents is unpredictable, *like* yet *unlike* those who have brought it into the world. That mix of kinship and difference is an essential feature of human relationships. It is the basis of a key belief of Judaism, that each individual is unique, non-substitutable, and irreplaceable. In a famous mishna, the sages taught: "When a human being makes many coins in a single mint, they all come out the same. God makes every human being in the same image, His image, yet they all emerge different."[5]

The glory of creation is that unity in heaven creates diversity on earth. God wants every human life to be unique. As Harvard philosopher Hilary Putnam put it: "Every child has the right to be a complete

3. See Matt Ridley, *The Red Queen: Sex and the Evolution of Human Nature* (London: Penguin, 1994); David M. Buss, *The Evolution of Desire* (New York: Basic Books, 1994).

4. To be sure, this would not be applicable to all cases of cloning, most notably to situations in which this is the only way in which a couple can have a child. Under such circumstances, halakha might well permit such a procedure.

5. Mishna, *Sanhedrin* 4:5.

surprise to its parents" – which means the right to be no-one else's clone.[6] What would become of love if we knew that if we lost our beloved we could create a replica? What would happen to our sense of self if we discovered that we were manufactured to order?

The midrash about Abraham and Isaac does not bear directly on cloning. Even if it did, it would be problematic to infer halakha from *aggada*, that is, to derive a legal conclusion from a non-legal source (*aggada* is the general rabbinic term for anything that does not involve law). Yet the story is not without its ethical undertones. At first Isaac looked like a clone of his father. Eventually Abraham had to pray for the deed to be undone.

If there is a mystery at the heart of the human condition it is *otherness*: the otherness of man and woman, parent and child. It is the space we make for otherness that makes love something other than narcissism, and parenthood something greater than self-replication. It is this that gives every human child the right to be themselves, to know they are not reproductions of someone else, constructed according to a pre-planned genetic template. Without this, would childhood be bearable? Would love survive? Would a world of clones still be a human world? We are each in God's image but no one else's.

6. Hilary Putnam, "Cloning People," in Justine Burley (ed.), *The Genetic Revolution and Human Rights* (Oxford: Oxford University Press, 1999), 1–13.

The Future of the Past

*P*arashat Toledot opens with a forecast of the future, a revelation that casts its shadow over the tense, conflictual story that is about to unfold. Rebecca, hitherto infertile, becomes pregnant. Suffering acute pain, "she went to inquire of the Lord," *vatelekh lidrosh et Hashem* (25:22). The explanation she receives is that she is carrying twins who are contending with each other in her womb. They are destined to do so long into the future:

> Two nations are in your womb,
> And two peoples from within you will be separated;
> One people will be stronger than the other,
> And the older will serve the younger [*verav ya'avod tza'ir*]. (25:23)

Eventually the twins are born – first Esau, then Jacob, with his hand grasping his brother's heel. Perhaps mindful of the prophecy she has received, Rebecca favours the younger son, Jacob.[1] Years later, she

---

1. This may not be the only reason. The text goes on to say that "Jacob was a quiet man, staying among the tents," while Esau was a hunter. It then adds that Isaac loved Esau

persuades him to dress in Esau's clothes and take the blessing Isaac intended to give his elder son. One verse of that blessing is "May nations serve you and peoples bow down to you. Be lord over your brothers, and may the sons of your mother bow down to you" (27:29). The prediction has been fulfilled. Isaac's blessing can surely mean nothing less than what was disclosed to Rebecca before either child was born: the older will indeed "serve the younger." The story has reached closure – or so it seems.

But biblical narrative is not what it seems. Two events follow which subvert all that we had been led to expect. The first occurs when Esau arrives and discovers that Jacob has cheated him out of his blessing. Moved by his anguish, Isaac gives him a benediction, one of whose clauses is:

> You will live by your sword and you will serve your brother. But when you grow restless, you will throw his yoke from off your neck. (27:40)

This is not what we had anticipated. The older will not serve the younger in perpetuity.

The second scene, many years later, occurs when the brothers meet after a long estrangement. Jacob is terrified of the encounter. He had fled from home years earlier because Esau had vowed to kill him. Only after a long series of preparations and a lonely wrestling match at night, is he able to face Esau with some composure. He bows down to him seven times. Five times he calls him "my lord." Twice he refers to himself as "your servant." The roles have been reversed. Esau does not become the servant of Jacob. Instead, Jacob speaks of himself as the servant of Esau.

It seems a contradiction. The words heard by Rebecca when "she

---

but Rebecca loved Jacob (25:27). It may be that Rebecca loved Jacob because of his character. Yet it seems unlikely that the revelation given to her before the birth played no part in her decision to persuade Jacob to engage in deception in order to take Isaac's blessing. Evidently she believed that Jacob was destined to prevail over his brother.

went to inquire of the Lord" suggested precisely the opposite, that "the older will serve the younger." We are faced with cognitive dissonance.

More precisely, we have here an example of one of the most remarkable of all the Torah's narrative devices – the power of the future to transform our understanding of the past. This is the essence of midrash. New situations retrospectively disclose new meanings in the text.[2] The present is never fully determined by the present. Sometimes it is only later that we understand now.

This is the significance of the great revelation of God to Moses, where He says "you will see My back; but My face shall not be seen" (Exodus 33:33) – meaning, God's presence can be seen only when we look back at the past; it can never be known or predicted in advance. The indeterminacy of meaning at any given moment is what gives the biblical text its openness to ongoing interpretation.

This was not an idea invented by the sages. It already exists in the Torah itself. The words Rebecca heard seemed to mean one thing at the time. It later transpires that they might have meant something else.

The words *verav ya'avod tza'ir* seem simple: "the older will serve the younger." Returning to them in the light of subsequent events, though, we discover that they are anything but clear. They contain multiple ambiguities.

The first (noted by Radak and Rabbi Joseph ibn Kaspi) is that the word *et*, signalling the object of the verb, is missing. Normally in biblical Hebrew the subject precedes the verb, and the object follows – but not always. In Job 14:19 for example, the words *avanim shaḥaku mayim* mean "water wears away stones," not "stones wear away water." Thus, while the phrase told to Rebecca might mean "the older shall serve the younger," it could also mean "the younger shall serve the older." To be sure, the latter would be poetic Hebrew rather than conventional prose style, but that is what this utterance is: a poem.

---

2. On midrash generally see Michael Fishbane, *The Midrashic Imagination: Jewish Exegesis, Thought, and History* (Albany: State University of New York Press, 1993). On the use of midrash to find new meanings in past events, see the work of Mordechai Rotenberg, especially *Re-Biographing and Deviance: Psychotherapeutic Narrativism and the Midrash* (New York: Praeger, 1987); also available as *Rewriting the Self: Psychotherapy and Midrash* (New Brunswick, NJ: Transaction, 2004).

The second ambiguity is that *rav* and *tza'ir* are not opposites, a fact disguised by the English translation of *rav* as "older." The opposite of *tza'ir* ("younger") is *bekhir* ("older" or "firstborn").[3] *Rav* does not mean "older." It means "great" or possibly "chief." This linking together of two terms as if they were polar opposites, when in fact they are not – the opposites would have been *bechir/tza'ir* or *rav/me'at* – further destabilises the meaning. Who was the *rav*? The elder? The leader? The chief? The more numerous? The word might mean any of these things.

The third ambiguity is not part of the text but of later tradition: the musical notation. The normal way of notating these three words would be *merkha-tipḥa-sof pasuk*. This would support the reading, "the older shall serve the younger." However, they are notated *tipḥa-merkha-sof pasuk* – suggesting, "the older, shall the younger serve"; in other words, "the younger shall serve the older."

A later episode within Genesis adds yet another retrospective element of doubt. Another pair of twins is born in Genesis 38:27–30. The passage is clearly reminiscent of the story of Esau and Jacob:

> When her [Tamar's] time was come, there were twins in her womb. While she was in labour one of them put out a hand. The midwife took a scarlet thread and fastened it round the wrist, saying, "This one appeared first." No sooner had he drawn back his hand, than his brother came out, and the midwife said, "What! You have broken a breach for yourself!" So he was named Perez. Soon afterwards his brother was born with the scarlet thread on his wrist, and he was named Zerah.

Who then was the elder? And what does this imply in the case of Esau and Jacob?[4]

These multiple ambiguities are not accidental, but integral to the text. The subtlety is such, that we do not notice them at first. Only later,

---

3. So it is, for example, in Genesis 29:26, when Laban justifies his deception in giving Leah, not Rachel, to Jacob in marriage: "It is not our custom here to give the younger [*hatze'ira*] before the older [*habekhira*]".
4. See Rashi, 25:26, who suggests that Jacob was in fact the elder.

when the narrative does not turn out as expected, are we forced to go back and notice what at first we missed: that the words Rebecca heard may mean "the older will serve the younger" or "the younger will serve the older," and that the identity of younger and older is not at all obvious.

A number of things now become clear. The first is that the initial revelation is a rare example in the Torah of an oracle as opposed to a prophecy.[5] Oracles – a familiar form of supernatural communication in the ancient world – were normally obscure and cryptic, unlike the normal form of Israelite prophecy. This may well be the technical meaning of the phrase "she went to inquire of the Lord" which puzzled the medieval commentators.[6]

The second – and this is fundamental to an understanding of Genesis – is that the future is never as straightforward as we are led to believe. Abraham was promised many children but had to wait years before Isaac was born. The patriarchs were promised a land but did not acquire it in their lifetimes. The Jewish journey, though it has a destination, is long and has many digressions and setbacks. Will Jacob serve or be served? We do not know. Only after a long, enigmatic struggle alone at night does Jacob receive the name Israel, meaning, "he who struggles with God and with men and prevails" (32:28).

The significance of this strange, ambiguous, passage is both literary and theological. The future affects our understanding of the past. We live our lives toward the future, but we understand our lives only in retrospect. Only looking back can we see whether we took the right road, whether a certain decision was justified, whether our dreams were intimations or illusions. Life involves risk, which is why we need faith, and the courage to which faith gives rise. We are part of a story whose last chapter has not yet been written. That rests with us, as it rested with Jacob.

5. "Oracles" are in fact the probable meaning of the word *ḥidot* in Numbers 12:8: "With him [Moses] I speak mouth to mouth, openly and not in *ḥidot*" – usually translated as "dark speeches" or "riddles."
6. Rashi says it means that she went to the school of Shem, the son of Noah. Rashbam says that she went to a prophet. Neither opts for the obvious reading, which is that she besought God directly through prayer.

The Courage of Persistence

There is a strange passage in the life of Isaac, ominous in its foreshadowing of much of later Jewish history. Like Abraham, Isaac finds himself forced by famine to go to Gerar, in the land of the Philistines. There, like Abraham, he senses that his life may be in danger because he is married to a beautiful woman. He fears that he will be killed so that Rebecca can be taken into the harem of king Avimelekh. The couple pass themselves off as brother and sister. The deception is discovered, Avimelekh is indignant, explanations are made, and the moment passes. Genesis 26 reads almost like a replay of Genesis 20, a generation later.

In both cases Avimelekh promises the patriarchs security. To Abraham he said, "My land is before you; live wherever you like" (20:15). About Isaac, he commands, "Anyone who molests this man or his wife shall surely be put to death" (26:11). Yet in both cases, there is a troubled aftermath. In Genesis 21 we read about an argument that arose over a well that Abraham had dug: "Then Abraham complained to Avimelekh about a well of water that Avimelekh's servants had seized" (21:25). The two men make a treaty. Yet, as we now discover, this was not sufficient to prevent further difficulties in the days of Isaac:

Isaac planted crops in that land and the same year reaped a hundredfold, because the Lord blessed him. The man became rich, and his wealth continued to grow until he became very wealthy. He had so many flocks and herds and servants that the Philistines envied him. So all the wells that his father's servants had dug in the time of his father Abraham, the Philistines stopped up, filling them with earth.

Then Avimelekh said to Isaac, "Move away from us; you have become too powerful for us."

So Isaac moved away from there and encamped in the Valley of Gerar and settled there. Isaac reopened the wells that had been dug in the time of his father Abraham, which the Philistines had stopped up after Abraham died, and he gave them the same names his father had given them.

Isaac's servants dug in the valley and discovered a well of fresh water there. But the herdsmen of Gerar quarrelled with Isaac's herdsmen and said, "The water is ours!" So he named the well Esek, because they disputed with him. Then they dug another well, but they quarrelled over that one also; so he named it Sitnah. He moved on from there and dug another well, and no one quarrelled over it. He named it Rehovot, saying, "Now the Lord has given us room and we will flourish in the land." (26:12–22)

There are three aspects of this passage worthy of careful attention. The first is the intimation it gives us of what will later be the turning point of the fate of the Israelites in Egypt. Avimelekh says, "you have become *too powerful* for us." Centuries later, Pharaoh says, at the beginning of the book of Exodus, "Behold, the people of the children of Israel are greater in number and *power* than we are. Come on, let us deal wisely with them, lest they multiply and it come to pass, when there befall any war, that they join also with our enemies and fight against us, and so get them up out of the land" (1:9–10). The same word, *atzum*, "power/powerful," appears in both cases. Our passage signals the birth of one of the deadliest of human phenomena, anti-Semitism.

Anti-Semitism is in some respects unique. It is, in Robert

Wistrich's phrase, the world's longest hatred.[1] No other prejudice has lasted so long, mutated so persistently, attracted such demonic myths, or had such devastating effects. But in other respects it is not unique, and we must try to understand it as best we can.

One of the best books about anti-Semitism, is in fact not about anti-Semitism at all, but about similar phenomena in other contexts, Amy Chua's *World on Fire*.[2] Her thesis is that any conspicuously successful minority will attract envy that may deepen into hate and provoke violence. All three conditions are essential. The hated group must be *conspicuous*, for otherwise it would not be singled out. It must be *successful*, for otherwise it would not be envied. And it must be a *minority*, for otherwise it would not be attacked.

All three conditions were present in the case of Isaac. He was conspicuous: he was not a Philistine, he was different from the local population as an outsider, a stranger, someone with a different faith. He was successful: his crops had succeeded a hundredfold, his flocks and herds were large, and the people envied him. And he was a minority: a single family in the midst of the local population. All the ingredients were present for the distillation of hostility and hate.

There is more. Another profound insight into the conditions that give rise to anti-Semitism was given by Hannah Arendt in her book *The Origins of Totalitarianism* (the section has been published separately as *Anti-Semitism*).[3] Hostility to Jews becomes dangerous, she argued, not when Jews are strong, but when they are weak.

This is deeply paradoxical because, on the face of it, the opposite is true. A single thread runs from the Philistines' reaction to Isaac and Pharaoh's to the Israelites, to the myth concocted in the late nineteenth century, known as *The Protocols of the Elders of Zion*.[4] It says that Jews

1. Robert S. Wistrich, *Anti-Semitism: The Longest Hatred* (New York: Schocken, 1991).
2. Amy Chua, *World on Fire: How Exporting Free Market Democracy Breeds Ethnic Hatred and Global Instability* (New York: Anchor Books, 2004).
3. Hannah Arendt, *Anti-Semitism* (part one of *The Origins of Totalitarianism*), (Harcourt Brace and Company, 1979).
4. *The Protocols of the Elders of Zion* was a forgery, produced by a Russian journalist at the end of the nineteenth century, claiming that there was a Jewish conspiracy to

are powerful, too powerful. They control resources. They are a threat. They must be removed.

Yet, says Arendt, anti-Semitism did not become dangerous until they had lost the power they had once had:

> When Hitler came to power, the German banks were already almost *Judenrein* (and it was here that Jews had held key positions for more than a hundred years) and German Jewry as a whole, after a long steady growth in social status and numbers, was declining so rapidly that statisticians predicted its disappearance in a few decades.[5]

The same was true in France:

> The Dreyfus affair exploded not under the Second Empire, when French Jewry was at the height of its prosperity and influence, but under the Third Republic when Jews had all but vanished from important positions.[6]

Anti-Semitism is a complex, protean phenomenon because anti-Semites must be able to hold together two beliefs that seem to contradict one another: Jews are so powerful that they should be feared, and at the same time so powerless that they can be attacked without fear.

It would seem that no one could be so irrational as to believe both of these things simultaneously. But emotions are not rational, despite the fact that they are often rationalized, for there is a world of difference between *rationality* and *rationalization* (the attempt to give rational justification for irrational beliefs).

So, for example, in the twenty-first century we can find that (a)

achieve world domination. The classic work on the subject is Norman Cohn, *Warrant for Genocide: The Myth of the Jewish World-Conspiracy and the Protocols of the Elders of Zion* (New York: Harper & Row, 1966). See also Hadassa Ben-Itto, *The Lie That Wouldn't Die: The Protocols of the Elders of Zion* (London: Vallentine Mitchell, 2005).
5. Ibid., 4.
6. Ibid., 4–5.

Western media are almost universally hostile to Israel, and (b) otherwise intelligent people claim that the media are controlled by Jews who support Israel: the same inner contradiction of perceived powerlessness and ascribed power.

Arendt summarizes her thesis in a single, telling phrase which links her analysis to that of Amy Chua. What gives rise to anti-Semitism is, she says, the phenomenon of "wealth without power." That was precisely the position of Isaac among the Philistines.

There is a second aspect of our passage that has had reverberations through the centuries: the self-destructive nature of hate. The Philistines did not ask Isaac to share his water with them. They did not ask him to teach them how he (and his father) had discovered a source of water that they – residents of the place – had not. They did not even simply ask him to move on. They "stopped up" the wells, "filling them with earth." This act harmed them more than it harmed Isaac. It robbed them of a resource that would, in any case, have become theirs, once the famine had ended and Isaac had returned home.

More than hate destroys the hated, it destroys the hater. In this case too, Isaac and the Philistines were a portent of what would eventually happen to the Israelites in Egypt. By the time of the plague of locusts, we read:

> Pharaoh's officials said to him, "How long will this man be a snare to us? Let the people go, so that they may worship the Lord their God. *Do you not yet realize that Egypt is ruined?*" (Exodus 10:7)

In effect they said to Pharaoh: you may think you are harming the Israelites. In fact you are harming us.

Both love and hate, said Rabbi Shimon bar Yoḥai, "upset the natural order" (*mekalkelet et hashurah*).[7] They are irrational. They make us do things we would not do otherwise. In today's Middle East, as so often before, those intent on destroying their enemies end by doing great harm to their own interests, their own people.

7. *Bereshit Raba* 55:8.

Third, Isaac's response remains the correct one today. Defeated once, he tries again. He digs another well; this too yields opposition. So he moves on and tries again, and eventually finds peace.

How fitting it is that the town that today carries the name Isaac gave the site of this third well, is the home of the Weizmann Institute of Science, the Faculty of Agriculture of the Hebrew University, and the Kaplan hospital, allied to the Medical School of the Hebrew University. Israel Belkind, one of the founders of the settlement in 1890, called it Reḥovot precisely because of the verse in our *parasha*: "He named it Reḥovot, saying, Now the Lord has given us room and we will flourish in the land."

Isaac is the least original of the three patriarchs. His life lacks the drama of Abraham or the struggles of Jacob. We see in this passage that Isaac himself did not strive to be original. The text is unusually emphatic on the point: Isaac "reopened the wells that had been dug in the time of his father Abraham, which the Philistines had stopped up after Abraham died, and he *gave them the same names* his father had given them."

Normally we strive to individuate ourselves by differentiating ourselves from our parents. We do things differently, or even if we don't, we give them different names. Isaac was not like this. He was content to be a link in the chain of generations, faithful to what his father had started.

Isaac represents the faith of persistence, the courage of continuity. He was the first Jewish child, and he represents the single greatest challenge of being a Jewish child: to continue the journey our ancestors began, rather than drifting from it, thereby bringing the journey to an end before it has reached its destination. And Isaac, because of that faith, was able to achieve the most elusive of goals, namely peace – because he never gave up. When one effort failed, he began again. So it is with all great achievement: one part originality, nine parts persistence.

I find it moving that Isaac, who underwent so many trials, from the binding when he was young, to the rivalry between his sons when he was old and blind, carries a name that means, "He will laugh." Perhaps the name – given to him by God Himself before Isaac was born – means what the psalm means when it says, "Those who sow in tears will reap with joy" (126:5). Faith means the courage to persist through all the setbacks, all the grief, never giving up, never accepting defeat. For at the end, despite the opposition, the envy and the hate, lie the broad spaces, Reḥovot, and the laughter, Isaac: the serenity of the destination after the storms along the way.

The Other Face of Esau

The Torah is an understated text, sparse in its details, elusive and allusive about the inner life of its characters. Yet in *Parashat Toledot* we are shown one of the most emotionally affecting scenes in the Torah. Jacob, dressed in Esau's clothes, has taken Esau's blessing. He leaves, and shortly thereafter:

> ...his brother Esau came in from hunting. He too had prepared some tasty food and brought it to his father. Then he said to him, "My father, sit up and eat some of my game, so that you may give me your blessing."
>
> His father Isaac asked him, "Who are you?"
>
> "I am your son," he answered, "your firstborn, Esau."
>
> Isaac trembled violently and said, "Who was it, then, that hunted game and brought it to me? I ate it just before you came and I blessed him – and indeed he will be blessed."
>
> When Esau heard his father's words, he cried a loud and bitter cry and said to his father, "Bless me – me too, my father."
>
> But he said, "Your brother came deceitfully and took your blessing."

Esau said, "Is he not rightly named Jacob [= heel-grasper], for he has supplanted me these two times: He took my birthright, and now he has taken my blessing." Then he asked, "Haven't you kept any blessing for me?"

Isaac answered Esau, "I have made him lord over you and have made all his brethren his servants, and I have sustained him with corn and new wine. What then can I do for you, my son?"

Esau said to his father, "Do you have only one blessing, my father? Bless me too, my father." Then Esau lifted his voice and wept. (27:30–38)

What is remarkable is less what happens than how the Torah describes it, its use of language and narrative art. In general the Torah is sparing in its details, especially about the emotional state of its characters. Its descriptions are minimalist, leaving the reader to supply what the text omits: what the characters look like, their location, body language and so on. Emmanuel Levinas was surely correct[1] in seeing this as an invitation to midrash, summoning the reader to complete the text in dialogue with the written word – the Torah is more like radio than television, actively enlisting the imaginative participation of its hearers. This is, then, a passage unusual in its literary explicitness and psychological depth of drama.

As readers, we feel with and for Isaac and Esau. We are drawn into their subjective states. We enter into Isaac's dawning realisation that he has been deceived. We identify too with Esau, whose first thought is not betrayal or desire for revenge but simple, sharp and shocking pain ("Bless me – me too, my father"). Then comes Isaac's helplessness ("What then can I do for you, my son?") and Esau's agonized weeping – all the more poignant given what we know of him, that he is a man of the fields, rough in some ways, impetuous in others, not a man given (as Joseph will later be) to tears. The scene of the two of them together, father and son, deceived and disappointed, robbed of what should have been a moment of great tenderness and intimacy – son feeding father,

---

1. Emmanuel Levinas, "Revelation in the Jewish tradition," in Sean Hand (ed.), *The Levinas Reader* (Oxford: Blackwell, 1989), 190–210.

father blessing son) – is deeply affecting. We can imagine the painting Rembrandt might have made of it.

The question is why this level of detail is necessary. In Torah, form follows function. Nothing is accidental. If there is a marked stylistic feature to a given section, it is there for a reason. Here, the Torah wants our sympathies to be drawn, throughout the chapter, to Esau rather than to Jacob. It is not that we feel that Esau was the rightful heir of the covenant; that history had taken a wrong turn; that things should have been otherwise. Manifestly this is not so. Rebecca favours Jacob, and in Genesis, mothers know their children better than their fathers do. Esau – the hunter, the man who "despised his birthright" (25:34) once he had sold it – was clearly not destined to be the faithful follower of an invisible, transcendent God. The Abrahamic covenant must surely pass through Jacob, the child described as "a quiet man, staying among the tents" (25:27). Yet nonetheless, the Torah goes out of its way, using unusual devices of style, to enlist our sympathies with Esau, to make us enter his world and see things from his perspective. Why?

Before we can answer this, we must first take a wider look at what we know of Esau and his descendants from the rest of the Torah.

The first is that Esau does receive a blessing from Isaac:

> The fat places of the earth will be your dwelling. [You can still have] the dew of heaven. But you shall live by your sword. You may have to serve your brother, but when your complaints mount up, you will throw his yoke off your neck. (27:39–40)

The "fat places of the earth" and the "dew of heaven" are not so circumscribed, implies Isaac, that there will not be enough for both of you. This is a blessing both sons can enjoy without the one diminishing the other. As for Jacob's supremacy, it will last only as long as he does not misuse it. If he acts with unwarranted high-handedness, Esau will simply "throw his yoke off" his neck. There is a basis here for coexistence.

The second insight comes when Esau "marries out," taking two Hittite girls as wives. This is "a source of bitterness" (26:35) to Isaac and Rebecca, and provides Rebecca with the necessary pretext to reconcile Isaac with Jacob, as well as giving Jacob a legitimate excuse to leave home ("I am disgusted with life because of those Hittite women," she tells Isaac, "If Jacob marries such a Hittite girl from the daughters of this land, why should I go on living?" [27:46]). Esau's reaction is interesting. He "understood that the Canaanite girls were displeasing to his father Isaac" (28:8) and tries to ameliorate the situation by taking a third wife – Maḥlat, daughter of Ishmael. The gesture fails for two obvious reasons: he does not divorce the other wives, and he has not internalised the fact that Ishmael too has been rejected as an heir to the Abrahamic covenant. Esau is not overly endowed with intelligence, but he cares for his father and does not wish to cause him distress.

The third glimpse into Esau's character is offered when the brothers finally meet again twenty-two years later. This is one of the great passages of the Torah, full of depths and resonances. But the surface narrative is clear, and there is a rabbinic principle: "Scripture does not depart from its plain meaning."[2] Jacob is full of fear in advance of the encounter – fear that leads him to make elaborate preparations involving "prayer, diplomacy and war."[3] The night before the fateful meeting he wrestles alone with an unnamed adversary. Yet when the brothers finally meet, Esau runs to meet Jacob, embraces him, weeps, and shows none of the hostility he had once harboured. The internal drama is played out entirely within the soul of Jacob. Esau, it seems, is swift to anger, equally swift to forget. When Jacob, pleading with him to accept a gift of cattle and flocks, uses the deeply significant phrase, "please accept my blessing" (33:11) – an implicit reference to that event twenty-two years earlier – Esau shows no sign of understanding at what he is hinting. Esau does not harbour a grudge, not because he forgives but because he forgets.

The fourth passage, Genesis 36, is the list of Esau's descendants. At first glance it is no different from the many other genealogies in Genesis, but it contains two significant pieces of information, one explicit, the other implicit. The first is the statement, "These are the kings who ruled in the Land of Edom before any king reigned in Israel" (36:31). The second is the contrast between the closing verse of chapter 36 and the opening verse of chapter 37: "These are the tribes of Esau, each with its

2. *Shabbat* 63a.
3. *Pesikta deRav Kahana* 19.

own settlements in its hereditary lands [*eretz aḥuzatam*] … Meanwhile, Jacob lived in the land where his father had lived as an alien [*be'eretz megurei aviv*]." The implication could not be clearer. Esau's descendants establish themselves geographically and politically long before Jacob's. Not for them the twists and turns of covenantal history – exile, slavery, redemption and the wilderness years. While both twins may eventually inherit the fat places of the earth and the dew of heaven, for one the route is straightforward, for the other, anything but.

The fifth element that must be taken into account is the shape of the relationship between the Israelites and Edomites. God instructs the Israelites:

> You are passing by the borders of your brothers, the descendants of Esau, who live in Seir. Although they fear you, be very careful not to provoke them. I will not give you even one foot of their land, since I have given Mount Seir as Esau's inheritance. (Deuteronomy 2:4–5)

No less emphatic is the command:

> Do not abhor an Edomite, since he is your brother. (Deuteronomy, 23:7)

There is nothing in these commands to remind us of the eternal strife between the two nations predicted before their birth ("Two nations are in your womb… one people will be stronger than the other, and the older will serve the younger" [25:22–23]). During the biblical era there were periodic tensions and shifting fortunes in the relationship between Edom and Israel, but normatively, the Israelites were commanded to respect both the Edomites and their land.[4]

Combining all these elements, we can make several inferences. At the simplest level, there is a humanity here that defies all stereotypes and conventional categorisations. Esau is a child loved by his father and loving him in return. This is so striking that, despite the generally

---

4.   See for example, II Samuel 8:14; II *Melakhim* 8:20.

negative evaluation of Esau in the midrashic literature, this fact shines through:

> Rabbi Shimon ben Gamliel said: no man ever honoured his father as I did mine, yet I found that Esau honoured his father even more than I did.[5]

There is at times a tendency on the part of the midrash to separate biblical characters into the wholly good and wholly bad, and for this there are good pedagogic reasons, as Rabbi Zvi Hirsch Chajes points out.[6] To serve effectively as role models, biblical heroes must be seen as consistently heroic, non-heroes as systematic villains.

Yet beneath this overlay of midrash, the Torah teaches a different and equally important message, albeit one that demands a certain maturity to appreciate: even heroes have their faults and non-heroes their virtues, and these virtues are important to God. "The Holy One, blessed be He, does not withhold the reward of any creature" said the sages.[7] The Esau who emerges from the Torah has none of Abraham's faith, Isaac's steadfastness or Jacob's persistence. He is carved of an altogether coarser grain. But he is not without his humanity, his filial loyalty and a decent if quick-tempered disposition.

This too is part of the Torah's message. Just as we cannot predict God's actions in advance ("I will be who I will be," "I will have mercy and show kindness to whomever I desire"),[8] so we cannot predict in advance where God's image will shine in the affairs of mankind. It was the sectarians of Qumran, not the rabbis, who divided mankind into the "children of light" and the "children of darkness." Such anthropological dualism is as alien to Judaism as is theological dualism.

There is, however, something far more fundamental at stake in the story of Esau. It has to do with the very concept of chosenness itself. The book of Genesis is, among other things, a profound meditation on

5. *Devarim Raba* 1:15.
6. In *Mavo HaAggadot*, printed at the beginning of standard editions of *Ein Yaacov*.
7. *Pesaḥim* 118a.
8. Exodus 3:14; 33:19.

what it is to be chosen and what it is not to be chosen. There can be no doubt that chosenness has deep psychological consequences on both sides of the equation. To be chosen means – as Jacob discovers – a life of high demands and great hardship – "Few and evil have been the days of my life" (47:9), he says to Pharaoh. But not to be chosen is also deeply disturbing. We see this time and again – on the two occasions in which Hagar is sent away, in the relations between Joseph and his brothers, but most explicitly in the case of Leah and Rachel:

> [Jacob] also married Rachel, and he loved Rachel more than Leah … [God] saw that Leah was hated [*senua*] … (29:30)

I have translated this last phrase literally to give it its full, shocking force in the Hebrew. Leah, of course, was not hated – she was loved, Rachel was only loved *more*.[9] Yet the sense of rejection cuts deep, so deep that the Torah does not hesitate to compare it to the feeling of being hated. And one who feels rejected may hate in return. That is why the brothers "hate" Joseph (the verb is used three times – a significant repetition – in chapter 37).

Love chooses. But choice creates estrangement, which leads to tension, which can sometimes erupt into conflict and violence – potential or actual. This is a theme signalled almost at the beginning of the biblical narrative, where God's choice of Abel's offering and not Cain's leads to fratricide.

Something of the deepest possible consequence is being intimated in the story of Esau. The choice of one does not mean the rejection of another. Esau is not chosen, but he is also not rejected. He too will have his blessing, his heritage, his land. He too will have children who become kings, who will rule and not be ruled. He too will have his virtues recognized, above all his love and respect for his father. Not

---

9. Both Ramban and Radak point out that the verb *s-n-'*, which usually means "to hate," has a different meaning in biblical Hebrew when contrasted with the verb "to love." This too is its meaning in Devarim 25:15, "If a man has two wives, one loved, the other hated [*senua*] …" Here again, the meaning is not "hated" but "less loved." See also essay "Hearing the Torah," p. 203.

accidentally are our sympathies drawn to him. The Torah is saying for all time to all humanity – not all are chosen for the rigors, spiritual and existential, of the Abrahamic covenant, but all are precious to God, each has his or her place in the scheme of things, each has his or her virtues, talents, gifts, and each is precious in the eyes of God.[10] In the words

10. To be sure, there is the seemingly contrary view in Malachi: "I have loved you," says the Lord. "But you ask, 'How have You loved us?'" The Lord says "Was not Esau Jacob's brother? Yet I have loved Jacob, but Esau I have hated…" (Malachi 1:2–3). However, there is the remarkable comment by the Vilna Gaon that the phrase, "Esau I have hated" refers only to "the peripheral part of Esau" not his essence.

The verse in Malachi refers to particular historical circumstances. During the First Temple period there were conflicts and wars between the Israelites and Edomites. The prophet Amos attributes particular cruelty to Edom: "He pursued his brother with a sword, stifling all compassion, because his anger raged continually and his fury flamed unchecked" (Amos 1:11). Malachi is speaking about a specific historical era, not eternity.

The issue has larger significance because, for the rabbis, Esau/Edom symbolised the Roman Empire, and then (after the conversion of Constantine), Christianity. Ishmael was the Arab world and later, Islam. On the basis of the Vilna Gaon's comments, Rav Kook wrote this about the relationship between Judaism and these two other faiths:

> Noteworthy in this respect is the statement of Rabbi Eliahu Gaon on the verse, "But Esau I hated" – "this refers to the peripheral part of Esau, but the essential part of him, his head, was interred with the patriarchs." It is for this reason that the man of truth and integrity, Jacob, said [on his reunion with Esau], "I have seen you, and it is like seeing the face of God" (33:10). His word shall not go down as a vain utterance. The brotherly love of Esau and Jacob, Isaac and Ishmael, will assert itself above all the confusion that the evil brought on by our bodily nature has engendered. It will overcome them and transform them into eternal light and compassion. (*Letters*, 1, 112)

Rav Kook believed that just as in the Torah, Jacob and Esau, Isaac and Ishmael, were eventually reconciled, so will Judaism, Christianity and Islam be in future. They will not cease to be different, but they will learn to respect one another.

We believe as a matter of principle that "the righteous of the nations have a share in the world to come" (*Ḥullin* 92a). When Jacob was chosen, Esau was not rejected. God does not reject. "Though my mother and father might abandon me, the Lord will take me in" (Psalms 27:10). Chosenness means two things: intimacy and responsibility. God holds us close and makes special demands on us. Beyond that, God is the God of all mankind – the Author of all, who cares for all.

God will later say to Jonah: "You are concerned about this vine, though you did not tend it or make it grow... Nineveh has more than a hundred and twenty thousand people who cannot tell their right hand from their left, and many cattle as well. Should I not be concerned about that great city?" (Jonah 4:10). Or as Psalms puts it: "The Lord is good to all; He has compassion on all He has made" (145:9).

To be chosen does not mean that others are unchosen. To be secure in one's relationship with God does not depend on negating the possibility that others too may have a (different) relationship with Him. Jacob was loved by his mother, Esau by his father; but what of God who is neither father nor mother but both and more than both?

In truth, we can only know our own relationship with our parents. We can never know another's. Am I loved more than my brothers or sisters? Less? Once asked, the question cannot but lead to sibling rivalry – which is one of the central themes of Genesis. But the question is not a valid question. It should not be asked. A good parent loves all his or her children and never thinks of more or less. Love is not quantifiable. It rejects comparisons. Jacob is Jacob, heir to the covenant. Esau is Esau, doing what he does, being what he is, enjoying his own heritage and blessing. What a simple truth and how beautifully, subtly, it is conveyed. It is one of the Torah's most profound messages to humanity – and how deeply, in an age of "the clash of civilizations," the world needs to hear it today.

Vayetzeh
ויצא

Jacob leaves home in flight from Esau who had sworn to kill him, only to find himself in a fraught relationship with Laban, his uncle, with whom he takes refuge. He falls in love with Laban's younger daughter Rachel, and agrees to work the seven years to earn her hand in marriage. When the wedding eventually takes place, Jacob wakes the next morning to discover that Laban has substituted the elder, Leah, in place of Rachel. Jacob later marries Rachel as well, but there is tension between the sisters. Leah, unloved, is blessed with children; Rachel, loved, is not. Interwoven with this is another tension between Jacob and Laban – about flocks, wages and ownership – which eventually leads Jacob to flee again, this time homeward. The *parasha* is framed by these two journeys.

The first three of the following essays are about different aspects of Jewish prayer in the light of Jacob's vision of a ladder between earth and heaven, one of the supreme metaphors of prayer. The fourth is about Jacob's love for Rachel, while the fifth examines the plight and pathos of Leah, and its message that God loves those who feel unloved.

Encountering God

It is one of the great visions of the Torah. Jacob, alone at night, fleeing from the wrath of Esau, lies down to rest, and sees not a nightmare but an epiphany:

> And he lighted upon a certain place [*vayifga bamakom*] and stayed for the night for the sun had set. Taking one of the stones of that place, he put it under his head and lay down to sleep. And he dreamed, and behold a ladder resting on the earth, with its top reaching heaven. God's angels were ascending and descending on it. And there above it stood God...
>
> Jacob awoke from his sleep and said, "God is truly in this place, and I knew it not." He was afraid and said, "How awesome is this place! This is none other than the house of God and this is the gate of heaven." (28:11–17).

On the basis of this passage the sages assert that "Jacob instituted the evening prayer."[1] The inference is based on the word *vayifga* which

---

1. *Berakhot* 26b.

denotes not only, "he came to, encountered, happened upon" but also "he prayed, entreated, pleaded" as in Jeremiah 7:16, "Neither lift up cry nor prayer for them nor make intercession to Me [*ve'al tifga bi*]." The sages also understood the word *bamakom*, "the place" to mean "God," for God is the "place" of the universe.[2]

Thus Jacob completed the cycle of daily prayers. Abraham instituted *shaharit*, the morning prayer; Isaac *minha*, the afternoon prayer; and Jacob *ma'ariv*, the prayer of night time.

This is a striking idea, implying that though each of the weekday *Amida*-prayers is identical in wording, each bears the character of one of the patriarchs. Abraham represents morning. He is the initiator, the one who introduced a new religious consciousness to the world. With him a day begins. Isaac represents afternoon. He initiates no major transition from darkness to light or light to darkness. Indeed, as we have seen, many of the incidents in Isaac's life recapitulate those of his father's: Famine forces him, as it did Abraham, to go to the land of the Philistines; He re-digs his father's wells. Isaac's is the quiet heroism of continuity. He is a link in the chain of the covenant, joining one generation to the next. He is steadfastness, loyalty, the determination to continue. Without these virtues Judaism would not have survived. Jacob represents night. He is the man who discovers God in the midst of fear.

Abraham is morning: the dawn of a new faith. It was he who broke his father's idols, recognizing the inner contradictions of polytheism and paganism. His religious career began with a journey away from home, birthplace and his father's house to a new and unknown destination. Abraham represents beginning – a new chapter in the religious history of mankind.

Isaac is afternoon. There is nothing spectacular about the afternoon, no qualitative change from dark to light or day to night. Instead there is a slow transition, an almost imperceptible shift. Isaac is the bridge between day and night, between Abraham and Jacob, two lives fraught with drama. His own life is relatively uneventful and passive. He is not the prime mover of events. Yet without a bridge we cannot cross from one domain to another. If Abraham is the iconoclast, Isaac

2. *Bereshit Raba* 68:9.

represents the courage of continuity, without which the entire project of the covenant would die.

Jacob is night. He sees his great vision of the ladder and angels at night. He struggles with an unknown adversary at night. He ends his days in exile, at the beginning of the long, dark night of slavery. Jacob's great strength is that he does not let go. He is born holding his brother's heel. He refuses to let go of the stranger wrestling with him. If Abraham is originality and Isaac continuity, then Jacob represents tenacity.

There is, however, a difficulty with the idea that Jacob introduced the evening prayer. In a famous episode in the Talmud, Rabbi Yehoshua takes the view that, unlike *shaḥarit* or *minḥa*, the evening prayer is not obligatory (though, as the commentators note, it has become so through the acceptance of generations of Jews).[3] Why, if it was instituted by Jacob, was it not held to carry the same obligation as the prayers of Abraham and Isaac? Tradition offers three answers.

The first suggests that the view that *ma'ariv* is non-obligatory was held only by those who maintained that the daily prayers are based not on the patriarchs, but on the sacrifices that were offered in the Temple. There was a mandatory morning and afternoon offering, but there was no evening sacrifice. Thus, the two approaches to the source of the prayers lead to divergent practical implications: for those who trace prayer to sacrifice, the evening prayer is voluntary, whereas for those who base it on the patriarchs, it is obligatory.

The second approach points to the law that those on a journey are exempt from prayer until three days thereafter. In the days when journeys were hazardous – when travellers were in constant fear of attack by raiders – it was impossible to concentrate while in transit, and prayer requires concentration (*kavanah*). Therefore Jacob was exempt from prayer, and offered up his entreaty not as an obligation but as a voluntary act – and so it remained.

The third approach bases itself on the tradition that, as Jacob was travelling, "the sun set suddenly" – not at its normal time.[4] Jacob had intended to say the afternoon prayer, but found, to his surprise, that

---

3. *Berakhot* 27a.
4. *Sanhedrin* 95b.

night had fallen. *Ma'ariv* did not become an obligation, since Jacob had not meant to say an evening prayer at all.

There is, however, a more profound explanation. Note that a different linguistic construction is used for each of the three occasions that the sages site as the basis of prayer. Abraham "rose early in the morning to the place where he had stood before God" (19:27). Isaac "went out to meditate [*lasuaḥ*] in the field towards evening" (24:63). Jacob "met, encountered, came across" God (*vayifga bamakom*). These are different kinds of religious experience.

Abraham initiated the quest for God. He was a creative religious personality – the father of all those who set out on a journey of the spirit to an unknown destination, armed only with the trust that those who seek, find. Abraham sought God before God sought him.

Isaac's prayer is described as a *siḥa*, literally, a conversation or dialogue. There are two parties to a dialogue – one who speaks and one who listens, and having listened, responds. Isaac represents the religious experience as conversation between the word of God and the word of mankind.

Jacob's prayer is very different. He does not initiate it. His thoughts are elsewhere – on Esau from whom he is escaping, and on Laban to whom he is journeying. Into this troubled mind comes a vision of God and the angels and a stairway connecting earth and heaven. He has done nothing to prepare for it. It is unexpected. Jacob literally "encounters" God as we can sometimes encounter a familiar face among a crowd of strangers. This is a meeting brought about by God, not man. That is why Jacob's prayer could not be made the basis of a regular obligation. None of us knows when the presence of God will suddenly intrude into our lives.

There is an element of the religious life that is beyond conscious control. It comes out of nowhere, when we are least expecting it. If Abraham represents our journey towards God, and Isaac our dialogue with God, Jacob signifies God's encounter with us – unplanned, unscheduled, unexpected; the vision, the voice, the call we can never know in advance but which leaves us transformed. As for Jacob, so for us, it feels as if we are waking from sleep and realizing, as if for the first time, that "God is truly in this place, and I knew it not." The place has not changed, but we have. Such an experience can never be made the subject of an obligation. It is not something we do. It is something that happens to us. *Vayfiga bamakom* means that, thinking of other things, we find that we have walked into the presence of God.

Such experiences take place, literally or metaphorically, at night. They happen when we are alone, afraid, vulnerable, close to despair. It is then that, when we least expect it, we can find our lives flooded by the radiance of the divine. Suddenly, with a certainty that is unmistakable, we know that we are not alone, that God is there and has been all along, but that we were too preoccupied by our own concerns to notice Him. That is how Jacob found God – not by his own efforts, like Abraham; not through continuous dialogue, like Isaac; but in the midst of fear and isolation. Jacob, in flight, trips and falls – and finds he has fallen into the waiting arms of God. No one who has had this experience ever forgets it.

"Now I know that You were with me all the time but I was looking elsewhere" – that was Jacob's prayer. There are times when we speak and times when we are spoken to. Prayer is not always predictable, a matter of fixed times and daily obligation. It is also an openness, a vulnerability. God can take us by surprise, waking us from our sleep, catching us as we fall.

The Ladder of Prayer

At the opening of *Parashat Vayetzeh*, having "gone out" of the familiar world of his parents home in Be'er Sheva, Jacob, finds himself in what is known as liminal space – the space between[1] – between the home he is escaping and the destination he has not yet reached, between the known danger of his brother Esau from whom he is in flight, and the as yet unknown danger of Laban from whom he will eventually suffer great wrongs.

As will happen again twenty-two years later on his return, when

---

1. On liminality, see Arnold van Gennep, *The Rites of Passage* (London: Routledge & Paul, 1960); Victor Turner, *The Ritual Process: Structure and Anti-Structure* (London: Routledge & Paul, 1969). Liminality is the space between two states or territories, between where you are coming from and where you are going to. It represents transition, and is marked by uncertainty and vulnerability. Turner argues that liminality sheds light on the basic distinction between society – a place of structure and hierarchy where everyone has their roles – and "communitas" – a community and communion of equal individuals. Liminality is an experience of communitas, where role, rank, status and office, fall away and we are left bereft of externalities, as souls, selves, without masks or ascribed identities. Hence liminal experiences tend to combine humility and sacredness, a beautiful description of Jacob's encounter with God, and of our experience of prayer.

he encounters and wrestles with a stranger, Jacob has his most intense experiences alone, at night, in the middle of a journey. It is in these transitional travels, when he is most open to the unexpected, that Jacob is defined, through liminal encounters that border dream and reality. On his journey home he emerges a new man, injured and limping, yet with a victorious new name. In this, the first of his visions:

> He dreamed, and behold a ladder resting on the earth, with its top reaching heaven. God's angels were ascending and descending on it. And there above it stood God... (28:12–13)

What does this vision signify? There are many interpretations given by the sages and commentators, but the simplest is that it has to do with the encounter between the human soul and God, the encounter that later generations would know as prayer.

> Jacob awoke from his sleep and said, "God is truly in this place, and I knew it not." He was afraid and said, "How awesome is this place! This is none other than the house of God and this is the gate of heaven." (28:16–17).

The House of God came to refer to the synagogue, for prayer is the gate of heaven. And when we have truly prayed, the most profound result is that we too are conscious of the feeling: "God is truly in this place, and I knew it not."

The *Zohar* (1, 201b) identifies the ladder in Jacob's vision with prayer: we who pray stand on earth, yet our prayers reach heaven, as is said: "May You hear from heaven, Your dwelling place" (1 Kings 8:39) – Solomon's prayer about prayer at the dedication of the Temple.

I would like to suggest that this primal vision did not merely give us a paradigm of prayer: its impact extends to influence the very *structure* of Jewish liturgy. If we examine Jewish prayer carefully, we will see that its shape precisely reflects the model of a ladder on which angels ascend and descend.

A close study of the liturgy reveals a prevalent symmetrical three-part structure, A-B-A, which has the following form: (a) ascent, (b) standing in the Presence, (c) descent. For example, *shaharit*, the morning service, begins with (a) *pesukei dezimra*, a series of Psalms which constitute a preparation for prayer. It moves on to (b) prayer-proper: the *Shema* with its three blessings, and the *Amida*, standing prayer. It ends with (c) a series of concluding hymns including *Ashrei*, itself a key element of *pesukei dezimra*.

The basis of this threefold structure is a statement in the Talmud (*Berakhot* 32b) that "the early pious men used to wait for an hour before praying, then they would pray for an hour, and then they would wait for another hour." The Talmud queries the basis of this custom, and answers by citing the verse *Ashrei* itself: "Happy are those who sit in Your house." Clearly this is what is known as an *asmakhta*, a supporting verse, rather than the origin of the custom itself (this passage, though, is undoubtedly the reason that *Ashrei* is said in the first and third sections).

The three-fold pattern of *shaharit* is repeated in the microcosm in the structure of the *Amida*. It too follows a three-part pattern: (a) *shevah*, praise, the first three blessings; (b) *bakasha*, request, the middle blessings, and (c) *hodaya*, "thanks" or "acknowledgement," the last three blessings. On Shabbat and Yom Tov, the middle section is replaced by usually one – on Rosh Hashanah three – blessings relating to "the holiness of the day" on the grounds that we do not make requests on days of rest.

Shevah is a preparation. It is our entry to the Divine Presence. *Hodaya* is a leave-taking. We thank God for the goodness with which He has favoured us. *Bakasha*, the central section, is standing in the Presence itself. We are like supplicants standing before the King, presenting our requests. The spiritual form of the first and last actions – entry and leave-taking – are dramatized by taking three steps forward, and at the end, three steps back. This is the choreography of ascent and descent.

This pattern appears yet again in the *kedusha* – a prayer formed around verses taken from the mystical visions of the prophets, which makes explicit reference to angels. Its key verses are the words Isaiah and Ezekiel heard the angels saying as they surround the Throne of Glory. We speak of the angels at this point: the Serafim, Cherubim, Ofanim and holy Ḥayot. The *kedusha* is said three times in the morning service.[2] The first, known as *kedushat yotzer*, appears in the blessings before the Shema; the third, *Kedusha DeSidra*, is said in the concluding section of the prayers, beginning *Uva leTzion*. The middle *kedusha* is in the reader's repetition of the *Amida*.

There are obvious differences between the first and last versions of the *kedusha*, on the one hand, and the second on the other. The first and third do not need a quorum, a *minyan*. They can be said privately. They do not need to be said standing. The second requires a *minyan* and must be said standing.

Maimonides explains the difference. In the first and third, we are *describing* what the angels do when they praise God. In the second, we are *enacting* what they do. In other words, the first and third are preparation for, and reflection on, an event. The second is the event itself, as we relive it.[3]

There are other examples, but these will suffice.

The daily prayers, as we now have them, evolved over a long period of time. The sages tell us that the first architects were the men of the Great Assembly in the days of Ezra and Nehemiah, the fifth century B.C.E. There was a further intensive process of composition and canonization in the days of Rabban Gamliel at Yavneh. Shaping and reshaping continued until the first prayer books, those of Rav Amram Gaon and Rav Saadiah Gaon, in the ninth and tenth centuries C.E.

What we see from the above examples is that there is a basic shape – a deep grammar – of prayer. It consists of ascent – standing in the Presence – descent. The inspiration for this cannot have been anything other than Jacob's vision.

Prayer is a ladder stretching from earth to heaven. On this ladder of words, thoughts and emotions, we gradually leave earth's gravitational

2. On Shabbat, the third *kedusha* is transferred to the afternoon service, because the morning service is more than usually long. However, its proper place is in *shaharit*.

3. Cited in *Ḥiddushim* at the beginning of *Ma'aseh Roke'aḥ*, 1. See R. Nahum Rabinovitch, *Yad Peshuta* to Rambam, *Mishneh Torah* (Hilkhot Tefilla 7:17), *Sefer Ahava*, vol. 1 (Jerusalem: Maaliyot, 1984), 294–5; also cited in *Rambam LaAm* (Jerusalem: Mossad HaRav Kook, 1958), ad loc.

field. We move from the world around us, perceived by the senses, to an awareness of that which lies beyond the world – the earth's Creator.

At the end of this ascent, we stand, as it were, directly in the conscious presence of God – which Maimonides defines as the essential element of *kavana*, the intentional state essential to prayer.[4]

We then slowly make our way back to earth again – to our mundane concerns, the arena of actions and interactions within which we live. But if prayer has worked, we are not the same afterward as we were before. For we have seen, as Jacob saw, that "God is truly in this place, and I knew it not."

If the first stage is the climb, and the second standing in heaven, then the third is bringing a fragment of heaven down to earth. For what Jacob realized when he woke from his vision is that God is in *this* place. Heaven is not somewhere else, but is here – even if we are alone and afraid – if only we realized it. And we can become angels, God's agents and emissaries; we can ultimately even struggle "with God and with men" (32:28), if, like Jacob, we have the ability to pray and the strength to dream, and the openness to see the transformations that can happen in the difficult spaces between.

---

4. Maimonides, *Mishneh Torah, Hilkhot Tefilla veNesiat Kapayim* 4:15–16.

When the "I" is Silent

We return to the powerful, primal vision of prayer: Jacob, alone and far from home, lies down for the night, with only stones for a pillow, and dreams of a ladder set on earth but reaching heaven, with angels ascending and descending. This is the initial encounter with the "house of God" that would one day become the synagogue, the first dream of a "gate of heaven" that would allow access to a God that stands above, letting us know finally that "God is truly in this place."

There is, though, one nuance in the text that is lost in translation, and it took the Hassidic masters to remind us of it. Hebrew verbs carry with them, in their declensions, an indication of their subject. Thus the word *yadati* means "I knew," and *lo yadati*, "I did not know." When Jacob wakes from his sleep, however, he says, "Surely the Lord is in this place *ve'anokhi lo yadati.*" *Anokhi* means "I," which in this sentence is superfluous. To translate it literally we would have to say, "And I, I knew it not." Why the double "I"?

To this, Rabbi Pinchas Horowitz (*Panim Yafot*) gave a magnificent answer. How, he asks, do we come to know that "God is in this place"? "By *ve'anokhi lo yadati* – not knowing the I." We know God when we forget the self. We sense the "Thou" of the Divine Presence when we move beyond the "I" of egocentricity. Only when we stop thinking about ourselves do we become truly open to the world and the Creator.

In this insight lies an answer to some of the great questions about prayer: What difference does it make? Does it really change God? Surely God does not change. Besides which, does not prayer contradict the most fundamental principle of faith, which is that we are called on to do God's will rather than ask God to do ours? What really happens when we pray?

Prayer has two dimensions, one mysterious, the other not. There are simply too many cases of prayers being answered for us to deny that it makes a difference to our fate. It does. I once heard the following story. A man in a Nazi concentration camp lost the will to live – and in the death camps, if you lost the will to live, you died. That night he poured out his heart in prayer. The next morning, he was transferred to work in the camp kitchen. There he was able, when the guards were not looking, to steal some potato peelings. It was these peelings that kept him alive. I heard this story from his son.

Perhaps each of us has some such story. In times of crisis we cry out from the depths of our soul, and something happens. Sometimes we only realise it later, looking back. Prayer makes a difference to the world – but how it does so is mysterious.

There is, however, a second dimension which is non-mysterious. Less than prayer changes the world, it changes us. The Hebrew verb *lehitpalel*, meaning "to pray," is reflexive, implying an action done to oneself. Literally, it means "to judge oneself." It means, to escape from the prison of the self and see the world, including ourselves, from the outside. Prayer is where the relentless first person singular, the "I," falls silent for a moment and we become aware that we are not the centre of the universe. There is a reality outside. That is a moment of transformation.

If we could only stop asking the question, "How does this affect me?" we would see that we are surrounded by miracles. There is the almost infinite complexity and beauty of the natural world. There is the divine word, our greatest legacy as Jews, the library of books we call the Bible. And there is the unparalleled drama, spreading over forty centuries, of the tragedies and triumphs that have befallen the Jewish people. Respectively, these represent the three dimensions of our knowledge of God: creation (God in nature), revelation (God in holy words) and redemption (God in history).

Sometimes it takes a great crisis to make us realise how self-centred we have been. The only question strong enough to endow existence with meaning is not, "What do I need from life?" but "What does life need from me?" That is the question we hear when we truly pray. More than an act of speaking, prayer is an act of listening – to what God wants from us, here, now. What we discover – if we are able to create that silence in the soul – is that we are not alone. We are here because someone, the One, wanted us to be, and He has set us a task only we can do. We emerge strengthened, transformed.

More than prayer changes God, it changes us. It lets us see, feel, know that "God is in this place." How do we reach that awareness? By moving beyond the first person singular, so that for a moment, like Jacob, we can say, "I know not the I." In the silence of the "I," we meet the "Thou" of God.

On Love and Justice

The story of Jacob's love for Rachel is one of the most romantic in the Torah. Yet it is full of hidden depths and ambiguities, reversals and unexpected turns. It begins, as do other Torah narratives of man-meets-future-wife, with a scene at a well. The shepherds have gathered there to water their flocks, but the well is covered with a large stone which they will not remove until all the local shepherds have arrived. The text does not tell us why. It may be that the stone is too large to be moved except by all the shepherds together, or it may be a local custom to ensure a fair distribution of the water. At that moment, however, Rachel arrives. Jacob knows – the shepherds have told him – that she is the daughter of his uncle Laban with whom he has come to seek refuge. Immediately, Jacob moves into action:

> Now while he was still speaking with them, Rachel came with her father's sheep, for she was a shepherdess. And it came to pass, when Jacob saw Rachel the daughter of Laban his mother's brother, and the sheep of Laban his mother's brother, that Jacob went near and rolled the stone from the well's mouth, and watered

the flock of Laban his mother's brother. Then Jacob kissed Rachel, and lifted up his voice and wept. (29:9–11)

We notice the sharp contrast with the earlier scene at which Abraham's servant sought a wife for his master's son at a well. Here it is Jacob, not the woman, who is active. Rolling the stone off the well is a feat of considerable strength, as well as a daring defiance of local custom, not attributes we have hitherto associated with the quiet son of Isaac. Evidently, Jacob is seized with strong emotion. He kisses Rachel; he weeps. The text at least raises the possibility that he has performed his act of bravado to impress her with both his strength and his kindness. It may be love at first sight.

For several verses we are kept in suspense. The subject changes to Laban, and Jacob's desire to stay with him for a while. After a month, Laban asks Jacob what he would like his wages to be in return for the work he expects from him. Only now does the text make clear what we suspected at the outset. Jacob has indeed fallen in love with Rachel:

> Laban had two daughters: the name of the elder was Leah, and the name of the younger was Rachel. Leah was tender-eyed, but Rachel was of beautiful form and beautiful appearance. Jacob loved Rachel, and said, "I will serve you seven years for Rachel your younger daughter." Laban said, "It is better that I give her to you than that I should give her to another man: stay with me." (29:16–19)

The word *rakot*, translated as "tender" may mean "weak, sensitive, clouded." It could also mean "attractive," but the implied contrast with Rachel who was doubly beautiful, in form and appearance, makes this unlikely.

Jacob has fallen in love with Rachel because she is beautiful: so the text implies. This is highly significant. We are told that Sarah and Rebecca were also beautiful, but in both cases the text says so in the context of a temporary location among strangers. Abraham has travelled to Egypt, Isaac to the land of the Philistines, because of famine. They ask their wives to say that they are their sisters, because both fear that otherwise they will be killed so that their wives can be taken into the royal harem. It is as if, hearing that Sarah and Rebecca are beautiful, we see them through Egyptian or Philistine eyes. This is the first time physical beauty is associated with love and a reason for marriage.

Jacob is following his eyes, not generally considered a good thing in Tanakh. Eve followed her eyes in desiring the forbidden fruit (3:6). Samuel, seeing the sons of Jesse, among whom God has told him is Israel's future king, initially chooses Eliav, who looks the part. He is told by God that he has judged wrongly: "Do not consider his appearance or height, for I have rejected him. The Lord does not look at the things man looks at. Man looks at the outward appearance, but the Lord looks at the heart" (1 Samuel 16:7).

Yet Jacob is deeply in love. The Torah tells us this in one of its most beautiful lines:

> Jacob served seven years for Rachel; and they seemed to him but a few days, because of the love he had for her. (29:20)

He is oblivious to both labour and time. Not before and not afterward do we find in the Torah such romantic passion. The years pass and the moment for which Jacob has been waiting arrives:

> Jacob said unto Laban, "Give me my wife, for my days are fulfilled, that I may go in unto her." (29:21)

Laban gathered together all the men of the place, and made a feast.

> It came to pass in the evening, that he took Leah his daughter, and brought her to him; and he went in to her. Laban gave to his daughter Leah, Zilpah his maid as a handmaid. It came to pass, that in the morning, behold, it was Leah: and he said to Laban, "What is this you have done to me? Did not I serve you for Rachel? Why have you deceived me?" But Laban said, "It is not done in our place to give the younger before the firstborn." (29:22–26)

It is an astonishing reversal. Jacob has been tricked. Laban has taken advantage of night and the cover of darkness to substitute Leah for

Rachel. He has also made it impossible for Jacob to backtrack. He had invited "all the men of the place" to be witnesses to the marriage celebration. They could not have known that in fact he had promised that the bride would be Rachel. They would have assumed, Laban implies, that it would be Leah, since the local custom is that the elder is married first. Besides which, had Laban in fact promised Rachel? His answer, seven years earlier, when Jacob had first asked for Rachel, was curiously evasive and oblique: "It is better that I give her to you than that I should give her to another man: stay with me" (29:19). It may be that he had already formed the intention to deceive.

So Jacob, trusting Laban, marries what in his eyes is the wrong woman. Eventually, as we go on to read, he marries Rachel as well, but the damage has been done. The result is lingering tragedy. Rachel has beauty; Leah has children, six boys, half the twelve tribes of Israel. Each wife is a source of pain to the other: Rachel because she lacks children, Leah because she feels herself unloved. The tragedy continues into the next generation when the other children first envy, then come to hate, Jacob's favourite son Joseph, child of his beloved Rachel.

The details of the story are clear. What is unclear is its message. Is it to show us the cunning and calculating nature of Laban? Certainly the text supports this reading, but Laban is a secondary character in this drama of Jacob and his two wives.

Is it to provide justification for a later law in the book of Leviticus: "Do not take a woman as a rival wife to her sister, uncovering her nakedness while her sister is still alive" (18:18)? This too is possible. Law and narrative are often connected in the Torah. As for the problem that the sages believed the patriarchs kept the Torah before it was given, and here Jacob is acting against the law, Nahmanides answers that the patriarchs kept the Torah only when they were in Israel, not, as here, in exile.[1]

Is it that Jacob is being punished, or corrected, for following his eyes and judging his future wife by her appearance instead of putting character first? The text, as we have seen, is suggestive of this, but other than these hints, there is nothing to make this reading the most likely.

If we listen carefully to the text another possibility presents itself.

1. Ramban, commentary to *Bereshit* 26:5.

The word Jacob uses to Laban, "Why did you deceive me [*rimitani*]?" is the very word Isaac used to describe Jacob's behaviour in taking Esau's blessing: "Your brother came in deceit [*mirma*]" (27:35).

The word Laban uses to describe the younger sibling is *tze'ira*, the word that appears in Rebecca's oracle about Jacob and Esau: "the elder will serve the younger [*tza'ir*]" (25:23).

Even the sentence Laban uses to justify the deception – "It is not done *in our place*, to give the younger before the firstborn" – is deeply ironic. Did Laban know that this, in effect, was what Jacob had done in another place? The irony may be unintentional. Laban may not have known, but we, the readers, do. And so surely did Jacob himself.

If these hints are signalling how the passage should be read, then the narrative is an example, unparalleled in its drama, of the single most fundamental moral axiom of the torah, *midda keneged midda*, measure for measure.[2] What we do will be done to us. "He who sheds the blood of man, by man shall his blood be shed" (Genesis 9:6) as God says in the covenant with Noah. Those who deceive will be deceived. That is what happens to Jacob.

One midrash is explicit:

> "In the morning, and behold it was Leah." – He said to her, "Deceiver, daughter of a deceiver, did I not call you Rachel last night, and you answered me?" She replied, "Is there a master without students? Did your father not call you Esau and you answered him?"[3]

Here it is Leah who makes the connection. In general, the midrash did not take this route. Midrash emphasizes the virtues of the patriarchs and the vices of others. The latter is not hard to do in this case, for Laban is anything but a noble character concerned with justice. He is a devious man concerned with his own advantage. But the story is too precise a mirror image of the scene in chapter 27 where Jacob pretends to be Esau, taking his blessing by taking his place, for the connection to be

2. *Shabbat* 105b.
3. *Bereshit Raba* 70:17.

accidental. As we have seen, the Torah gives us three linguistic cues that take us back to that earlier episode. What we do to others will one day be done to us. In a later age, Hillel once saw a skull floating on the water and said: "Because you drowned others, they drowned you, and those who drowned you will themselves eventually be drowned" (*Avot* 2:7).

There may be a yet deeper principle at stake. The verb "to love" does not appear often in Genesis. The emotions of its characters are often hidden from us, so that when they are revealed, they have great literary force. So it is notable that the word "love" appears three times in relation to Jacob's feelings for Rachel: "Jacob loved Rachel" (29:18). The seven years seemed like a few days "because of the love he had for her" (29:20). Jacob "loved Rachel more than Leah" (29:30). We will later discover the same about Jacob's feelings for Rachel's son Joseph: three times the text speaks of his love for him, one of which is, as with Rachel, comparative: just as he loved Rachel more than Leah, so he "loved Joseph more than any of his other sons" (37:3).

Love is an emotion; love is a virtue; love is the ultimate bond between soul and soul. But without justice, love alone is insufficient to sustain the world, insufficient even to maintain peace within a family. Jacob's love for Rachel, and later Joseph, is the cause of conflict between his two wives and their sons, and Jacob paid heavily for it. How heavily he did so he makes clear many years later, speaking to Pharaoh in Egypt where his long lost son is now a man of power. "Few and evil have been the days of the years of my life" (47:9), he says. There is no other statement quite like this in Genesis and it is all the more striking given the fact that Jacob had just been reunited with Joseph, whom he once thought he would never see again. Love is not enough, for it leaves the less loved feeling unloved, and the result is conflict and sometimes tragedy.

If this is so, then it has immense significance for the relationship between Judaism and Christianity. Christian writers often drew a contrast between the New Testament "God of love" and the Old Testament "God of justice." This cannot be right, for Christianity holds that they are the same God. What is more, when the New Testament refers to the imperative of love, it does so by quoting two verses from the Torah itself, "Love your neighbour as yourself" and "Love the Lord your God with all your heart, soul and might," as central to Judaism as they are to Christianity.

What the story of Jacob, his wives and their children tells us is that love alone is not enough. There must be justice, fairness, a regard for how your sentiments impact on others. In the end it was Leah, the less loved, who gave Israel its holy tribe, Levi, and its kings, descendants of Judah.

Weaving together these two strands of love (Jacob's intense feelings for Rachel) and justice (the deceiver deceived), the story of Jacob, Rachel and Leah turns out to be an essential prelude to the book of Exodus and the covenant between God and Israel, based on love and justice. For without justice, love is blind; and without love, justice is impersonal and cold. Jacob's family needed both, and so do we.

Hearing the Torah

The *parashot* are inextricably linked to and defined by *keriat haTorah*, what we commonly think of as the public reading of the Torah in the synagogue. Yet the phrase *keriat haTorah* does not simply mean "reading the torah." In biblical Hebrew the verb *likro* means not "to read" but "to call." The phrase *mikra'ei kodesh*, "festivals," literally means "holy convocations," days on which the people were called or summoned together. Every seven years the king was commanded to "read aloud [*tikra*] this Torah before them in their hearing [*be'aznehem*]," in the ceremony of *hakhel* that called together man, woman and child. In the historic gathering of those who had returned from Babylon, Ezra "read [the Torah] aloud [Leviticus] from daybreak till noon, in the presence of the men, women and others who could understand, and all the people listened attentively [literally, the ears of all the people were directed] to the book of the Torah." (Nehemiah 8:3)

Keriat haTorah therefore means not reading, but *proclaiming* the Torah, reading it aloud. The one who reads it has the written word in front of him, but for the rest of the gathering it is an experience not of the eye, but of the ear. The divine word is something heard rather than seen. Indeed, it was only with the spread of manuscripts, and the invention of printing in the fifteenth century, that reading become a visual rather than auditory experience. To this day the primary experience of *keriat haTorah* involves listening to the reader declaim the words from the Torah scroll, rather than following them in a printed book. We miss some of the most subtle effects of Torah if we think of it as the text seen, rather than the word heard.

There are many differences between sound and sight. I would like to focus on the element of time. We can see – but not hear – a sentence at a single glance. Seeing is often instantaneous. Listening is a process extended through time. Halfway through a sentence, we can guess what will come next, but we cannot be sure until we have actually heard the words. That is why, for example, jokes are more powerful when heard rather than read. Crucial to a joke is the element of surprise. If we can guess the punchline, the joke is not successful. Listening, we are kept in suspense. Reading, we can go directly to the last sentence.

Torah is written to be read aloud, and several of its literary devices are based on the timed sequence of the audial. Time and again, the Torah makes use of the fact that a later word has the power to confound expectations that have been formed based on what has been heard thus far. Sometimes the result is humorous, at others the opposite, but in all cases it makes us sit up and pay attention. One of the most striking examples occurs in *Parashat Vayetzeh*.

Jacob, in flight from Esau's anger, has travelled to the house of Laban. Arriving, he meets Laban's younger daughter Rachel and falls in love with her. Laban proposes a deal: work for me for seven years and I will give her to you in marriage. Jacob does so, but on the wedding night Laban substitutes Leah for Rachel. The next morning, when Jacob discovers the deception, he protests, "Why did you deceive me?" Laban pointedly replies, "It is not the done thing in our place to give the younger before the elder." Laban agrees, however, that in return for a further seven years' labour, Jacob may marry Rachel. He will not have to wait until the seven years are complete, but only until the end of the seven days of Leah's wedding celebration (an early example of a custom we still keep: the week of *sheva berakhot*). The seven days pass. Jacob marries Rachel. We then are told the following:

He also [*gam*] married Rachel, and he also [*gam*] loved Rachel...
(29:30)

The implication at this point is clear. The repeated *gam*, "also," leads us
to believe that the two sisters are equal in Jacob's eyes. The story of the
deception has – or so we must suppose on the basis of what we have so
far heard – a happy ending after all. Jacob has married both. He loves
them both. The sibling rivalry that is so pronounced a theme of Genesis,
from Cain and Abel, to Isaac and Ishmael, and on to Jacob and Esau,
seems to finally be reaching a positive resolution. It is possible to love
two siblings equally.

The next word sends our expectation crashing to the ground:

...more than Leah (29:30)

This is an ungrammatical construction. The words "also" and "more than"
do not belong together in the same sentence. Either one loves X and also
Y, or one loves X more than Y, but not both. The effect – like a sudden
discord in the middle of a Mozart symphony – is strident and shocking.
Jacob does not love the two sisters equally. He may love them both, but
his passion is for Rachel. The next verse contains an even sharper discord:

God saw that Leah was hated [*senua*]...

This is a phrase that cannot be understood literally. The previous verse
has just said that Leah was not hated but loved. The commentators and
translators wrestled with this difficulty. Nahmanides (in his second
interpretation) and Radak both read the word *senua* not as "hated" but
as "[relatively] unloved."[1]

---

1. Ramban and Radak, commentaries to *Bereshit* 29:31. In one interpretation, Ramban
    suggests that Jacob hated Leah because of the deception she had practiced on him.
    But he also offers the possibility that one's first love is usually the deepest. Jacob had
    met and fallen in love with Rachel at the well, before he had met Leah (Ramban to
    Bereshit 29:30).

Yet though the text is semantically strange, is it psychologically lucid. Leah knew that Jacob's heart was elsewhere. She may have been loved but she felt the lesser love as a rejection. The words "God saw" mean that God felt her sense of humiliation. Laban's deception had human consequences, and they were tragic. Leah weeps inwardly for the husband she acquired as a result of her father's wiles, whose love is for someone else.

Only now, perhaps, do we understand the significance of the Torah's introduction of Leah:

> Now Laban had two daughters; the name of the older was Leah, and the name of the younger was Rachel. The eyes of Leah were weak (*rakot*), but Rachel was lovely in form, and lovely in appearance. (29:17)

The word *rakot*, as we mentioned in the previous essay, could mean "unattractive, weak." Netziv suggests that it means "sensitive": Leah was unable to go out with the flocks because the bright sunlight hurt her eyes.[2] The ambiguity is deliberate. Only rarely and sparingly does the Torah give us physical descriptions of its characters, and always for a reason that will eventually be disclosed (so, for example, we hear in II Samuel 14 about Absolom's hair; four chapters later we discover why: it became caught in a tree, which led to his death).

One of the meanings of the phrase "Leah's eyes were *rakot*," is, as Rashi, Radak and various midrashic traditions explain, "Leah was easily moved to tears."[3] She was emotionally vulnerable. She had none of the resilience that might have carried her through her husband's attachment to her younger sister. She was thin-skinned, sensitive, attuned to nuance, easily hurt. She knew she was Jacob's lesser love, and it caused her pain.

The subtlety with which all this is conveyed is remarkable. The Torah has sketched Leah's portrait in a few deft strokes, each of which we will hear only if we are listening carefully. Nor has this been done for the sake of description. Rather, it has set the scene for the drama that is

2. Netziv, *Ha'amek Davar* to *Bereshit* 29:17.
3. Rashi, Radak, commentaries to *Bereshit* 29:17; Midrash, *Bereshit Raba* 70:16.

about to unfold – and once again we find it done with the utmost brevity and delicacy. In fact, unless we are paying the closest of attention we will not notice it at all.

What follows next is, on the face of it, a simple account of the birth of four children. Beneath the surface, however, these verses are as eloquent as any in the entire Torah:

> God saw that Leah was hated, and He opened her womb. Rachel remained barren. Leah became pregnant and gave birth to a son. She named him Reuben, saying: "God has seen (*ra'ah*) my troubles. Now my husband will love me." She became pregnant again and had a son. "God has heard (*shama*) that I was unloved," she said, "and has given me also this son." She named the child Shimon. She became pregnant again and had a son. "Now my husband will become attached (*lava*) to me," she said, "because I have given him three sons." Therefore he named the child Levi. She became pregnant again and had a son. She said, "This time let me praise (*odeh*) God," and she named the child Judah. She then stopped having children. (29:31–35)

Read superficially, these verses are no more than a genealogy, a list of births, of the kind of which there are many in Genesis. Heard while attuned to Leah's plight, however, what we hear is heartbreaking.

Leah is pleading for attention. Each of the names of her first three children is a cry to her husband Jacob – to see, to listen, to be attached, to notice, to love her. Significantly, it is she, not Jacob, who names three of the children.[4]

Sadly, the lack of relationship between Jacob and Leah at the birth of her children is carried through in the years to come. Jacob's relationship with Reuben, Shimon and Levi breaks down completely,

---

4. The exception is Levi. However, while commentators who emphasise the plain sense of the text, Rashbam and Radak, assume that the "he" who names Levi is Jacob, Rashi, whose commentary goes deeper, says, on the basis of midrashic tradition, that it was an angel. Rashi understood and emphasized that a key fact about the four births is the absence of Jacob.

with Reuben after the episode of Bilhah's couch, with Shimon and Levi after the incident with Shechem. On his death-bed he curses instead of blesses them. Yet it is from Levi that Israel's spiritual leaders will eventually come – Moses, Aaron, Miriam, and eventually the *kohanim* and *levi'im* (priests and Levites); it is from Judah that will come its kings, David and his descendants.

What is going on in this intense and sometimes tragic drama between Leah and Jacob?

Jacob is unlike the other patriarchs. If the ideas that come to mind in relation to Abraham are kindness and hospitality, and to Isaac, sacrifice and fear, the idea that characterises Jacob is struggle.

Already in the womb he struggles with his brother. He competes with him for the birthright and the blessing. The defining scene in his life is his wrestling match at night with an unnamed adversary. Both his names – Jacob, "he who grasps by the heel," and Israel, "he who struggles with God and man and prevails" – convey a sense of conflict.

While Abraham and Isaac represent modes of being, Jacob stands for becoming. The gifts he has, he has fought for. None have come naturally. Jacob is the supreme figure of persistence. He is the man who said to the angel, "I will not let you go until you bless me." More than Abraham and Isaac, Jacob is the person who wrestles with life and refuses to let go.

The Torah describes Jacob as an *ish tam*, sometimes translated as "a simple man" but better understood (according to Rabbi Samson Raphael Hirsch) as "a single-minded man." Associated by the prophet Micah with truth – "You give truth to Jacob, kindness to Abraham" (Micah 7:20), Jacob's life embodies the fact that truth must be fought for with single-minded determination. It rarely comes without a struggle and the pain of experience.

There are many truths at stake in Jacob's life, but the central motif is a truth about love. One of the most striking facts about the Jacob narrative is the frequency with which the word "love" appears. While it figures once in the story of Abraham (Genesis 22:2), and twice in the life of Isaac (24:67, 25:28),[5] it figures seven times in the case of Jacob

5. There are, however, also three references to Isaac's love of a particular kind of food: 27:4,9,14.

(29:18, 20, 30, 32; 37:3,4; 44:20). Jacob loves more than any other figure in Genesis.

But through painful experience, Jacob must learn a truth about love: it not only unites, it also divides. It did so in his childhood, when Isaac loved Esau and Rebecca loved Jacob. It did so again when he married two sisters. It did so a third time when he loved Rachel's child Joseph more than his other sons. What Jacob learned – and what we learn, hearing his story – is that love is not enough. We must also heed those who feel unloved. Without that, there will be conflict and tragedy. But to heed the unloved requires a specific capacity: the ability to listen – in Jacob's case, to the unspoken tears of Leah and her feeling of rejection, made explicit in the names she gave her sons.

I began by pointing out that the Torah was a text intended to be read aloud and listened to. It is the single greatest expression of faith in a God we cannot see, but only hear. Judaism is supremely a religion of the ear, unlike all other ancient civilizations, which were cultures of the eye. This is more than a metaphysical fact. It is a moral one as well. In Judaism the highest spiritual gift is the ability to listen – not only to the voice of God, but also to the cry of other people, the sigh of the poor, the weak, the lonely, the neglected and, yes, sometimes the un- or less-loved. That is one of the meanings of the great command *Shema Yisrael*, "Listen, O Israel." Jacob's other name, we recall, was Israel.

Jacob wrestles with this throughout his life. It is not that he has a moral failing. To the contrary, he is the most tenacious of all the patriarchs – and the only one whose children all become part of the covenant. It is rather that every virtue has a corresponding danger. Those who are courageous are often unaware of the fears of ordinary people. Those of penetrating intellect are often dismissive of lesser minds. Those who, like Jacob, have an unusual capacity to love must fight against the danger of failing to honour the feelings of those they do not love with equal passion. The antidote is the ability to listen. That is what Jacob discovered in the course of his life – and why he, above all, is the role model for the Jewish people – the nation commanded to listen.

How beautiful it is that this message – one of the deepest and most subtle in the Torah – is conveyed in a series of passages whose meaning does not lie on the surface of the text, but discloses itself only to those who listen to what is going on beneath the words: the unspoken cry, the implicit appeal, the unheard tears, the unarticulated pain. Those who wish to learn to listen to God must learn to listen to other people – to the *kol demama daka*, "the still, small voice" of those who need our love.

Vayishlaḥ
וישלח

Vayishlḥ tells the story of the meeting, after an estrangement that lasted twenty-two years, between Jacob and Esau. Hearing that his brother is coming to meet him with a force of four hundred men, Jacob is "greatly afraid and distressed." He divides his camp into two, sends gifts to Esau, and prays. That night he wrestles with a mysterious stranger, in an episode that ends with his being given a new name, Israel, meaning "one who struggles with God and men and prevails." The next day the two brothers meet, not in violence but in peace. They embrace and then go their separate ways. The *parasha* ends with the death of Isaac and a genealogy of the descendants of Esau.

The first of the following studies examines Jacob's state of mind before the meeting, exploring the difference between (physical) fear and (moral) distress. The second analyzes the wrestling match with the stranger and what it tells us about Jacob's inner struggle of identity and self-image. The third relates Jacob's struggle to our own responses to crisis, and the fourth asks what it means to be a descendant of a man whose name means "one who struggles with God and men," arguing that Judaism is the countervoice in the conversation of humankind.

Physical Fear, Moral Distress

Twenty-two years have passed since Jacob fled his brother, penniless and alone; twenty-two years have passed since Esau swore his revenge for what he saw as the theft of his blessing. Now the brothers are about to meet again. It is a fraught encounter. Once, Esau had sworn to kill Jacob. Will he do so now – or has time healed the wound? Jacob sends messengers to let his brother know he is coming. They return, saying that Esau is coming to meet Jacob with a force of four hundred men – a contingent so large it suggests to Jacob that Esau is intent on violence. Jacob's response is immediate and intense:

Then Jacob was greatly afraid and distressed ... (32:8)

The fear is understandable, but his response contains an enigma. Why the duplication of verbs? What is the difference between fear and distress? To this a midrash gives a profound answer:

Rabbi Judah bar Ilai said: Are not fear and distress identical? The meaning, however, is that "he was afraid" that he might be killed; "he was distressed" that he might kill. For Jacob thought: If he prevails against me, will he not kill me; while if I prevail against him, will I not kill him? That is the meaning of "he was afraid" – lest he should be killed; "and distressed" – lest he should kill.[1]

The difference between being afraid and distressed, according to the midrash, is that the first is a physical anxiety, the second a moral one. It is one thing to fear one's own death, quite another to contemplate being the cause of someone else's. Jacob's emotion, then, was twofold, encompassing the physical and psychological, the moral and the material.

However, this raises a further question. Self-defence is permitted in Jewish law.[2] If Esau were to try to kill Jacob, Jacob would be justified in fighting back, if necessary at the cost of Esau's life. Why then should this possibility raise moral qualms? This is the issue addressed by Rabbi Shabbetai Bass, author of the commentary on Rashi, *Siftei Ḥakhamim*:

> One might argue that Jacob should surely not be distressed about the possibility of killing Esau, for there is an explicit rule: "If someone comes to kill you, forestall it by killing him." Nonetheless, Jacob did have qualms, fearing that in the course of the fight he might kill some of Esau's men, who were not themselves intent on killing him but merely on fighting his men. And even though Esau's men were pursuing Jacob's men, and every person has the right to save the life of the pursued at the cost of the life of the pursuer, nonetheless there is a condition: "If the pursued could have been saved by maiming a limb of the pursuer, but instead the rescuer killed the pursuer, the rescuer is liable to capital punishment on that account." Hence Jacob feared that, in the confusion of battle, he might kill some of Esau's men when he might have restrained them by merely inflicting injury on them.[3]

The principle at stake, according to the *Siftei Ḥakhamim*, is the minimum use of force. The rules of defence and self-defence are not an open-ended

1. Rashi to 32:8; *Bereshit Raba* 76:2.
2. *Sanhedrin* 72a.
3. *Siftei Ḥakhamim* to 32:8.

permission to kill. There are laws restricting what is nowadays called "collateral damage," the killing of innocent civilians even if undertaken in the course of self-defence. Jacob was distressed at the possibility that in the heat of conflict he might kill some of the combatants when injury alone might have been all that was necessary to defend the lives of those – including himself – who were under attack.

A similar idea is found in the midrash's interpretation of the opening sentence of Genesis 15. Abraham had just fought a victorious war against the four kings, undertaken to rescue his nephew Lot, when God suddenly appeared to him and said: *"Do not be afraid, Abram, I am your shield. Your reward will be very great'"* (Genesis 15:1). The verse implies that Abraham was afraid, but of what? He had just triumphed in the military encounter. The battle was over. There was no cause for anxiety. On this, the midrash comments:

> Another reason for Abram's fear after killing the kings in battle was his sudden realisation: "Perhaps I violated the divine commandment that the Holy One, blessed be He, commanded the children of Noah, 'He who sheds the blood of man, by man shall his blood be shed.' For how many people I killed in battle."[4]

Or, as another midrash puts it:

> Abraham was filled with misgiving, thinking to himself, Maybe there was a righteous or God-fearing man among those troops which I slew.[5]

There is, however, a second possible explanation for Jacob's fear – namely that the midrash means what it says, no more, no less: Jacob was distressed at the possibility of being forced to kill *even if it were entirely justified*.

What we are encountering here is the concept of a moral

4. Solomon Buber, comp., Tanhuma, *Lekh Lekha* 19 (Vilna, 1885).
5. *Bereshit Raba* 44:4.

dilemma.[6] This phrase is often used imprecisely, to mean a moral problem, a difficult ethical decision. But a dilemma is not simply a conflict. There are many moral conflicts. May we perform an abortion to save the life of the mother? Should we obey a parent when he or she asks us to do something forbidden in Jewish law? May we desecrate the Shabbat to extend the life of a terminally ill patient? These questions have answers. There is a right course of action and a wrong one. Two duties conflict and we have meta-halakhic principles to tell us which takes priority. There are some systems in which all moral conflicts are of this kind. There is always a decision procedure and thus a determinate answer to the question, "What should I do?"

A dilemma, however, is a situation in which there is no right answer. It arises in cases of conflict between right and right, or between wrong and wrong – where, whatever we do, we are doing something that in other circumstances we ought not to do.

The *Talmud Yerushalmi* (*Terumot* 8) describes one such case, where a fugitive from the Romans, Ulla bar Koshev, takes refuge in the town of Lod. The Romans surround the town, saying: Hand over the fugitive or we will kill you all. Rabbi Yehoshua ben Levi persuades the fugitive to give himself up. This is a complex case, much discussed in Jewish law, but it is one in which both alternatives are tragic. Rabbi Yehoshua ben Levi acts in accordance with halakha, but the prophet Eliyahu asks him: "Is this the way of the pious? [*Vezu mishnat haHasidim*]"

Moral dilemmas are situations in which doing the right thing is not the end of the matter. The conflict may be inherently tragic. Jacob, in this *parasha*, finds himself trapped in such a conflict: on the one hand, he ought not allow himself to be killed; on the other, he ought not kill someone else; but he must do one or the other. The fact that one principle (self-defence) overrides another (the prohibition against killing) does not mean that, faced with such a choice, he is without qualms, especially given the fact that Esau is his twin brother. Despite their differences, they grew up together. They were kin. This intensifies the dilemma yet more. Sometimes being moral means that one experi-

6. See Christopher Gowans (ed.), *Moral Dilemmas* (Oxford: University Press, 1987), for a collection of philosophical essays on this subject.

ences distress at having to make such a choice. Doing the right thing may mean that one does not feel remorse or guilt, but one still feels regret or grief about the action that needs to be taken.

A moral system which leaves room for the existence of dilemmas is one that does not attempt to eliminate the complexities of the moral life. In a conflict between two rights or two wrongs, there may be a proper way to act – the lesser of two evils, or the greater of two goods – but this does not cancel out all emotional pain. A righteous individual may sometimes be one who is capable of distress even while knowing that they have acted correctly. What the midrash is telling us is that Judaism recognises the existence of dilemmas. Despite the intricacy of Jewish law and its meta-halakhic principles for deciding which of two duties takes priority, we may still be faced with situations in which there is an ineliminable cause for distress. It was Jacob's greatness that he was capable of moral anxiety even at the prospect of doing something entirely justified, namely defending his life at the cost of his brother's.

This characteristic – distress at violence and potential bloodshed even when undertaken in self-defence – has stayed with the Jewish people ever since. One of the most remarkable phenomena in modern history was the reaction of Israeli soldiers after the Six Day War in 1967. In the weeks preceding the war, few Jews anywhere in the world were unaware that Israel and its people faced terrifying danger. Troops – Egyptian, Syrian, Jordanian – were massing on all its borders. Israel was surrounded by enemies who had sworn to drive its people into the sea. And yet it won one of the most stunning military victories of all time. The sense of relief was overwhelming, as was the exhilaration at the reunification of Jerusalem and the fact that Jews could now pray (as they had been unable to do for nineteen years) at the Western Wall. Even the most secular Israelis admitted to feeling intense religious emotion at what they knew was a historic triumph.

Yet, in the months after the war, as conversations took place throughout Israel, it became clear that the mood among those who had taken part in the war was anything but triumphal.[7] It was sombre,

---

7. See Abraham Shapira (ed.), *The Seventh Day: Soldiers Talk About the Six Day War* (London: Andre Deutsch, 1970).

reflective, even anguished. That year, the Hebrew University in Jerusalem gave an honorary doctorate to Yitzhak Rabin, Chief of Staff during the war. During his speech of acceptance he said:

> We find more and more a strange phenomenon among our fighters. Their joy is incomplete, and more than a small portion of sorrow and shock prevails in their festivities, and there are those who abstain from celebration. The warriors in the front lines saw with their own eyes not only the glory of victory but the price of victory: their comrades who fell beside them bleeding, and I know that even the terrible price which our enemies paid touched the hearts of many of our men. It may be that the Jewish people has never learned or accustomed itself to feel the triumph of conquest and victory, and therefore we receive it with mixed feelings.[8]

These mixed feelings were born thousands of years earlier, when Jacob, father of the Jewish people, experienced not only the physical fear of defeat but the moral distress of victory. Only those who are capable of feeling both, can defend their bodies without endangering their souls.

8. Martin Gilbert, *Israel: A History* (London: Doubleday, 1998), 395.

Wrestling Face to Face

Jacob is about to meet his brother Esau after an estrangement that has lasted twenty-two years. In a way unparalleled anywhere else in Genesis, the narrative builds up suspense. Jacob is afraid and distressed. He divides his camp into two, that at least one may survive. He prays. He sends emissaries with gifts. He takes his family and possessions across the river. He has made every possible preparation, taken every possible precaution. Yet still we sense his disquiet. It is then that one of the most haunting scenes in the Torah takes place:

> And Jacob was left alone; and there wrestled a man with him until the breaking of the day. And when he saw that he prevailed not against him, he touched the hollow of his thigh ... (32:24–25)

This story of Jacob's wrestling match with an unnamed adversary is deeply enigmatic. Everything about it is mysterious. It takes place at a liminal time between night and dawn, at an unspecified location, with no explanation. We do not even know who the adversary was. The text itself calls him "a man"; according to the prophet Hosea, it was an angel;[1] for the sages, it was the guardian angel of Esau.[2] Jacob himself had no doubt. It was God. He called the place of the encounter Peni'el, "because I saw God face to face, and yet my life was spared" (32:30). The adversary himself implies as much when he gives Jacob the name Israel: "for you have struggled with God and with man and have overcome." Hitherto, we have seen Jacob struggle with human beings, with Esau and Laban. Now, the text seems to suggest, he has struggled with God Himself.

The passage resists easy interpretation, yet it holds the key to understanding Jewish identity. It is not we, the readers, who give it this significance but the Torah itself. For it was then, as dawn was about to break, that Jacob acquired the name that his descendants would bear throughout eternity. The people of the covenant are not the children of Abraham or Isaac but "the children of Israel." It was only with the division of the kingdom and the Assyrian conquest of the north, that those who remained were called generically Judah (the Southern Kingdom), and thus *Yehudim* or, in English, Jews.

Names in the Torah – especially a new name given by God – are not mere labels but signals of character or calling. The moment at which Jacob became Israel contains the clue to who we are. To be sure, our ancestors were later called on to be "a kingdom of priests and a holy nation" but we never lost that earlier appellation. *We are the people who struggled with God and with man and yet survived.* What does this mean?

One way into the text (to be sure, only one of many) is to ask: what happened next? By reasoning backwards, from effect to cause, we may gain an insight into what transpired that night.

The events of the next day are little short of astonishing, especially when juxtaposed to the battle of the night before. The narrative has prepared us to expect a tense encounter. We have read how Jacob was afraid and distressed, and how he made elaborate preparations. Jacob's wrestling match with the adversary further prepares us for a fraught and possibly violent confrontation.

Yet when Esau finally appears, all the fears turn out to be

---

1. Hosea 12:4.
2. *Bereshit Raba* 77:3; cited in Rashi to 32:24.

unfounded. He "runs" to meet Jacob, throws his arms around his neck, kisses him and weeps. There is no anger, animosity or threat of revenge in Esau's behaviour.[3] That is not to say that Jacob's fears were irrational. They were not. After all, Esau had vowed revenge twenty-two years before ("The days of mourning for my father are near; then I will kill my brother Jacob" [27:41]). Esau, however, turns out to be an impulsive man who lives in the mood of the moment. He has none of Cassius's' "lean and hungry look" or Iago's cold calculation. He is quick to anger, quick to forget. The anticlimax when the brothers meet is consistent with Esau's character, if not with Jacob's fears.

More consequential and unexpected is Jacob's behaviour when the brothers meet. First, he "bowed down to the ground seven times," prostrating himself before Esau. Each of his family members does likewise: "Then the maidservants approached, they and their children, and bowed themselves. Next Leah and her children came and bowed themselves. And after came Joseph and Rachel, and they too bowed themselves" (33:6–7). The threefold repetition is significant.

No less striking is Jacob's use of language. Five times he calls Esau *adoni*, "my lord" (in the previous chapter he tells his servants three times to use the same word to Esau). Twice he calls himself Esau's *eved*, "servant" (and four times in the previous chapter tells his servants to do likewise). As with his physical gesture of sevenfold prostration, so with his sevenfold use of the words *adon* and *eved*, this is the choreography of self-abasement.

How are we to connect this with the wrestling match of the previous night? Surely Jacob had won a victory over his adversary. At the very least he had refused to let him go until he received a blessing. The new name implied that henceforth Jacob should have no doubts about his ability to survive any conflict. A man who has "wrestled with God and with men and has overcome" is not one who needs to bow down to anyone or call him "my lord." We would have expected Jacob to show a newfound confidence rather than a wholly surprising servility.

---

3. To be sure, there is a midrashic tradition (*Bereshit Raba* 78:9) that says that Esau "tried to bite" Jacob – a play on the words *n-sh-k*, "to kiss" and *n-sh-kh*, "to bite." We are concerned here, however, only with the plain sense of the text.

Perhaps an answer lies in Jacob's words on first meeting Esau. Esau at first refuses Jacob's gifts, saying "I have plenty [*yesh li rav*], my brother; let what is yours be yours." Jacob's reply is enigmatic, harking back to the mysterious struggle of the previous night, while raising yet more questions:

> "No, please, if I have found favour in your eyes, accept this gift [*minḥa*] from my hand, for to see your face is like seeing the face of God, now that you have received me favourably. Please accept the present [*birkhati*, literally "my blessing"] that was brought to you, for God has been gracious to me and I have everything [*yesh li khol*]." (33:10–11)

Why has the "gift" become a "blessing"? In what conceivable way is seeing the face of Esau like "seeing the face of God"? And what exactly does Jacob mean by altering Esau's words, "I have plenty," into his own "I have everything"? If we could understand these words, perhaps we could understand the link between the wrestling match and the subsequent meeting.

There are many resonances in the passage. The most significant has to do with the word *panim*, "face." Jacob's words to Esau, "to see your *face* is like seeing the *face* of God," clearly echo his remark after the wrestling match, "He called the place Peni'el, saying, 'It is because I saw God *face* to *face*, and yet my life was spared'" (32:31). Altogether, chapters 32 and 33 (the preparations for the meeting, the night-time struggle, and the meeting itself) echo time and again with variants on the word *panim*. This is missed in translation, because *panim* has many forms in Hebrew not evident in English. To take one example, chapter 32, verse 21 is translated:

> [Jacob said to his servants,] "You shall say, 'Your servant Jacob is coming behind us,'" for he thought, "I will pacify him with these gifts I am sending on ahead; later, when I see him, perhaps he will receive me."

There is nothing here to suggest that, in fact, the word *panim* appears *four times* in this verse alone (literally, the second half of the verse should be translated: "for he thought, 'I will wipe [the anger from] his *face* with the gift that goes ahead of my *face*; afterward, when I see his *face* perhaps he will lift up my *face*...'"). There is a drama here and it has to do with faces: the face of Esau, of Jacob, and of God Himself. What is going on?

The clue lies in Jacob's use of the word "blessing." This takes us back twenty-two years to another fateful moment (Genesis chapter 27) in which Jacob, dressed in Esau's clothes, takes his brother's blessing (whether by accident or design, the term *b-r-kh*, "bless" or "blessing," occurs exactly twenty-two times in that chapter). Let us remind ourselves of what the blessing was:

> May God give you of the dew of heaven
> And the richness of the earth –
> An abundance of corn and new wine.
> May nations serve you
> And peoples bow down to you.
> Be lord over your brothers, and may the sons
> of your mother bow down to you.
> May those who curse you be cursed
> And those who bless you be blessed.

The plain sense of these words is clear. They imply *wealth* and *power*. This is the blessing Jacob took, dressed in Esau's clothes, taking Esau's place.

Yet we must remember that there was also a *later* blessing, in Genesis 28. Esau had married two Hittite women, which was "a grief of mind to Isaac and Rebecca" (26:35). Rebecca takes this as an opportunity to send Jacob away to her brother Laban, where he will be safe from Esau's desire for revenge. Before Jacob leaves, Isaac blesses him with these words:

> May God Almighty bless you and make you fruitful and increase your numbers until you become a community of peoples. May He give you and your descendants the blessing of Abraham, so that you may take possession of the land where you now live as an alien, the land God gave to Abraham. (28:3–4)

This second blessing is completely different: it focuses on *children* and a *land*, the two key elements God had repeatedly promised Abraham. These are the "covenantal blessings" which dominate the book of Genesis, and have nothing to do with wealth or power. God promised Abraham that he would have children who would continue the covenant, and a land in which to do so. God never promises Abraham "the dew of heaven and the richness of the earth," nor does He use the language of power, "Be lord over your brothers, and may the sons of your mother bow down to you." Before sending him away from home, Isaac gives Jacob the Abrahamic blessings, saying to him in so many words: it will be you who will continue the covenant into the future.

It is significant to note that at the time of the blessings, Isaac was blind. Jacob's impersonation of Esau was possible only because his father could not see. Genesis 27 is almost an essay on the senses. Deprived of one (sight), Isaac uses the other four. He *tastes* the food, *touches* Jacob's hands (which Rebecca has covered with goatskins to make them feel rough) and *smells* his clothes ("Ah, the smell of my son is like the smell of the field that the Lord has blessed" [27:27]). He also *hears* his voice ("The voice is the voice of Jacob, but the hands are the hands of Esau" [27:22]). Eventually, after considerable doubt, Isaac trusts the evidence of taste, touch and smell over that of sound, and gives Jacob Esau's blessing. He does so only because *he cannot see Jacob's face.* These three elements are enough to allow us to decipher the mystery of the meeting between Jacob and Esau twenty-two years later.

The patriarchs were more than just founders of a new faith. They were also role models. Their lives are significant not only for what they tell us about the past but also for what they tell us about the present – for their challenges are ours.

Abraham was the man who had the strength of conviction to stand apart from the culture of his time – to be different, to refuse to worship the idols of the age, and to listen instead to the inner voice of the one God, even when it meant setting out on a long and risk-laden journey. What carried him through was love (*ḥesed*) – love of God and, yes, the love of humanity that shines through all his deeds and words.

Isaac was the man who knew the reality of sacrifice. He lived, he survived, but not without seeing the knife lifted against him. He knew to the core of his being that to be a child of the covenant is neither easy nor safe. What carried him through was courage (*gevura*) – and for whatever reason, the historical record is clear: to remain Jewish takes courage.

In connection with Jacob, though, the prophet Micah speaks of *truth* ("You will give truth to Jacob" [7:20]). This does not imply truth in a cognitive sense (What are the facts? What is ultimately real?), but rather truth in an existential sense (Who am I? To which story do I belong and what part am I called on to play?). The search for cognitive truth – scientific, metaphysical, artistic – is not specific to the Abrahamic covenant. It is the heritage of all mankind. There is no such thing as Jewish science or economics or psychology. What is, is; and it is given to Homo sapiens as such to discover it (Rashi translates the phrase "Let us make man in our image, *after our likeness*" to mean "with the capacity to understand and discern").[4] The truth with which Jacob spent much of his life wrestling was quite different. It was a truth about identity. Central to it are the words *face* (in which mirror do I look to see who I am?), *name* (by which term do I know myself?) and *blessing* (to what destiny am I called?).

One thing stands out about the first phase in Jacob's life. He longs to be Esau – more specifically, he desires to occupy Esau's place. He struggles with him in the womb. He is born holding on to Esau's heel (this is what gives him the name *Jacob*, "heel-grasper"). He buys Esau's birthright. He dresses in Esau's clothes. He takes Esau's blessing. When the blind Isaac asks him who he is, he replies, "I am Esau, your firstborn" (27:19).

Why? The answer seems clear. Esau is everything Jacob is not. He is the firstborn. He emerges from the womb red and covered in hair (Esau means "fully made"). He is strong, full of energy, a skilled hunter, "a man of the fields." More importantly, he has his father's love. Esau is *Homo naturalis*, a man of nature. He knows that *homo homini lupus est*, "man is wolf to man." He has the strength and skill to fight and win in the Darwinian struggle to survive and the Hobbesian war of "all against all." These are his natural battlegrounds and he relishes the contest.

Esau is the archetypal hero of a hundred myths and legends of the

4. Rashi, 1:26.

ancient world (and of action movies today). He is not without dignity, nor does he lack human feelings. His love for his father Isaac is genuine and touching. The midrash, for sound educational reasons, turned Esau into a bad man. The Torah itself is altogether more subtle and profound. Esau is not a bad man; he is a natural man, celebrating the Homeric virtues and the Nietzschean will to power.

It is not surprising that Jacob's first desire was to be like him. That was the face he first saw in the mirror of his imagination, the face he presented to the blind Isaac when he came to take the blessing. But the face was not the face of Jacob, any more than were the hands.

Nor was the blessing he took the one that was destined for him. The true blessing was the one he received later, when Isaac *knew* he was blessing Jacob, not thinking him to be Esau.

Jacob's blessing had nothing to do with wealth or power. It had to do with children and a land – children he would instruct in the ways of the covenant and a land in which his descendants would strive to construct a covenantal society based on justice and compassion, law and love. To receive that blessing Jacob did not have to dress in Esau's clothes. Instead he had to be himself, not a man of nature, but a person whose ears were attuned to a voice beyond nature, the call of the Author of all to be true to that which cannot be bought by wealth or controlled by power, namely, the human spirit as the breath of God and human dignity as the image of God.

It should now be clear exactly what Jacob was doing when he met Esau twenty-two years later: He was giving back the blessing he had taken all those years before. The herds and flocks he sent to Esau represented wealth ("the dew of heaven and the richness of the earth"). The sevenfold bowing and calling himself "your servant" and Esau "my lord" represented power ("Be lord over your brothers, and may the sons of your mother bow down to you"). Jacob no longer wanted or needed these things. "I have everything" he says – meaning, "I no longer need either wealth or power to be complete." He makes this explicit in the words "Please take [not just 'my gift' but also] *'my blessing.'*" He now knows the blessing he took from Esau was never meant for him, and he is returning it.

It is equally clear what was transacted in the wrestling match the previous night. It was Jacob's inner battle with existential truth. Who was he? The man who longed to be Esau? Or the man called to a different destiny, "the road less travelled," the Abrahamic covenant? "I will not let you go until you bless me," he says to his adversary. The unnamed stranger responds in a way that defies expectation. He does not give Jacob a conventional blessing (You will be rich, or strong, or safe). Nor does he promise Jacob a life free of conflict. The name *Jacob* signifies struggle; the name *Israel* also signifies struggle. But the terms of the conflict have been reversed.

It is as if the man said to him, "In the past, you struggled to be Esau. In the future you will struggle *not to be Esau* but to be yourself. In the past you held on to Esau's heel. In the future you will hold on to God. You will not let go of Him; He will not let go of you. Now let go of Esau so that you can be free to hold on to God." The next day, Jacob does so. He lets go of Esau by giving him back his blessing. And though Jacob had now renounced both wealth and power, and though he still limped from the encounter the night before, the passage ends with the words, *Vayavo Ya'akov shalem*, "And Jacob emerged complete." That is the stunning truth at which Jacob finally arrived, and to which the name Israel is testimony. To be complete we do not need Esau's blessings of wealth and power. Ours is another face, an alternative destiny, a different blessing. The face we bear is the image we see reflected in the face of God when we wrestle with Him and refuse to let go.

Not by accident was this episode the birth of our identity (our "name") as Israel. At almost every significant juncture in our history we have wrestled with civilizations who worshipped the gods of nature: wealth ("the dew of heaven and the richness of the earth") or power ("may nations serve you and peoples bow down to you"). Israel never knew the wealth of ancient Greece or Rome, Renaissance Italy or aristocratic France. It never knew the power of great empires, their invincible armies and weapons of destruction. When it longed for those things, as in the days of Solomon, it lost its way.

Israel's strength never lay in itself but in that which was other and greater than itself: the power that transcends all earthly powers, and the wealth that is not physical but spiritual, a matter of mind and heart. Jews have often wished to be someone else, the Esaus of the age. Too often, they knew what it was, in Shakespeare's words, to

> ...look upon myself, and curse my fate,
> Wishing me like to one more rich in hope,
> Featur'd like him, like him with friends possess'd,
> Desiring this man's art, and that man's scope,
> With what I most enjoy contented least.
>
> (Sonnet XXIX 4–8)

That is a feeling we must ultimately reject. The Torah does not ask us to think badly of Esau. To the contrary, it commands us: "Do not hate an Edomite [i.e., a descendant of Esau], for he is your brother" (Deuteronomy 23:7). It did however ask us to wrestle, as did Jacob, alone, at night, in the depths of our soul, and discover the face, the name and the blessing that is ours. Before Jacob could be at peace with Esau he had to learn that he was not Esau but Israel – he who wrestles with God and never lets go.

Surviving Crisis

T he Torah is not just a book to read; it is a book to live by. In that spirit, I want to reflect in this essay on how the story of Jacob's wrestling match with the angel can help us survive crisis, when we, like our ancestor, feel ourselves alone, afraid and in distress. It can happen in many ways: we can lose our job, our savings, our self respect. We can suffer bereavement and feel ourselves surrounded by a cloud of grief. We can find ourselves in the midst of controversy, subject to the sometimes brutal criticism of others. We can feel ourselves to be a failure. These are terrifying moments when life seems drained of meaning, when we can no longer concentrate or connect with others, when we find it hard to sleep at night or stay awake during the day, when mere existence seems a burden we lack the strength to carry.

At such times, it can sometimes help to retrace the steps of our ancestors when they faced similar situations. One of the most beautiful aspects of Genesis, often lost when we read the stories through the lens of midrash, is that its heroes and heroines are recognizably human. They too have fears and doubts, none more so than Jacob, the man whose name, Israel, we bear. Often it is argued that we should not read the text at its surface meaning, precisely because this would make them seem mere mortals like us, and there is much to be said for this point of view. But there is a contrary case. The Torah portrays the patriarchs and matriarchs in all their human complexity so that we can identify with them and take strength from their stories rather than seeing them as impossibly remote from all we know and are. What follows is what I have learned from Jacob's night-time struggle.

And Jacob was left alone: The wrestling match with the stranger takes place after the most elaborately conceived and executed preparations for any event in Genesis. Jacob had prepared himself for three things: diplomacy, war and prayer. He sent huge gifts of cattle to appease Esau's anger. He divided his camp in two so that even if one were destroyed the other might survive. He prayed to God. He covered every eventuality, adopted every strategy, anticipated every outcome – except the one that actually happened, the appearance of an unnamed adversary who fought with him.

Crises happen, and there is no way we can make ourselves immune to them. That is the human condition and we cannot escape it. We live toward an unknown, unknowable future. Even the answer God gives Moses when he asks Him His name – "I will be what I will be" – tells us this. God is saying, "You will not know what, where or how I will be until the moment comes." Faith is not certainty: it is the courage to live with uncertainty. Indeed that is why we need faith, because life is uncertain. Even in the twenty-first century when we know so much about the universe, cosmology, the human genome and the workings of the human brain, there is one thing we do not know and never will: what tomorrow will bring.

And a man wrestled with him: We do not know who this stranger was, a man, an angel or God Himself. What we surely do know is that the wrestling match was an externalisation of Jacob's inner conflict, the result of his fear and distress. However we construe the passage, Jacob was wrestling with himself, and that is where the real battle takes place. If we can win the struggle "in here," we can win it "out there," and if we cannot win the struggle with ourselves, we will eventually lose our struggle with the world.

The late Viktor Frankl, a psychotherapist, was a prisoner in Auschwitz, and it was there that he discovered his vocation. He saw how difficult it was to sustain the will to live, and those who lost it, died. He took it as his mission to give people back the will to live. He would talk to them to discover whether they had an unfulfilled dream or a task to complete. Once he found it he was able to give them a reason to survive. Something was calling to them from the future, and this was sometimes enough to give them the inner strength to keep going. After the war he founded a new school of psychotherapy – he called it Logotherapy – based on what he called "Man's search for meaning," the power of which he had seen in the camp.[1]

Crisis can challenge us at the deepest level of the self, threatening our self-confidence and self-respect. That is where we need to concentrate our effort and focus our energies. We are here because someone, the One, wanted us to be. He loves us, understands us, forgives us when we acknowledge our mistakes, and believes in us more than we believe in ourselves. That is where true self-confidence is born: the faith that lights the way in the heart of darkness. "The Lord is with me; I will not be afraid. What can man do to me?" (Psalms 118:6). "The Lord is my light and my salvation – whom shall I fear? The Lord is the stronghold of my life – of whom shall I be afraid?" (27:1).

Rashi's grandson Rashbam gives an extraordinary interpretation of Jacob's wrestling match.[2] Fearing the confrontation with Esau, Jacob wanted to run away, and God sent an angel to wrestle with him to stop him doing so. On this reading, God was teaching Jacob how to wrestle with his fears and defeat them. "Who is strong?" asked Ben Zoma. Not one who can defeat his enemies but one who "who masters his impulses."[3] Ben Zoma's proof text was a verse from Proverbs: "He who is slow to anger is better than the mighty, and he who rules over his spirit than he who conquers a city" (16:22).

What actually happened the next day, when Jacob finally came face to face with Esau? Instead of attacking him, Esau ran to meet him

1. See Viktor E. Frankl, *Man's Search for Meaning: An Introduction to Logotherapy* (New York: Simon & Schuster, 1984); *The Doctor and the Soul* (New York: Vintage Books, 1986); *The Will to Meaning* (New York: New American Library, 1988).
2. Rashbam, commentary to *Bereshit* 32. Rashbam compares Jacob to Jonah, who also tried to flee.
3. *Avot* 4:1.

and embraced him (32:1). There was no anger, no violence, no lingering trace of resentment. Everything Jacob feared, failed to happen. Was
this mere coincidence, happenstance? Were Jacob's fears simply mis-
placed? I believe the Torah is teaching a deeper truth, that once Jacob
had resolved the conflict within himself he had removed the source of
tension between himself and Esau. Even animals sense fear. Predators
chase those who run away. The way of safety is to stay calm and still.

An inner sense of self-confidence and trust does not mean that
one will never have to fight battles. Economics and politics are intrinsically conflictual. Much of life is a zero-sum competition for scarce
goods in which some win, some lose. But spiritual goods – love, trust,
friendship, the pursuit of knowledge – are not zero-sum. The more we
share, the more we have. That I win does not mean that you lose, and
vice versa. So my self-respect never needs to be purchased at the cost of
yours. I can respect you without denigrating myself. I can make space
for you without denying myself. So our deepest psychological and spiritual goods need never be bought at the cost of others. That knowledge
alone – that Jacob and Esau can each have their own blessings without
envying one another – is enough to remove many, even most, of the
conflicts by which people cause one another pain.

The sun rose upon him as he passed Penu'el, limping because of his
hip (32:31): Jacob limped after the fight. Crisis is real; the suffering to
which it gives rise can cut deep; even when you survive, you limp; long
afterwards, perhaps for a lifetime, you bear the scars. But they are hon-
ourable scars. They tell that you fought and won, and greater is one who
fought and won that one who, fearing confrontation, takes the path of
least resistance and submits.

I will not let you go until you bless me: These words of Jacob to
the angel lie at the very core of surviving crisis. Each of us knows from
personal experience that events that seemed disappointing, painful,
even humiliating at the time, can be the most important in our lives.
Through them we learned how to try harder next time; or they taught
us a truth about ourselves; or they shifted our life into a new and more
fruitful direction. We learn, not from our successes but from our failures. We mature and grow strong and become more understanding and
forgiving through the mistakes we make. A protected life is a fragile and

superficial life. Strength comes from knowing the worst and refusing to give in. Jacob/Israel has bequeathed us many gifts, but few more valuable than the obstinacy and resilience that can face hard times and say of them: "I will not let you go until you bless me." I will not give up or move on until I have extracted something positive from this pain and turned it into blessing.

That is how the story of Jacob's struggle has helped me, and it serves to emphasize how important it is not to lose sight of the biblical text by burying it under layers of midrashic reinterpretation. What Genesis tells us is that the heroes of our faith did not live charmed lives. They suffered exiles, knew danger, had their hopes disappointed and their expectations delayed. They fought, they struggled, but they neither gave in nor gave up. They were not serene. Sometimes they laughed in disbelief; there were times when they feared, trembled, wept and even gave way to anger. For they were human beings, not angels; they were people with whom we can identify, not saints to be worshipped. Jacob taught us that we cannot pre-empt crisis, nor should we minimise it, but we can survive it, thus becoming worthy of bearing the name of one who struggled with God and with men and prevailed.

Jacob's Destiny, Israel's Name

The two previous essays reflected on Jacob's nighttime struggle with the angel. In this essay I want to look at the aftermath, for it was as a result of this encounter that the Jewish people acquired its name, Israel, meaning "one who has struggled with God and with men and has overcome." It is, by any standards, a strange, unconventional, thought-provoking name.

Jacob is not, at first glance, the most obvious figure in Tanakh to represent and epitomize the Jewish people. There are other compelling alternatives: Abraham, who began the journey; Isaac, the first Jewish child; Moses, who took the people from slavery to freedom and gave them its most precious possession, the Torah; David, Israel's greatest king and poet; even Isaiah, its greatest visionary of hope.

Nor is the phrase "one who has struggled with God and with men and has overcome" the most natural characterization of Jewish identity. We can think of others. In Exodus God summons Israel to be "a kingdom of priests and a holy nation." Isaiah speaks of Israel as "a covenant for the people and a light for the nations" (Isaiah 42:6). Zechariah gives one of the most concise summaries of the Jewish experience: "Not by might nor by power, but by My spirit, says the Lord Almighty" (Zechariah 4:6). So why Israel, with its implication of ceaseless struggle?

A fascinating possibility is raised by the writings of a critic of Judaism, Nikolai Berdyaev. Berdyaev (1874–1948) was a Russian intellectual. Initially a Marxist, he broke with the movement after the Russian revolution and its aftermath, the death of freedom. He became an unconventional Christian – he had been charged with blasphemy for criticizing the Russian Orthodox Church in 1913 – and went into exile, eventually settling in Paris.

In *The Meaning of History*, Berdyaev wrote one of the most remarkable tributes to Judaism:

> I remember how the materialist interpretation of history, when I attempted in my youth to verify it by applying it to the destinies of peoples, broke down in the case of the Jews, where destiny seemed absolutely inexplicable from the materialistic standpoint.... Its survival is a mysterious and wonderful phenomenon demonstrating that the life of this people is governed by a special predetermination, transcending the processes of adaptation expounded by the materialistic interpretation of history. The survival of the Jews, their resistance to destruction, their endurance under absolutely peculiar conditions and the fateful role played by them in history: all these point to the particular and mysterious foundations of their destiny.[1]

Yet Berdyaev believed that Jews and Judaism were profoundly wrong about the central question of human life. They were, he says, "obsessed by the passionate idea of justice and its terrestrial fulfilment." They believed that redemption could be achieved on earth. The "intense Jewish striving after truth, justice and happiness" was responsible for the perennial restlessness of the Jewish spirit and its often revolutionary expression. Berdyaev regarded Marxism as a secularised version of the Jewish belief in the messianic age.

His own view was that this is an error and an impossibility.

---

1. Nikolai Berdyaev, *The Meaning of History* (New Jersey: Transaction, 2006), 86–87.

Human destiny, "whose pains and torments can in no wise be redeemed within the narrow limits of a single life, finds its fulfilment in another life." Truth, justice, and happiness belong to heaven, not earth; the world to come, not this world; the immortal soul, not the mortal body. "He who believes in immortality ought to look soberly on terrestrial life and realise that it is impossible to achieve a conclusive victory on earth over the dark irrational principle; and that sufferings, evil and imperfections are the inevitable lot of man."[2]

Berdyaev, I believe, framed the alternatives sharply and correctly. The classic function of religion throughout history has been to reconcile people to the random brutalities of fate, the injustices of society, the triumph of might over right, the brevity of life itself and the pains and disappointments with which it is fraught. In a thousand different ways, religion has represented an alternative reality, a "haven in a heartless world," an escape from the strife and conflict of everyday life into the quiet spaces of the soul, or the thought of life beyond death. Religion, faith, spirituality – these words conjure up ideas of peace, serenity, inwardness, meditation, calm, acceptance, consolation, bliss.

Judaism is, intellectually, spiritually and emotionally, the great exception.

For we believe that sufferings, evil and imperfections are *not* the inevitable lot of man; they are not woven into the fabric of the universe that God created and pronounced seven times "good." Justice, freedom, human dignity, equality of respect, integrity and compassion are to be fought for *here*, not in heaven. The sages said that when Moses ascended to heaven to receive the Torah, the angels objected. How could God entrust His most precious possession to mere mortals? Are there murderers among you, said Moses to the angels, that you need the command, "You shall not kill"? Are there adulterers among you that you need to be told, "You shall not commit adultery"?[3] The Torah was not given to the ministering angels, but to humans, because humans need it. And in giving human beings freewill, God expressed His faith that one day

2. Ibid., 87–107.
3. *Shabbat* 88b-89a.

they would learn to use it responsibly and morally and thus create a world of societal beatitude.

Berdyaev's view represents the perennial temptation known as Gnosticism, a complex doctrine that can nonetheless be summarized as "this world, bad; the world to come, good." Ultimately Gnosticism is incompatible with monotheism, for why would a good God create a universe in which "sufferings, evil and imperfections are the inevitable lot of man"? Why create a species, Homo sapiens, in His own image and likeness, only to subject it to inescapable pain? Gnosticism played a considerable part in the early life of the Church; many previously lost Gnostic Gospels were rediscovered among the Nag Hammadi manuscripts, found in Egypt in 1945, two years before the discovery of the Dead Sea Scrolls. Gnostics in fact held that the physical universe was created by a demiurge, a lesser god, and that the true God, the God of the spirit, has no place on earth. It is a form of dualism – probably what the sages were referring to when they spoke of people who believed in *shetei reshuyot*, "two [divine] domains."[4]

Gnosticism sounds ancient and arcane, yet its appeal is timeless and powerful. It is not easy to reconcile the existence of God and the commands of faith with the world as we know it, fraught with tension and tragedy. Far easier intellectually and psychologically to think of religion and God as belonging to a different dimension altogether: in heaven, not earth; somewhere else not here; in life after death or the immortal soul, in meditative calm or mystical withdrawal. So religion can make us indifferent to the world or reconciled to it: indifferent because this is not where God is found, or reconciled because in some way human suffering is the will of God for which we will be rewarded in the world to come. That is what Karl Marx meant when he wrote his famous line, "Religion is the sigh of the oppressed creature, the heart of a heartless world, and the soul of soulless conditions. It is the opium of the people [*das Opium des Volkes*]."

Because we are so used to it, we forget how rare and difficult the

---

4. On Gnosticism, see Hans Jonas, *The Gnostic Religion* (London: Routledge, 1992); Elaine Pagels, *The Gnostic Gospels* (London: Penguin, 1990). On *shetei reshuyot*, see for example, *Berakhot* 33b.

Jewish approach is. Indeed Europe did not develop an activist approach toward poverty and suffering, freedom and democracy, industry, economic growth and the beginnings of a classless society until, in the seventeenth century, Christians began reading Tanakh again, made possible by the invention of printing and the availability of Bibles in vernacular translation. This gave rise to Calvinism, the closest Christianity came to Judaism, and it was responsible for the English revolution and the faith of the pilgrim fathers who created modern America.[5]

Berdyaev was right to see that the belief that redemption lies in this world, not the next, was responsible for all the features we associate with Jacob/Israel and the people who bear the name of one who struggled with God and with men and prevailed. If you believe that truth, justice and happiness are to be pursued in this world, then you must struggle with this world. Sometimes this meant wrestling with idolatry, superstition, paganism and the whole lexicon of ancient beliefs. Now it means wrestling with secularism, materialism and consumerism. There were times – until the nineteenth century – when much of Europe was illiterate and Jews alone practised universal education. There were others – the twentieth century, for example – when Jews became the targets of Fascism and Communism, systems that worshipped power and desecrated the dignity of the individual. Judaism is a religion of protest – the counter-voice in the conversation of mankind.

And it means struggling with God, as Moses and Jeremiah and Job struggled with God. In no other religious literature – certainly not Christianity or Islam – do human beings argue with God. Recall that it is not heretics who do this in Judaism, but the exemplars and role models of faith. They did so in the name of justice – recall Abraham's "Shall the Judge of all the earth not do justice?" For if justice belongs on earth, not just in heaven, then we may not accept seeming injustice, we

5. See Perry Miller, *The New England Mind: The Seventeenth Century* (Cambridge, MA: Harvard University Press, 1971); Michael Walzer, *The Revolution of the Saints: A Study in the Origins of Radical Politics* (London: Weidenfeld and Nicolson, 1966); Christopher Hill, *The English Bible and the Seventeenth-Century Revolution* (London: Penguin, 1994).

must protest it. Indeed, it was God Himself who empowered Abraham and Moses to do so.

Judaism is not an escape from the world, but an engagement with the world. It does not anaesthetise us to the pains and apparent injustices of life. It does not reconcile us to suffering. It asks us to play our part in the most daunting undertaking ever asked by God of mankind: to construct relationships, communities, and ultimately a society, that will create a home for the Divine Presence.[6] And that means wrestling with God and with men and refusing to give up or despair.

No one exemplifies this condition more profoundly than Jacob. Abraham symbolises faith as love. Isaac represents faith as fear, reverence, awe. But Jacob lives faith as struggle. Often his life seems to be a matter of escaping one danger into another. He flees from his vengeful brother only to find himself at the mercy of deceptive Laban. He escapes from Laban only to encounter Esau marching to meet him with a force of four hundred men. He emerges from that meeting unscathed, only to be confronted with the rape of his daughter Dina and the conflict between Joseph and his other sons. Alone among the patriarchs, he dies in exile. Jacob wrestles, as his descendants – the children of Israel – continue to wrestle with the world.

Yet Jacob never gives up, and is never defeated. He is the man whose greatest religious experiences occur when he is alone, at night, and far from home. Jacob wrestles with the angel of destiny and inner conflict and says, "I will not let you go until you bless me." That is how he rescues hope from catastrophe – as Jews have always done. Their darkest nights have always been preludes to their most creative dawns.

The ideals of Torah are high, and the story told by Tanakh and Jewish history is all too often suffused with failure and shortcomings. Yet Judaism produced generation after generation of prophets, sages, philosophers and poets, who never relinquished the dream, abandoned the ideals, or lowered their sights. They kept going, as Jacob kept going. There is grandeur in this refusal to abandon the struggle, this sustained reluctance to accept the world as it is, conforming to the conventional

---

6. See, for a fuller treatment, Jonathan Sacks, *To Heal a Fractured World* (London: Continuum, 2005; New York: Schocken, 2005).

wisdom, following the herd. Jews have always been pioneers of the spirit, disturbers of the peace.

The path chosen by Jacob/Israel is not for the fainthearted. *Zis schver zu sein a Yid*, they used to say: "It's hard to be a Jew." In some ways, it still is. It is not easy to face our fears and wrestle with them, refusing to let go until we have turned them into renewed strength and blessing. But speaking personally, I would have it no other way. Judaism is not faith as illusion, seeing the world through rose-tinted lenses as we would wish it to be. It is faith as relentless honesty, seeing evil as evil and fighting it in the name of life, and good, and God. That is our vocation. It remains a privilege to carry Jacob's destiny, Israel's name.

Vayeshev
וישב

With *Vayeshev*, the story shifts from Jacob to his children. The tension we have already sensed between Leah and Rachel is transferred to the next generation in the form of the rivalry between Joseph and his brothers, the story whose twists and turns take us to the end of Genesis.

Joseph is Jacob's favourite son, firstborn of his beloved Rachel. The envy and antagonism of his brothers leads them to sell Joseph into slavery in Egypt, an act that will many years later result in the entire family, by then a nation, being enslaved.

The Joseph story is full of fascinating vignettes, and in the studies that follow I look first at Reuben, Jacob's eldest son; then at Jacob's refusal to be comforted for the loss of Joseph; then at the relationship between Judah and Tamar, and lastly at Tamar and another biblical heroine, Ruth.

Common to them all is the power of the narrative to confound our expectations. Reuben, the firstborn, seems to suffer self-doubt that robs him of the courage to take decisive action. Jacob's interminable grief hides a refusal to give up hope. Tamar turns out to be a paradigm of moral sensibility and courage. Two unlikely women play a part in the lineage of David, Israel's greatest king. Part of the continuing power of these stories lies in their defiance of narrative convention. You can never predict in advance, the Torah seems to suggest, where virtue is to be found.

The Tragedy of Reuben

Reuben is the great might-have-been in the Torah. His father Jacob, in his dying words, the final blessings which tell us how he saw each of his sons, speaks of him thus:

> Reuben, you are my firstborn,
> My power and the beginning of my might,
> Pre-eminent in bearing
> Pre-eminent in strength.
> Unstable as water, you will not be pre-eminent. (49:3–4)

His is a story of potential unfulfilled, virtue not quite realized, greatness so close yet unachieved.

In *Parashat Vayeshev*, we are granted an insight into how such failure can happen. The Torah freeze-frames a critical juncture in Reuben's life, showing the diverging paths he faced when confronted with a fateful moral challenge.

The background to the scene is the story of the early years of Joseph, Jacob's child by his second wife and first love, Rachel. Jacob – the man who loves more than any other figure in Genesis – cannot help showing his favouritism, to the hurt and slight of his other sons. The vignettes we have of Joseph as an adolescent are (as Rashi notes) less than endearing.[1] He tells tales to his father about his brothers. He has dreams in which his family bows down to him, and worse – he reports them.[2] There is about him, the air of a spoiled child.[3] His father tolerates his behaviour and even gives him a richly embroidered cloak, the famous "coat of many colours," the sight of which acts as a constant provocation to the other sons.

One day, as his brothers are tending the flocks far from home, Jacob sends Joseph to see how they are doing. On this encounter, the whole future of the children of Israel will depend. The brothers see Joseph from afar, and the sight of the cloak enrages them. They realize that, alone, with no one to witness, they can kill Joseph and concoct a tale that will be impossible to refute. Only Reuben protests.

It is at this point that the Torah does something it does nowhere else: It makes a statement that, construed literally, is obviously false – indeed, the text goes on immediately to show that it was not quite so. The verse states: "Reuben heard and saved him [Joseph] from their hands" (37:21). He did not. The discrepancy is so obvious that most translations simply do not render the phrase literally. What Reuben actually did was to *attempt* to save him. The phrase "Reuben heard *and saved him*" tells us what might have been, not what actually was.

Reuben's plan was simple. He told the brothers not to kill Joseph but to let him die, thus averting the immediate danger:

1. See Rashi, commentary to *Bereshit* 37:2 on the phrases *Vehu na'ar* and *Veet dibatam ra'ah*. Ramban explains that Joseph was hated by the sons of the handmaids because "he brought ill report of them to their father" (37:2), and by the sons of Leah because "they saw that their father loved him more than all his brothers" (37:4), reminding them that their father had loved Joseph's mother Rachel more than theirs.
2. The text says "And they hated him yet more because of his dreams and his words" (37:8). *Keli Yakar* (R. Ephraim Solomon of Luntshits, 1550–1619) explains the double hate: (1) they resented him for dreaming that he would rule over them, and (2) they were angered at the fact that he reported the dream to them when they did not wish to speak to him at all.
3. Rashi, on the basis of *Bereshit Raba*, takes the phrase *Vehu na'ar* (37:2), usually translated as "he was a lad," to mean "he acted childishly."

"Let's not take his life," he said. "Don't shed any blood. Throw him into this cistern here in the desert, but don't lay a hand on him." (37:22)

The text then – again unusually, for it is rare for the Torah to describe a person's thoughts – explains Reuben's intent: "[Reuben said this] *in order to save him from their hand* and take him back to his father." Reuben had no intention of letting Joseph die. His plan was to persuade the brothers to leave Joseph in the pit so that, when their attention was elsewhere, he could come back to it, lift him out and take him home.

What happens next is obscure, though the outcome is clear. While Reuben was somewhere else, Joseph was taken from the pit and sold to a passing caravan of merchants who carry him to Egypt to be sold as a slave. The text itself makes it impossible to determine whether this was done by the other brothers at the suggestion of Judah, or by passing Midianites.[4] Reuben, unaware of all this, returns to the pit to rescue Joseph but finds him gone. He is bereft. "When Reuben returned to the cistern and saw that Joseph was not there, he tore his clothes. He went back to his brothers and said, 'The boy is not! And I, where can I go?'" (37:29–30).

Commenting on this episode, the midrash states:

> If Reuben had only known that the Holy One, blessed be He, would write of him, "And Reuben heard and saved him from their hands," he would have picked Joseph up on his shoulders and carried him back to his father. [5]

This is a deeply puzzling assertion. Did Reuben really need the endorsement of Heaven to do the right thing? Did he need God's approval before rescuing his brother? Yet, as we will see, this holds the essential clue about Reuben's character. It tells us what stands between what might-have-been and what was.

---

4. See Nechamah Leibowitz, *Iyyunim beSefer Bereshit* (Jerusalem, 1972), 279–88, for a fine analysis of the various readings given by the commentators.
5. *Vayikra Raba,* 34:8.

Reuben is the Hamlet of Genesis, whose "native hue of resolution" is "sicklied o'er by the pale cast of thought." He is a person of good intentions. He cares. He thinks. He is not led by the crowd or by his darker instincts. He penetrates to the moral core of a situation. That is the first thing we notice about him. The second, however, is that somehow his interventions backfire. They fail to achieve their effect. Attempting to make things better, Reuben often makes them worse. The Torah clearly wants us to reflect on Reuben's character. To this end it paints a portrait of the young man in a series of rapidly sketched yet revealing vignettes.

In the first, we see him in the fields during the wheat harvest. He finds some mandrakes. From the context it appears that mandrakes were believed to be both an aphrodisiac and a fertility drug. His first thought is to give them to his mother Leah. This tells us something about Reuben. He is not thinking about himself but about her. He knows she feels unloved, and identifies with her anguish with all the sensitivity of an eldest child. He hopes that, with the aid of the mandrakes, Leah will be able to win Jacob's attention, perhaps even his love.

It is a strikingly mature and thoughtful act. Yet it has negative consequences. It provokes a bitter row between the two sisters, Leah and Rachel. Rachel sees the mandrakes and wants them for herself. The following exchange then takes place:

> Rachel said to Leah, "Please give me some of your son's mandrakes." But she said to her, "Wasn't it enough that you took away my husband? Will you take my son's mandrakes too?" (30:14–15)

This is the only time that angry words are reported between the two sisters. Reuben, seeking to help Leah, ends up creating a scene in which her bitterness rises to the surface.

We next see Reuben after Rachel's death. An obscure incident takes place which has tragic consequences. The biblical text is cryptic:

> So Rachel died and was buried on the way to Ephrath (that is, Bethlehem). Over her tomb Jacob set up a pillar, and to this day that pillar marks Rachel's tomb. Israel moved on again and pitched his tent beyond Migdal Eder. While Israel was living in

that region, Reuben went in and slept with his father's concubine
Bilhah, and Israel heard of it... (35:19–22)

Read literally, this suggests that Reuben took his father's place in Bilhah's
tent – an almost Oedipal act of displacement, as we discover later in the
Bible when Absolom does the same with his father David's concubine
(II Samuel 16:21). Rashi, following midrashic tradition, prefers a gentler
explanation. When Rachel died, Jacob, who had slept in her tent, moved
his bed to the tent of Bilhah, her handmaid. This, for Reuben, was an
unbearable provocation. It was bad enough that Jacob preferred Rachel
to her sister Leah, but intolerable to Reuben that he should prefer her
handmaid to his mother. Reuben therefore moved Jacob's bed from
Bilhah's tent to Leah's.

Even according to this interpretation, however, it is clear that
Jacob misunderstood the act and believed that his son had in fact usurped
his place. He never forgot or forgave the incident and on his death-bed
he reminds Reuben of it:

> Unstable as water, you will not be pre-eminent,
> For you went up onto your father's bed,
> Onto my couch and defiled it. (49:4)

Describing the event, the Torah uses an unusual stylistic device. After
the words, "And Israel heard of it," the Masoretic text indicates a para-
graph break in the middle of a sentence. The effect is to signal a silence,
a complete breakdown in communication. Hence the pathos of the
rabbinic interpretation of the passage, which certainly fits all we know
about Reuben. He was not seeking to displace Jacob but rather to draw
his father's attention to the hurt and distress of Leah. Yet Jacob says
nothing, giving Reuben no opportunity to clear his name or explain
why he did what he did. The result: a second tragedy.

Inevitably, we are drawn to yet another scene, chronologically
the first – Reuben's birth. One does not need to be a Freudian to hear,
in this passage, the key to Reuben's character. Leah, we recall, had been
substituted for Rachel on the wedding night. It was Rachel whom Jacob
loved and thought he was marrying, after seven years working for her

father Laban. The next morning, when Jacob discovers the identity of his new wife, there is an angry scene between the two men.

Jacob does marry Rachel a week later, and thereafter Leah must live with the knowledge that she was not her husband's choice. There then follows a passage of great pathos:

> When the Lord saw that Leah was not loved, he opened her womb, but Rachel was barren. Leah became pregnant and gave birth to a son. She named him Reuben ["see, a son"], for she said, "It is because the Lord has seen my misery. Surely my husband will love me now." She conceived again, and when she gave birth to a son she said, "Because the Lord heard that I am not loved, he gave me this one too." So she named him Shimon. (29:31–33)

Leah hoped that the birth of Reuben would make Jacob love her. But he does not – we know this because she is still voicing the same hope when Shimon is born. Reuben has to carry with him throughout his life the knowledge of his mother's slight and his father's lack of attention. Significantly, it is Leah, not Jacob, who gives both Reuben and Shimon their names. It is almost as if Jacob is not there.[6]

We now have a rich, penetrating portrait of Reuben – and we now know that the psychological key to his character is already given at his birth.

Jacob is a hero of faith, the man who gave Israel its name, the only patriarch whose children all remained within the covenant. Yet the complexity of Jacob's character is light years away from the idealised heroes

---

6. Incidentally, it is Rachel, not Jacob, who names her son Joseph (30:23). There is an extraordinary implication hinted at in the text, that Jacob failed not only to heed Leah's emotional state, but also Rachel's, despite his love for her. When Rachel, earlier in the story, cries to Jacob, "Give me children or else I die" (30:1), Jacob replies "Am I in place of God who has withheld from you the fruit of the womb?" On this, the midrash (*Bereshit Raba* 71:7) comments: "Is this the way to answer a woman in distress?" (and see Ramban ad loc.). A close reading of the Jacob narrative suggests that one of its themes is systemic failure of communication within the family. Alternatively, it may be that the text is suggesting that if you fail to heed those whom you do not love, you will eventually fail to heed those you do love.

of other religious traditions. In Jacob we discover that the life of faith is not simple. Not by accident does his name Israel mean "the one who wrestled with God and with men and prevailed." We discover something else as well. Every virtue carries with it a corresponding danger. The person who is over-generous may condemn his own family to poverty. The individual who, like Aaron, chooses peace at any price, can sometimes allow and abet those around him to make a golden calf. There is no single authoritative role model in Judaism. Instead there are many: Abraham, Isaac and Jacob; Moses, Aaron and Miriam; kings, prophets and priests; masters of halakha and *aggada*; sages and saints, poets and philosophers. The reason is that no one can embody all the virtues all the time. A strength here is a weakness there.

Jacob loved, passionately and deeply. That was his strength, but also his weakness. His love for Rachel meant that he could not bestow equal favour on Leah. His longing for a child by Rachel meant that there was something lacking in his relationship with Leah's firstborn, Reuben. Had he loved less, there might have been no problem. He might have divided his attention more equally. But had he loved less, he would not have been Jacob.

The result, however, is that Reuben carries with him a lack of confidence, an uncertainty, that at critical moments robs him of his capacity to carry through a course of action that he knows to be right. He begins well but does not drive the deed to closure. Returning with the mandrakes he might have bided his time until Leah was alone. After Rachel's death he might have spoken directly to his father instead of moving the beds. In the face of his brothers' murderous intentions toward Joseph he might, as the midrash says, have simply carried him home. Instead he hesitated, choosing to put off the moment until the brothers were elsewhere. The result was tragedy. It is impossible not to recognise in Reuben a person of the highest ethical sensibilities. But though he had conscience, he lacked courage. He knew what was right, but lacked the resolve to do it boldly and decisively. In that hesitation, more was lost than Joseph. Lost also was Reuben's chance to become the hero he might and should have been.

If Reuben had only known, says the midrash. If only he had known that the Torah would write of him, "And Reuben heard and saved him from their hands" – known that his intention was recognized and valued by God as if it were the deed – he might have found the courage to carry it through into action. But Reuben could not know. He had not read the story. None of us can read the story of our life – we can only live it. The result is that we live in and with uncertainty. Doubt can lead to delay until the moment is lost. In an instant of arrested intention, Reuben lost his chance of changing history.

Reuben could not read his story, but we can. If there is a single verse in Tanakh that stands as a commentary on his life it is the inexpressibly poignant line from Psalms 27:10: "Though my father and mother may forsake me, the Lord will receive me." Jacob, being human, loved some, not others. God, *not* being human, loves each of us, and that is our greatest source of strength. God heeds those not heard. He loves those whom others do not love. Reuben, still a young man, did not yet know this. But we, reading his story and the rest of Tanakh, do.

We are here for a reason, conceived in love, brought into being by the One who brought the universe into being, who knows our innermost thoughts, values our good intentions, and has more faith in us than we have in ourselves. That, if only we meditate on it, gives us the strength to turn intention into deed, lifting us from the person we might have been into the person we become.

Refusing Comfort, Keeping Hope

The deception has taken place. Joseph has been sold into slavery. His brothers dipped his coat in blood. They bring it back to their father, saying: "Look what we have found. Do you recognise it? Is this your son's robe or not?" Jacob recognises it and replies, "It is my son's robe. A wild beast has devoured him. Joseph has been torn to pieces." We then read:

> Jacob rent his clothes, put on sackcloth, and mourned his son for a long time. His sons and daughters tried to comfort him, but he *refused to be comforted*. He said, "I will go down to the grave mourning for my son." (37:34-35)

There are laws in Judaism about the limits of grief – *shiva, sheloshim*, a year. There is no such thing as a bereavement for which grief is endless. The Talmud says that God admonishes one who weeps beyond the appointed time, "You are not more compassionate than I."[1] And yet Jacob refuses to be comforted.

A midrash gives a remarkable explanation. "One can be comforted

1. *Mo'ed Katan* 27b.

for one who is dead, but not for one who is still living," it says. In other words, Jacob refused to be comforted *because he had not yet given up hope that Joseph was still alive.* That, tragically, is the fate of those who have lost members of their family (the parents of soldiers missing in action, for example), but have as yet no proof that they are dead. They cannot go through the normal stages of mourning because they cannot abandon the possibility that the missing person is still capable of being rescued. Their continuing anguish is a form of loyalty; to give up, to mourn, to be reconciled to loss is a kind of betrayal. In such cases, grief lacks closure. To refuse to be comforted is to refuse to give up hope.

Yet on what basis did Jacob continue to hope? Surely he had recognized Joseph's blood-stained coat – he said explicitly, "A wild beast has devoured him. Joseph has been torn to pieces." Do these words not mean that he had accepted that Joseph was dead?

The late David Daube made a suggestion that I find convincing.[2] The words the sons say to Jacob – *haker na*, literally "identify please" – have a quasi-legal connotation. Daube relates this passage to another, with which it has close linguistic parallels:

> If a man gives a donkey, an ox, a sheep or any other animal to his neighbour for safekeeping and it dies or is injured or is taken away while no one is looking, the issue between them will be settled by the taking of an oath before the Lord that the neighbour did not lay hands on the other person's property... If it [the animal] was torn to pieces by a wild animal, he shall bring the remains as evidence and he will not be required to pay for the torn animal. (Exodus 22:10–13)

The issue at stake is the extent of responsibility borne by a guardian (*shomer*). If the animal is lost through negligence, the guardian is at fault and must make good the loss. If there is no negligence, merely *force majeure,* an unavoidable, unforeseeable accident, the guardian is exempt from blame. One such case is where the loss has been caused by a wild animal. The wording in the law – *tarof yitaref,* "torn to pieces" – exactly

---

2. David Daube, *Studies in Biblical Law* (Cambridge: University Press, 1947).

parallels Jacob's judgment in the case of Joseph: *tarof toraf Yosef,* "Joseph has been torn to pieces."

We know that some such law existed prior to the giving of the Torah. Jacob himself says to Laban, whose flocks and herds had been placed in his charge, "I did not bring you animals torn by wild beasts; I bore the loss myself" (31:39). This implies that guardians even then were exempt from responsibility for the damage caused by wild animals. We also know that an elder brother carried a similar responsibility for the fate of a younger brother placed in his charge, as, for example, when the two were alone together. That is the significance of Cain's denial when confronted by God as to the fate of Abel: "Am I my brother's guardian [*shomer*]?" (4:9).

We now understand a series of nuances in the encounter between Jacob and his sons upon their return without Joseph. Normally they would be held responsible for their younger brother's disappearance. To avoid this, as in the case of later biblical law, they "bring the remains as evidence." If those remains show signs of an attack by a wild animal, they must – by virtue of the law then operative – be held innocent. Their request to Jacob, *haker na,* must be construed as a legal request, meaning, "Examine the evidence." Jacob has no alternative but to do so, and by virtue of what he has seen, to acquit them. A judge, however, may be forced to acquit someone accused of a crime because the evidence is insufficient to justify a conviction, while still retaining lingering private doubts. So Jacob was forced to find his sons innocent, without necessarily trusting what they said. In fact Jacob did not believe it, and his refusal to be comforted shows that he was unconvinced. He continued to hope that Joseph was still alive. That hope was eventually justified: Joseph *was* still alive, and father and son were ultimately reunited.

The refusal to be comforted sounded more than once in Jewish history. The prophet Jeremiah heard it in a later age:

> This is what the Lord says:
> "A voice is heard in Ramah,
> Mourning and great weeping,
> Rachel weeping for her children
> *Refusing to be comforted,*

Because her children are no more."
This is what the Lord says:
"Restrain your voice from weeping,
And your eyes from tears,
For your work will be rewarded," says the Lord.
"They will return from the land of the enemy.
So there is hope for your future," declares the Lord,
"Your children will return to their own land."

(Jeremiah, 31:15–17)

Why was Jeremiah sure that Jews would return? Because they refused to be comforted – meaning, they refused to give up hope.

So it was during the Babylonian exile, as articulated in one of the most paradigmatic expressions of the refusal to be comforted:

By the rivers of Babylon we sat and wept,
As we remembered Zion...
How can we sing the songs of the Lord in a strange land?
If I forget you, O Jerusalem,
May my right hand forget [its skill],
May my tongue cling to the roof of my mouth
If I do not remember you,
If I do not consider Jerusalem above my highest joy.

(Psalms 137:1–6)

It is said that Napoleon, passing a synagogue on the fast day of Tisha B'Av, heard the sounds of lamentation. "What are the Jews crying for?" he asked one of his officers. "For Jerusalem," the soldier replied. "How long ago did they lose it?" "More than 1,700 hundred years." "A people who can mourn for Jerusalem so long, will one day have it restored to them," the Emperor is reputed to have replied.

Jews are the people who refused to be comforted because they never gave up hope. Jacob did eventually see Joseph again. Rachel's children did return to the land. Jerusalem is once again the Jewish home. All the evidence may suggest otherwise: it may seem to signify irretrievable loss, a decree of history that cannot be overturned, a fate that must be accepted. Jews never believed the evidence because they had something else to set against it – a faith, a trust, an unbreakable hope that proved stronger than historical inevitability. It is not too much to say that Jewish survival was sustained in that hope. And that hope came from a simple – or perhaps not so simple – phrase in the life of Jacob. He refused to be comforted. And so – while we live in a world still scarred by violence, poverty and injustice – must we.

Flames and Words

Spliced within the story of Joseph – between his sale as a slave (chapter 37) and his arrival in Egypt (chapter 39) – is the story of Judah and the death of his children. Into this dark scenario enters one of the more unexpected heroines of the Torah, Tamar. The text gives us no inclination as to who she is, but from her entry into the narrative, this fascinating and mysterious figure begins to dominate the story.

The chapter opens by telling us that Judah had separated from his brothers, and married a Canaanite woman by whom he had three children. The eldest, Er, married Tamar. The plain implication is that Tamar too was a Canaanite. These were the people among whom Judah was living; and he was unlikely to have forbidden his son from marrying a local woman, given that he had done so himself.[1]

Er dies young, leaving Tamar a childless widow. Judah instructs his second son, Onan, to marry her, "to do his duty as the husband's brother and raise up offspring for his brother" (38:8). Realising that a child from the marriage would be regarded as belonging to his dead

---

1. Rabbinic tradition, though, identified Tamar as a daughter of Shem, and hence *not* a Canaanite, for they were descended from Shem's brother Ham.

brother rather than to himself, Onan is careful not to impregnate Tamar. This is a sin, and Onan too dies young. The proper thing would now be for Judah's third son, Shelah, to marry Tamar, but Judah is reluctant to let this happen, "for he was afraid that Shelah too might die like his brothers" (38:11). Instead, he tells Tamar to wait until Shelah grows up; but this is disingenuous. Judah has no intention of letting Shelah marry her.[2]

Operating throughout the story is a form of the law that later would became part of Judaism: *yibbum*, levirate marriage, the rule that a member of the dead husband's family should marry his childless widow "to perpetuate the dead brother's name so that it may not be blotted out from Israel" (Deuteronomy 25:6). Indeed, verse 8 explicitly uses the verb *y-b-m*. However, as Nahmanides points out – and this is crucial to the story – the pre-Mosaic law differed from its Mosaic successor. The law in Deuteronomy restricts the obligation to *brothers* of the dead husband. The earlier law included other members of the family as well.[3]

As the years pass, Tamar begins to realise that Judah has no intention of giving her his third son. She is now trapped as an *aguna*, a "chained woman," unable to marry Shelah because of Judah's fears, unable to marry anyone else because she is legally bound to her brother-in-law. Her plight concerns more than herself: it also means that she is unable to bear children who will carry on the name and line of her dead husband.

She decides on a bold course of action. Hearing that Judah is going to pass by on his way to the sheep-shearing, she removes her widow's weeds, puts on a veil, and sits at the crossroads. Judah sees her, does not recognise her, and takes her for a prostitute. They negotiate. Judah offers her a price – a young goat from the flock – but Tamar insists on security, a pledge: his seal and its cord, and his staff. Judah agrees, and they sleep together. The next day he sends a friend with the payment, but she is not to be found, and people tell him that there was

2. Rashi, commentary to 38:11.
3. Ramban, commentary to *Bereshit* 38:8. Some form of this extended familial obligation seems to have survived even after the giving of the Torah: it is presupposed in the story of Ruth (Ruth 4:5, 10). Ramban explains that "The ancient wise men of Israel…established it as a custom [marrying a childless widow who is part of the family] to be practiced among all those who inherit the legacy providing there is no probihition against the marriage."

no prostitute in the area. Judah shrugs off the episode, saying "Let her keep the pledge, or we shall be a laughing stock."

Three months later, people begin to notice that Tamar is pregnant. Since Shelah has been kept away from her, it can only mean that she has slept with someone else, and is thus guilty of adultery, a capital crime. Judah orders, "Bring her out so that she may be burnt" (38:24). Only then does the full subtlety of Tamar's strategy become apparent.

> As she was being brought out, she sent word to her father-in-law. "The father of my child is the man to whom these things belong," she said. "See if you recognise whose they are, this seal, the pattern of the cord, and the staff." Judah identified them and said, "She is more righteous than I am, because I did not give her to my son Shelah." (25–26)

With great ingenuity and boldness, Tamar has broken through the bind in which Judah had placed her. She has fulfilled her duty to the dead. But no less significantly, she has spared Judah shame. By sending him a coded message – the pledge – she has ensured that he will know that he himself is the father of the child, but that no one else will. To do this, she took the enormous risk of being put to death for adultery.

Her behaviour became a model. Not surprisingly, the rabbis inferred from her conduct a strong moral rule: "It is better that a person throw himself into a fiery furnace rather than shame his neighbour in public."[4] This acute sensitivity to humiliation displayed by Tamar permeates much of Rabbinic thought:

> Whoever shames his neighbour in public, is as if he shed his blood. (*Bava Metzia* 58b)

> One who publicly humiliates another, forfeits his place in the world to come. (*Bava Metzia* 59a)

> Rabbi Tanhuma taught: Know whom you shame, if you shame

4. *Bava Metzia* 59a.

your neighbour. [You shame God Himself, for it is written], "in the image of God, He made man." (*Bereshit Raba* 24:7)

When Rabbi Elazar ben Azariah was about to die, his disciples sat before him and asked, "Our teacher, teach us one [fundamental] thing." He replied, "My children, what can I teach you? Let every one of you go and be very careful of the dignity of others." (*Derekh Eretz Raba*, 3)

The Talmud even includes in the definition of *ona'at devarim*, "verbal oppression," the act of reminding a person of a past they may find shameful.

Judaism is a religion of words. God created the natural world with words. We create – and sometimes destroy – the social world with words. That is one reason why Judaism has so strong an ethic of speech. The other reason, surely, is its concern to protect human dignity. Psychological injury may be no less harmful – is often even more so – than physical injury. Hence the rule: never humiliate, never put to shame, never take refuge in the excuse that they were only words, that no physical harm was done.

I will never forget an episode that occurred when I was a rabbinical student in the mid-1970s, while I was attending a conference in Switzerland. A group of us, yeshiva students together with students from a rabbinical seminary, were praying together, in one of the rooms of the chateau where we were staying. A few minutes into the prayers, a new arrival entered: a woman Reform rabbi, wearing tallit and tefillin. She sat down among the men.

The students were shocked, and did not know what to do (among Orthodox Jews, the sexes are separated in prayer, and women do not normally wear tallit and tefillin). Should they ask her to leave? Should they go elsewhere to pray? They clustered around the rabbi leading the group – today a highly respected Rosh Yeshiva in Israel. He looked up, saw the situation, and without hesitation and with great solemnity recited to the students the law derived from Tamar: "It is better that a person throw himself into a fiery furnace than shame his neighbour in public." He told the students to go back to their seats and carry on praying. God forbid that they should shame the woman. The memory of that moment has stayed with me ever since.

It says something about the Torah and Jewish spirituality that we learn this law from Tamar, a woman at the very edge of Israelite society, who risked her life rather than put her father-in-law to shame. Psychological pain is as serious as physical pain. Loss of dignity is a kind of loss of life. It is perhaps no coincidence that it was this episode – Judah and Tamar – that began a family tree from which ten generations later David, Israel's greatest king, was born.

Tamar, a childless widow, unable to remarry, was a person without position or power. Was it this that gave her unusual insight into the fact that psychological pain can be as serious as physical pain, that loss of dignity is a kind of loss of life? It says something about the nature of Jewish spirituality that the Torah attributes this moral greatness to her and not to a direct member of the covenantal family – to one of Jacob's sons – and that the rabbis took her deed as a binding precedent for all of us.

Tamar took her sense of shame and used it to sensitize herself to avoiding shaming others. Can we, dare we, do less?

A Tale of Two Women

Tamar, whose story is told in Genesis 38, bears an uncanny resemblance to one other figure in Tanakh: Ruth, daughter-in-law of Naomi, eponymous heroine of one of the gentlest and loveliest books of the Hebrew Bible. The resemblances between their respective stories are many and striking.[1] These are some of them:

Both stories begin with a descent, literal or metaphorical: a journey from a Jewish to a gentile environment. In Genesis 38, Judah "went down from his brothers" to live among the Canaanites. In the book of Ruth, Elimelech takes his wife and sons to live in Moab. In both cases there is an "outmarriage." Judah marries a Canaanite woman; Elimelech's sons marry Moabite women. In both stories, two sons die: Judah's eldest, Er and Onan, and Elimelech's children, Mahlon and Khilyon. In both, the central figures, Tamar and Ruth, are left childless widows.

---

1. The connection is made explicitly in the *Zohar*: "There were two women – Tamar and Ruth – from whom the line of Judah was built, and from whom issued King David, King Solomon, and the Messiah. These two women were similar: after their first husbands died, they made efforts to win their second husbands. In doing so, both of them acted properly for the sake of kindness to the dead [by bearing children who would perpetuate their memory]" (*Zohar* 1:188b).

The prospect of widowhood plays a central part in each of their stories, though in different ways. Tamar is condemned to it, because she can only marry Judah's remaining son Shelah, and Judah withholds him, ostensibly on the grounds that he is too young, though actually because his previous two sons died after marrying Tamar:

> Judah said to his daughter-in-law Tamar, "Live as a widow in your father's house until my son Shelah grows up." For he thought, "He may die too, just like his brothers." So Tamar went to live in her father's house. (38:11)

It is opposite in the case of Ruth. Precisely because her mother-in-law Naomi finds herself a childless widow, she urges her daughters-in-law not to suffer the same fate, since they can avoid it by remaining in Moab:

> Naomi said, "Return home, my daughters. Why would you come with me? Am I going to have any more sons, who could become your husbands? Return home, my daughters; I am too old to have another husband. Even if I thought there was still hope for me – even if I had a husband tonight and then gave birth to sons – would you wait until they grew up? Would you remain unmarried for them? No, my daughters." (Ruth 1:11–13)

Tamar is thus an involuntary widow, an *aguna*; Ruth a voluntary one. But both are vulnerable, with neither husband nor children to provide for them or give them, as it were, a place, within a still tribal and familial society. Both were outsiders in another sense as well. Ruth was a Moabitess. The Moabites were longstanding enemies of Israel. As for Tamar, we noted in the previous study a rabbinic tradition that she was descended from Shem, son of Noah. Yet the absence of any genealogy in the text, and the fact that her appearance in the story occurs immediately after we have learned that Judah had left his brothers and married a Canaanite woman, suggests that that we are to assume that she too was a "stranger," in some sense not one of the covenantal family (Philo says that she was the child of idolaters).

Both women were driven by a specific kind of loyalty: the loyalty that motivates the biblical law of *yibbum*, levirate marriage. The Torah says about the childless widow who marries her brother-in-law and then has a child, "The first son that she bears shall be accounted to the dead brother, that his name may not be blotted out in Israel" (Deuteronomy 25:6). Likewise the book of Ruth explains, in the context of her marriage to Boaz, that "the name of the deceased shall not disappear from among his kinsmen" (Ruth 4:10). Both, in other words, keep faith with their dead husbands in seeking to have a child that will bear his name. Each, too, exhibits loyalty to their in-laws, Ruth in refusing to be parted from Naomi, Tamar in ensuring that she will not put her father-in-law Judah to shame.

At the critical point of the narrative, each engages in daring behaviour. Tamar disguises herself as a prostitute. Ruth waits until Boaz is asleep, then:

> Ruth approached quietly, uncovered his feet and lay down. In the middle of the night something startled the man, and he turned and discovered a woman lying at his feet. "Who are you?" he asked. "I am your servant Ruth," she said. "Spread the corner of your garment over me, since you are a kinsman-redeemer." (Ruth 3:7–9)

Naomi had suggested a different approach. She told Ruth to uncover Boaz's feet; "He will then tell you what you are to do" (3:4). Naomi assumed that it was for Boaz to take the initiative. Instead, by saying "Spread the corner of your garment over me," Ruth was initiating the proposal, telling Boaz that it was his duty to marry her (in Ezekiel 16:8, God says about the people Israel, "I spread the corner of My garment over you and covered your nakedness. I gave you My solemn oath and entered into a covenant with you … and you became Mine." The gesture was thus a proposal of marriage). In both cases, in other words, Tamar and Ruth boldly force the pace of events.

In both stories, an extended form of levirate marriage is involved, and in both cases, the man who becomes the father of the child or children – Judah and Boaz – is not the closest in line. For Tamar, this was Shelah, Judah's third son; for Ruth it was the anonymous Peloni-Almoni (this phrase has come, in Hebrew, to mean, "Mr So-and-so" or "Mr What's-his-name").

Finally, in both cases, the men pay tribute to the exemplary virtues of the women. Judah says of Tamar, "She has been more righteous than I" (Genesis 38:26). Boaz says of Ruth:

> I've been told all about what you have done for your mother-in-law since the death of your husband – how you left your father and mother and your homeland and came to live with a people you did not know before. May the Lord repay you for what you have done. May you be richly rewarded by the Lord, God of Israel, under whose wings you have come to take refuge. (Ruth 2:11–12)

And later: "This kindness is greater than that which you showed earlier: You have not run after the younger men, whether rich or poor" (3:10).

These similarities are surely too pronounced to be accidental, and it is the book of Ruth itself, in its closing lines, that provides the connection. When the elders give permission to Boaz to buy Naomi's field and marry Ruth, they pronounce this blessing:

> "May the Lord make the woman who is coming into your home like Rachel and Leah, who together built up the house of Israel... May your family be like that of Perez, *whom Tamar bore to Judah.*" (4:11–12)

There then follows a genealogy listing the ten generations from Perez to King David: The beginning of David's family tree is the son, Perez, born to Judah and Tamar. The seventh generation is the son, Oved, born to Ruth and Boaz. The family tree of Israel's great and future king includes both Tamar and Ruth, two women whose virtue and loyalty, kindness and discretion, surely contributed to David's greatness.

I find it exceptionally moving that the Bible should cast in these heroic roles two figures at the extreme margins of Israelite society:

women, childless widows, outsiders. Tamar and Ruth, powerless except for their moral courage, wrote their names into Jewish history as role models who gave birth to royalty – to remind us, in case we ever forget, that true royalty lies in love and faithfulness, and that greatness often exists where we expect it least.

Miketz
מקץ

Miketz is dominated by two of the great encounters in the Torah. The first is the reversal in Joseph's fortunes. Forgotten and abandoned in prison, he is brought out to interpret Pharaoh's dreams, which he does with ease. Having told Pharaoh that the dreams portend eventual drought and famine, he then articulates a solution to the problem. Pharaoh, impressed, appoints Joseph to high office in Egypt, second only to himself.

The second occurs when Joseph's brothers, driven by famine in Canaan, come to Egypt to buy food. They come before Joseph, but fail to recognise him as their brother, though he recognises them. Joseph, without disclosing his identity, sets in motion a complex scenario, designed to test his brothers, that reaches a climax in the next *parasha*.

The first two of the following studies look at the subtle interplay between human choice and divine intervention, traced more delicately and deeply in the Joseph story than anywhere else in Tanakh. The third explores the themes of particularity and universality in Judaism, as exemplified in the conversation between Pharoah and Joseph. The fourth sets the meeting between Joseph and his brothers in the context of three other narratives of recognition and non-recognition in Genesis. This turns out to be one of Genesis's major themes: appearance and reality in human interaction, the difference between who we seem to be and who we are.

These three tensions (freewill vs. providence, particular vs. universal, and appearance vs. reality) lie at the heart of Judaism, and they reach their fullest exposition in the story of Joseph.

Man Proposes, God Disposes

Nowadays we think of Genesis as a book, something we read in our own time, at our own pace, possibly in a single session. Listening to Torah in the synagogue, though, is a different kind of experience, and involves a different relationship to the text. There, the reading is public, not private. The words are sung, not spoken. We encounter the text through the listening ear more than through the seeing eye. And we do so section by section (each called a *parasha*), in weekly instalments. Genesis is divided into twelve such sections. The point at which Jewish custom makes the break is sometimes significant, and contributes to our understanding of the text.

Rarely is a break more subtle and suggestive than the one between *Vayeshev* and *Miketz*. *Vayeshev* ends with Joseph's bid for freedom. Having correctly interpreted the chief steward's dream – that in three days he would be restored to his position – Joseph pleads with him:

> "When all goes well with you, remember me and show me kindness; mention me to Pharaoh and get me out of this prison. For I was forcibly carried off from the land of the Hebrews, and even

here I have done nothing to deserve being put in a dungeon." (40:14–15)

The chief steward fails to do so. The last line of *Vayeshev* underlines the point by repeating it: "The chief steward, however, *did not remember* Joseph; he *forgot* him." On that dispiriting note, *Vayeshev* ends, and in the days before printing and the widespread availability of books, those who did not know the story had to wait a full week before discovering what happens next. The break is calculated to maximise suspense.

The opening words of *Miketz* are, "At the end of two full years." Our suspense, it now turns out, mirrors Joseph's. We have waited a week; he had to wait two years, his hope of release seemingly dashed. Then something happens to prompt the memory of the chief steward. Pharaoh dreams. Intuitively he senses that the dreams are significant, and he asks his *ḥartumim* (magicians, interpreters of mysteries) what they mean. Their explanations fail to satisfy him. Only then does the chief steward remember Joseph, who had so accurately interpreted his own dream two years earlier.

Joseph is then taken from jail, washed, dressed and brought before Pharaoh. He interprets the dreams, proposes a solution to the problem they foretell – seven years of famine, after seven years of plenty – and is made viceroy of Egypt, second in authority only to Pharaoh himself. The darkness of the last *parasha* ends, and from tragedy we move towards a fairy-tale ending.

But the initial impression of this *parasha* is not the happy conclusion, but the delay: "At the end of two full years." Joseph sought his freedom and he obtained it – yet he did not obtain it because he sought it. The steward forgot. Joseph had to wait. Something else – Pharaoh's dreams – had to intervene. There was a break between cause and effect – a break emphasised experientially by the *parasha* division, forcing us to relive, as it were, something of Joseph's sense of disappointment, of time passing, of the slow fading of hope. This, it transpires, is more than just a device of style, a way of maintaining the suspense. There is something more substantive at stake, a coded message we must decipher if we are to understand the full depth of the story.

The reason is that this is not the first time the Torah uses such a device in the Joseph narrative. Several chapters earlier there is an extremely enigmatic passage at the point where the brothers decide to sell Joseph into slavery:

> Then they sat down to a meal. Looking up, they saw a caravan of Ishmaelites coming from Gilead with camels laden with spices, balm and myrrh to be taken to Egypt. Then Judah said to his brothers, "What profit is it to us if we kill our brother and cover up his blood? Come, let us sell him to the Ishmaelites and not lay our hands upon him; for he is our brother, our own flesh." His brothers agreed. Then there passed by Midianite merchants, and they pulled Joseph up out of the pit and sold him for twenty shekels of silver to the Ishmaelites, who brought Joseph to Egypt. (37:25–28)

It is a confusing episode. *Who* pulled Joseph from the pit? Who sold him to the Ishmaelites? Was it the brothers or the Midianites? The subject, "they," is ambiguous.

The commentators offered many interpretations. Of these, the simplest is given by Rashbam, who reads it as follows: The brothers, having thrown Joseph into the pit, sat down some distance away to eat. Reuben sneaked back to rescue Joseph, but found the pit empty and cried, "The boy is not! And I, where can I go?" Rashbam points out that the brothers did not calm him by telling him they had sold Joseph. They seem as surprised as he was. It follows that the brothers, having seen the Ishmaelites in the distance, decided to sell Joseph to them, but before they had the chance to do so, a second group of travellers, the Midianites, heard Joseph's cries, saw the possibility of selling him to the Ishmaelites, and did so.

In other words, the brothers intended to sell Joseph, and Joseph was sold, but *not by the brothers.* They sought to do the deed, and the deed was done, but not by them.

That is precisely what happened in the case of Joseph's bid for freedom. He sought to be released from prison, and he was released from prison, but *not in the way he planned.* Two years had to pass. Some further, unexpected event – Pharaoh's dreams – had to happen. There is a break between cause and effect, between intention and outcome. The precise parallel between these two passages – the sale of Joseph, and his release from prison – is too marked to be accidental. The Torah is signalling something to the attentive reader.

It is telling us about the nature of divine providence. In both episodes, between intention and outcome, there was an intervention – in the first case, the appearance of the Midianites, in the second, Pharaoh's dreams. The Torah is giving us a rare glimpse of the workings of providence in individual lives. Nothing in the Joseph story happens by chance – and where an event most looks like chance, that is where divine intervention is most evident in retrospect.

The Joseph story is written to be read at two levels. On the surface it is a story about human beings and their relationships. It is not a happy story. Brothers are prepared to sell their own flesh and blood into slavery. The chief steward, released from prison, immediately forgets his fellow prisoner, failing to intercede on his behalf. People betray people. Dreams are mere dreams. Hopes are destined to be dashed on the rocks of reality. That is the point at which *Vayeshev* ends.

But as events unfold in *Miketz* we realise that at a deeper level some other force has been at work all along. God has been monitoring the entire sequence of events, arranging the necessary strategic interventions to ensure that the outcome will be as planned. This is not obvious, as it is, for example, in the story of the Exodus. There the hand of God, in the form of the plagues and the division of the Sea, is manifest. Here it is concealed. It takes reflection and the ability to read beneath the surface to sense it at all. The Joseph story is more than a story about Joseph. It is a story about each of us, and the subtle interweaving of apparent happenstance and divinely-scripted destiny.

We are at best co-authors of our lives. Not realizing it at the time, the very act the brothers did to *prevent* Joseph's dreams coming true was the first step in their coming true. As for Joseph, unbeknown to him, his life was part of a larger story – revealed by God to Abraham generations earlier when He told him that his children would suffer slavery in a land not their own.

Sometimes we too catch a glimpse of the workings of fate in our lives. Many times, I have had prayers answered – but never when I expected, nor in the way I imagined. In many cases, the answer came after I had given up hope. Providence exists. In Shakespeare's words "There's a divinity that shapes our ends, Rough-hew them how we will."[1] But there is a pause, an intervention, a break in the sequence of cause and effect, which says: things do not happen merely because we wish them, but because they are part of the larger scheme of things.

What Joseph discovered in the hiatus between the two *parashot* is that, in addition to initiative and enterprise, we also need patience, humility and trust. If our prayers are legitimate, God will answer them, but not necessarily when or how we think He will. That is the meaning of *Miketz* – "At the end of two full years." We must do our part; God will do His. Between them there is a gap, not just in time, but in consciousness. We learn that we are not sole masters of our fate. Sometimes it is only after many years that, looking back, we see the pattern in our life, and understand how Providence has shaped our destiny. *Miketz* is the space we make in our minds for the things not under our control. The name of that space is faith.

---

1.   *Hamlet*, act v, scene 2, 10–11.

Between Freedom and Providence

Ⅰn one of the great reversals in Tanakh, Joseph, whom we saw at the end of *Vayeshev*, languishing in prison, becomes in *Miketz* a ruler of Egypt, second only to Pharaoh. It happens with astonishing speed. Pharaoh has two disturbing dreams. None of the interpretations offered by his magi satisfy him. Pharaoh's chief steward remembers Joseph, his former fellow prisoner, who has an uncanny gift of deciphering dreams. Hurriedly, Joseph is taken from prison, given a wash and change of clothes, and brought before the ruler.

Not only does he interpret the dreams, he becomes, in effect, the world's first economist, inventing the theory of trade cycles: The dreams portend seven years of plenty followed by seven of scarcity. Having diagnosed the problem, Joseph immediately proceeds to solve it: store surplus grain in the years of plenty, then use these reserves in the years of famine. Pharaoh invites him to implement the strategy, giving him control of the Egyptian economy. Joseph moves from prisoner to prime minister in one effortless leap.

So enthralling is the story, and it moves at so brisk a pace, that we tend to miss one highly significant detail. Pharaoh has not one dream but two: one about cows, the other about ears of grain. Joseph explains that they are, substantively, the same dream, conveying the same message through different images. The reason that Pharaoh has had two dreams, not one, is because a twofold dream implies that "God is firmly resolved on this plan, and very soon He will put it into effect" (41:32).

In the immediate context, this is just another piece of information about Egypt and its future. Viewed within the full context of Joseph's life story, however, it changes our entire understanding of events. For it was not Pharaoh alone who had two dreams with a similar structure. Joseph did as well. At the very beginning of the story, he dreamed, once of sheaves of wheat bowing down to his sheaf, and then about the sun, moon and stars bowing down to him.

At that stage we had no idea what the dreams signified. Were they a prophecy, or the fruit of the fevered imagination of an over-indulged, overambitious boy? The tension of the Joseph narrative depends on this ambiguity. Only now, chapters and years later, are we given the vital information: a dream, repeated in different images, is not just a dream. It is a message sent by God about a future that will soon come to pass.

There are several possible reasons why we were not given this information earlier. It may be that it was only later that God disclosed this to Joseph. Or perhaps Joseph has only now come to understand it. Or it may simply be a literary device to create and maintain tension in the unfolding plot. It is also possible, though, that it signals something altogether deeper about the human condition seen through the eyes of faith.

It is only in retrospect that we understand the story of our life. Later events explain earlier ones. In the beginning, neither Joseph nor his brothers could know that his dreams were a form of prophecy, that he was indeed destined for greatness and that every misfortune he would suffer would play a part in the dreams coming true. At first reading, the Joseph story reads like a series of random happenings. Only later, looking back, do we see that each event was part of a precise, providential plan to lead a young man from a family of nomadic shepherds to become viceroy of Egypt.

This is a truth not about Joseph alone but about us as well. We live our lives poised between a known past and an unknown future. Linking them is a present in which we make our choices. We decide between alternatives. Ahead of us are several diverging paths, and it is up to us which we follow. Only looking back does our life take on the character of a story. Only many years later do we realise which choices were fateful, and which irrelevant. Things which seemed small at the time turn out to be decisive. Matters that once seemed important prove in retrospect to have been trivial. Seen from the perspective of the present, a life can appear to be a random sequence of disconnected events. It takes the passage of time for us to be able to look back and see the route we have taken, and the right and wrong turnings on the way.

The novelist Dan Jacobson puts this thought in the mind of the narrator of his novel, *The Confessions of Josef Baisz*:

> Told one way, looking forward as it were, and proceeding from one event to the next, my story may seem to be a mere sequence, without design or purpose. Told another way, looking backwards, it can be made to resemble a plot, a plan, a cunningly involuted development leading to a necessary conclusion. Being both narrator and subject, how am I to know which way to look?[1]

Whether in literature or in life, there is an intrinsic connection between time and meaning. The same series of events that once seemed mere happenstance becomes, with hindsight, the unfolding of a script.

This insight allows us to resolve one of the great paradoxes of the religious life – the seeming contradiction between divine providence and human free will. As Rabbi Akiva put it most famously: "All is foreseen, yet freedom of choice is given."[2]

On the face of it, these two propositions cannot both be true. If God knows in advance that we are going to do x, then we are not free not to do it. If, on the other hand, we are genuinely free, then no one can know what we will choose before we choose it.

---

1. Dan Jacobson, *The Confessions of Josef Baisz* (London: Secker and Warburg, 1977), 80.
2. Mishna, *Avot* 3:15.

The apparent paradox arises because of the nature of time. We live in time. God lives beyond it. Different time perspectives allow for different levels of knowledge. An analogy: imagine going to see a soccer match. While the match is in progress, you are on the edge of your seat. You do not know – no one knows – what is going to happen next. Now imagine watching a recording of the same match on television later that night. You know exactly what is going to happen next.

That knowledge does not mean that the players have had their freedom retroactively removed. All it means is that you are now watching the match from a different time perspective. When you were in the stadium, you were watching it in the present. On television you are watching it as an event in the past.

So it is with life itself. As we live it day by day, we choose in the present in order to shape what is for us an unknown, undetermined future. Only looking back are we able to see the consequences of our actions, and realize their part in the unfolding of our autobiography. It is then, with hindsight, that we begin to see how providence has guided our steps, leading us to where God needs us to be. That is one meaning of the phrase spoken by God to Moses "Then I shall take away My hand, and you will see My back, but My face cannot not be seen" (Exodus 33:23). Only looking back do we see God's providence interwoven with our life, never looking forward ("My face cannot not be seen").

How subtly and deftly this point is made in the story of Joseph – the supreme example of a life in which human action and divine intervention are inextricably entwined. It is all there in the verse about the doubling of Pharaoh's dream. By delaying this information until this point in Joseph's life, the Torah shows us how a later event can force us to reinterpret an earlier one, teaching us the difference between two time perspectives: the present, and the understanding that only hindsight can bring to the past. It does so not by expounding complex philosophical propositions, but by the art of story-telling – a far more simple and more powerful way of conveying a difficult truth.

These two time perspectives are embodied, in Judaism, in two different literatures. Through halakha, we learn to make choices in the present. Through *aggada*, we strive to understand the past. Together, these two ways of thinking constitute the twin hemispheres of the Jewish brain. We are free. But we are also characters in a divinely-scripted drama. We choose, but we are also chosen. The Jewish imagination lives in the tension between these two frames of reference: between freedom and providence, our decisions and God's plan.

The Universal and the Particular

The story of Joseph is one of those relatively rare narratives in Tanakh in which a Jew (Israelite/Hebrew) comes to play a prominent part in a gentile society – the others are, most notably, the books of Esther and Daniel. In one sense it is an obvious prelude to the reversal of fortune with which the book of Exodus begins. A new pharaoh, who "did not know Joseph" (Exodus 1:6), comes to the throne, and the pleasant interlude of life in Egypt turns into the nightmare of enslavement and oppression. Life in exile, the Torah is warning us, may begin innocently, but in the long run it is hazardous in the extreme.

There is a secondary theme, whose echoes continue to reverberate today. Can Jewish identity survive outside Israel? Specifically, can it survive freedom and equality? The irony is that under conditions of poverty and persecution, Jews tend to stay Jews. It is only when they are affluent and integrated that, in large numbers, they assimilate and abandon their identity. We see this in the Joseph story when, having been made second-in-command in Egypt, he names his firstborn child Menasheh, saying, "God has *made me forget* [*nasheh*] all my trouble and all my father's house" (41:51). The enduring hero of the patriarchal family is Judah (whose name we bear as *Yehudim*, "Jews"), not Joseph, the man of dual identity.[1] Judah's descendants survive the Babylonian exile; Joseph's disappear when the Northern Kingdom is conquered by the Assyrians.

I want here, however, to explore a third theme, no less fundamental to Judaism and Jewish identity through the ages. What is particular, and what is universal, in the religious life? Judaism occupies a unique position in the history of faith. On the one hand, the God of Abraham is, we believe, the God of everyone. We are all – Jew and non-Jew alike – made in God's image and likeness. On the other, the religion of Abraham is *not* the religion of everyone. It was born in the specific covenant God made with Abraham and his descendants. We say of God in our prayers that He "chose us from all the peoples." So when a member of Abraham's family, Joseph, meets a ruler of a quite different civilization, Pharaoh king of Egypt, what concepts do they share, and what remains untranslatable?

The Torah introduces this theme deftly and unobtrusively. When Joseph is brought from prison to interpret Pharaoh's dreams, both men refer to God. Three times the word *Elokim*, God, appears in Genesis 41. The first is when Joseph explicitly disavows any personal skill in interpreting dreams:

> "I cannot do it," Joseph replied, "But God [*Elokim*] will give Pharaoh the answer he desires." (41:16)

The second and third are uttered by Pharaoh himself, after Joseph has interpreted the dreams, stated the problem (seven years of famine), provided the solution (store up grain in the years of plenty), and advised him to appoint a "wise and discerning man" (41:33) to oversee the project:

> The plan seemed good to Pharaoh and all his officials. So Pharaoh asked them, "Can we find anyone like this man, in whom is the spirit of God [*Elokim*]?" Then Pharaoh said to Joseph, "Since

1. On this, see Aaron Wildavsky, *Assimilation versus Separation: Joseph the Administrator and the Politics of Religion in Biblical Israel* (New Jersey: Transaction Publications, 2001).

God [*Elokim*] has made all this known to you, there is no one so discerning and wise as you. You shall be in charge of my palace..." (41:37–39)

On the face of it, this is surprising. Pharaonic Egypt was not a monotheistic culture. On the contrary, it was a place of many gods and goddesses – the sun, the Nile, and so on. To be sure, there was a brief period under Ikhnaton (Amenhotep IV), when the official religion was reformed in the direction of monolatry (worship of one god without disputing the existence of others). But this was short-lived, and certainly not at the time of Joseph. The entire biblical portrayal of Egypt is predicated on their belief in many gods, against whom God "executed judgement" in the days of Moses and the plagues. Why then does Joseph take it for granted that Pharaoh will understand his reference to God – an assumption proved correct when Pharaoh twice uses the word himself? What is the significance of the word *Elokim*?

As we have noted elsewhere in these studies,[2] Tanakh generally and the Torah specifically have two primary ways of referring to God, the four-letter name we allude to as *Hashem* ("the name" par excellence) and the word *Elokim*.

The sages understood the difference in terms of the distinction between God-as-justice (*Elokim*) and God-as-mercy (*Hashem*). However, the philosopher-poet of the eleventh century, Judah HaLevi, proposed a quite different distinction, based not on ethical attributes but on modes of relationship[3] – a view revived in the twentieth century by Martin Buber in his distinction between I-It and I-Thou. HaLevi's view was this: the ancients worshipped forces of nature, which they personified as gods. Each was known as *El*, or *Eloah*. The word "El" therefore generically means "a force, a power, an element of nature."

The fundamental difference between those belief-systems and Judaism, was that Judaism believed that the forces of nature were not independent and autonomous. They represented a single totality, one creative will, the Author of being. The Torah therefore speaks of *Elokim*

2. See "Garments of Light" pp. 33–40
3. Judah HaLevi, *Kuzari*, book IV, para. 1.

in the plural, meaning, "the sum of all forces, the totality of all powers." *Elokim* is an abstract noun meaning "all that exists, and every cause that shapes their interactions, under the aspect of the single creative force that brought them into being." Moving from the ancient to the contemporary world, we might say that *Elokim* is God as He is disclosed by science: the Big Bang, the various forces that give the universe its configuration, and the genetic code that shapes life from the simplest bacterium to Homo sapiens.

Hashem is a word of different logical form. It is, according to HaLevi, God's proper name. Just as "the first patriarch" (a generic description) was called Abraham (a name), and "the leader who led the Israelites out of Egypt" (another description) was called Moses, so "the Author of being" (*Elokim*) has a proper name, *Hashem*.

The difference between proper names and generic descriptions is fundamental. *Things* have descriptions, but only *people* have proper names. When we call someone by name we are engaged in a fundamental existential encounter. We are relating to them in their uniqueness and ours. We are opening up ourselves to them and inviting them, in readiness and respect, to open themselves up to us. We are, in Kant's famous distinction, regarding them as *ends*, not *means*, as centres of value in themselves, not potential tools to the satisfaction of our desires. The word *Hashem* represents a revolution in the religious life of mankind. It means that we relate to the totality of being, not as does a scientist (seeing it as something to be understood and controlled) but as does a poet (standing before it in reverence and awe, addressing and being addressed by it).

Elokim is God as we encounter Him in nature. *Hashem* is God as we encounter Him in personal relationships, above all in that essentially human mode of relationship that we call speech, verbal communication, conversation, dialogue, words. *Elokim* is the aspect of God to be found in creation. *Hashem* is the aspect of God disclosed in revelation.

Hence the tension, within Judaism, between the universal and the particular. God as we encounter Him in creation is universal; God as we hear Him in revelation is particular. This is mirrored in the way the narrative of Genesis develops. It begins with characters and events whose significance is that they are universal archetypes: Adam and Eve,

Cain and Abel, Noah and the Flood, the builders of Babel. Their stories tell us about the human condition as such: obedience and rebellion, faith and fratricide, hubris and nemesis, technology and violence, the order God makes and the chaos we create. Not until the twelfth chapter of Genesis does the Torah turn to the particular, to one family, that of Abraham and Sarah, and the covenant God enters into with them and their descendants.

That duality and its sequence – from the universal to the particular – is not marginal to Judaism. One might almost call it the basic structure, the depth grammar, of the Jewish mind. Two examples will illustrate the point.

The first is *birkat hamazon*, "grace after meals." It begins with a blessing that is completely universal. We speak of God who "feeds the whole world with grace," who "provides food for all creatures" and who "feeds and sustains all." The second blessing is saturated with singularity. It talks of the things that are specific to Judaism and the Jewish people: the *"land"* (Israel) He has given us as a heritage; the *history* of our ancestors ("for having brought us out … of the land of Egypt and freed us from the house of bondage"); the *covenant* (*brit*) He has "sealed in our flesh," and "Your *Torah* which You have taught us." These are not universal. They are what make Jews and Judaism different.

The second example is the blessings we say before the *Shema*, morning and evening. In both cases, the first blessing is universal. It speaks of nature and the cosmos, light and darkness, and the cycle of time as it moves from day to night or night to day. There is nothing here about Jews and Judaism, Israel and its covenant with God. The second blessing, however, is about the special relationship between God and Israel. In exquisite poetry it speaks about the love of God for this people, and the expression of that love in the Torah He has given us. Here prayer rises to heights at once poetic and passionate. This is the supreme language of I-Thou.

The duality has legal-theological expression in the form of two covenants, the first with Noah and all humanity after the Flood, the second with Abraham and his descendants, given detailed articulation at Mount Sinai and during the wilderness years. On the one hand there is the Noahide covenant with its seven commands: not to murder, steal, commit adultery, blaspheme, worship idols or practise needless cruelty against animals, together with a positive command to establish a system of justice. These are the minimal and basic requirements of humanity as such, the foundations of any stable and morally acceptable society. On the other is the richly detailed code of 613 commandments that form Israel's constitution as "a kingdom of priests and a holy nation" (Exodus 19:6).

Not only is the duality worked out in the form of law and ethics, covenant and command. It is also expressed in Judaism's dual epistemology, its twofold scheme of human knowledge. This is given lucid expression in a midrash: "If you are told, 'There is wisdom [*hokhma*] among the nations,' believe it. If you are told, 'There is Torah among the nations,' do not believe it."[4]

Torah and *hokhma* are both biblical categories. Torah is to be found primarily in the five books of Moses generically known by that name. *Hokhma* is to be found primarily in the book of Proverbs, but also in Ecclesiastes and Job. The word *hokhma* appears thirty-seven times in Proverbs, eighteen times in Job, twenty-five times in Ecclesiastes – and only thirty-five times in the entirety of the rest of Tanakh.

The difference between them is this: *hokhma* is the truth we discover; Torah is the truth we inherit. *Hokhma* is the universal heritage of mankind, by virtue of the fact that we are created in God's "image and likeness" (Rashi translates "in our likeness" as "with the capacity to understand and discern").[5] Torah is the specific heritage of Israel ("He has revealed His word to Jacob, His laws and decrees to Israel. He has done this for no other nation" [Psalms 147:19]). *Hokhma* discloses God in creation. Torah is the word of God in revelation. *Hokhma* is ontological truth (how things are); Torah is covenantal truth (how things ought to be). *Hokhma* can be defined as anything that allows us to see the universe as the work of God, and humanity as the image of God. Torah is God's covenant with the Jewish people, the architecture of holiness and Israel's written constitution as a nation under the sovereignty of God.

Though the sages valued Torah above all else, they had a high

---

4. Midrash, *Eikha Raba* 2: 13.
5. Rashi to Bereshit 1: 26.

regard for *ḥokhma*. They instituted a special blessing for *ḥokhmei umot olam* ("the sages of the nations" or, as the Singer's Prayer Book translates it, persons "distinguished in worldly learning"): "Blessed are You ... who has given of His wisdom to flesh and blood." Consistent with the pattern established in the Grace after Meals and the blessings before the *Shema*, the *Amida* prayer speaks first of universal wisdom ("You favour man with knowledge and teach mankind understanding") and only then of the particular heritage of Israel ("Bring us back, O our Father, to Your Torah").

So there are the universals of Judaism – creation, humanity as God's image, the covenant with Noah and knowledge-as-*ḥokhma*. There are also its particularities – revelation, Israel as God's "firstborn child," the covenants with Abraham and the Jewish people at Sinai, and knowledge-as-Torah. The first represents the face of God accessible to all mankind (creation); the second, that special, intimate and personal relationship He has with the people He holds close, as disclosed in the Torah (revelation) and Jewish history (redemption). The word for the first is *Elokim*, and for the second, *Hashem*.

We can now understand why it is that Genesis works on the assumption that one aspect of God, *Elokim*, is intelligible to all human beings, regardless of whether they belong to the family of Abraham or not. So, for example, *Elokim* comes in a vision to Avimelekh, King of Gerar, despite the fact that he is a pagan. Abraham himself, defending the fact that he has told a half-truth in calling Sarah his sister, says to Avimelekh, "I said to myself, There is surely no fear of God [*Elokim*] in this place, and they will kill me because of my wife." The Hittites call Abraham "a prince of God [*Elokim*] in our midst." Jacob, in his conversations with Laban and later with Esau uses the term *Elokim*. When he returns to the land of Canaan, the Torah says that "the terror of God [*Elokim*]" fell on the surrounding towns. All these cases refer to individuals or groups who are outside the Abrahamic covenant. Yet the Torah has no hesitation in ascribing to them the language of *Elokim*.

That is why Joseph is able to assume that Egyptians will understand the idea of *Elokim*, even though they are wholly unfamiliar with the idea of *Hashem*. This is made clear in two pointed contrasts. The first occurs in Genesis 39, the passage that describes Joseph's experience in the house of Potiphar. The chapter consistently and repeatedly uses the word *Hashem* in relation to Joseph ("*Hashem* was with Joseph... *Hashem* gave him success in everything he did" [39:2, 5]), but when Joseph speaks to Potiphar's wife, who is attempting to seduce him, he says, "How then could I do such a wicked thing and sin against *Elokim*" (30:9). The second lies in the contrast between the Pharaoh who speaks to Joseph and twice uses the word *Elokim*, and the Pharaoh of Moses's day, who says, "Who is *Hashem* that I should obey Him and let Israel go? I do not know *Hashem* and I will not let Israel go" (Exodus 5:2). An Egyptian can understand *Elokim*, the God of nature. He cannot understand *Hashem*, the God of personal relationship.

Judaism was – and to this day remains – unique in its combination of universalism and particularism. We believe that God is the God of all humanity. He created all. He is accessible to all. He cares for all. He has made a covenant with all.

Yet there is also a relationship with God that is unique to the Jewish people. It alone has placed its national life under His direct sovereignty. It alone has risked its entire being on a divine covenant. It alone testifies in its history to the presence within it of a Presence beyond it. As Tolstoy put it:

> The Jew is that sacred being who has brought down from heaven the everlasting fire and has illuminated with it the entire world. He is the religious source, spring and fountain out of which all the rest of the peoples have drawn their beliefs and their religions...
>
> The Jew is the emblem of eternity. He whom neither slaughter nor torture of thousands of years could destroy, he whom neither fire nor sword nor inquisition was able to wipe off the face of the earth, he who was the first to produce the oracles of God, he who has been for so long the guardian of prophecy, and who has transmitted it to the rest of the world – such a nation cannot be destroyed. The Jew is as everlasting as eternity itself.[6]

6. Letter found in the archives of the Bulgarian statesman F. Gabai. The text appears in Allan Gould, *What Did They Think of the Jews?* (Northvale, NJ: Jason Aronson, 1991), 180–181.

As we search in the twenty-first century for a way to avoid a "clash of civilizations," it seems to me that humanity can learn much from this ancient and still compelling way of understanding the human condition. We are all "the image and likeness" of God. There are basic, non-negotiable principles of human dignity. They are expressed in the Noahide covenant, in human wisdom (*ḥokhma*), and in that aspect of the One God we call *Elokim*. But there are many ways, each distinct and unique, in which different cultures and civilizations define their relationship with the Author of all being. We do not presume to judge them, except insofar as they succeed or fail in honouring the basic, universal principles of human dignity (the sanctity of life, the integrity of the family and property, the fundamentals of justice and so on). We as Jews are (or should be) secure in our relationship with God, the God who has revealed Himself in the intimacy of love, whose expression is Torah. The challenge of faith in its particularity and universality is therefore today what it was in the days of Abraham and Sarah: to be true to our particular heritage while being a blessing to others, whatever their heritage. That is a formula for peace and graciousness in an era badly in need of both.

Behind the Mask

J oseph is now the ruler of Egypt. The famine he predicted has come
to pass. It extends beyond Egypt to the land of Canaan. Seeking to
buy food, Joseph's brothers make the journey to Egypt. They arrive at
the palace of the man in charge of grain distribution:

> Now Joseph was governor of all Egypt, and it was he who sold
> the corn to all the people of the land. Joseph's brothers came and
> bowed to the ground before him. Joseph recognized his brothers
> as soon as he saw them, but he behaved like a stranger and spoke
> harshly to them...Joseph recognized his brothers, but they did
> not recognize him. (42:6–8)

There is something familiar about this situation. Once more we are in
the realm of disguises and mistaken identities which so define the early
history of Jacob and his family.

Here we encounter what Robert Alter defines as a *type-scene*, a
drama enacted several times with variations. These are particularly in
evidence in the book of Genesis. There is no universal rule as to how to
decode the significance of a type-scene. One example is boy-meets-girl-

at-well, an encounter that takes places three times in the Torah: between Abraham's servant and Rebecca, Jacob and Rachel, and Moses and the daughters of Jethro. Here, the setting is probably not significant (wells are where strangers met in those days, like the water-dispenser in a New York office). Rather what we must attend to in these three episodes is their variations: Rebecca's activism, Jacob's show of strength, Moses's passion for justice. How people act toward strangers at a well is, in other words, a test of their character.

In some instances, however, a type-scene seems to indicate a recurring theme. That is the case here. If we are to understand what is at stake in the meeting between Joseph and his brothers, we have to see it in the context of three other episodes, all of which occur in Genesis.

Scene one takes place in Isaac's tent. The patriarch is old and blind. He tells his elder son to go out into the field, trap an animal and prepare a meal so that his "soul may bless him" (27:4). Surprisingly soon, Isaac hears someone enter. "Who are you?" he asks. "I am Esau, you firstborn," the voice replies. Isaac is not convinced. "Come close and let me feel you, my son. Are you really Esau or not?" He reaches out and feels the rough texture of the skins covering his son's arms. Still unsure, he asks again, "But are you really my son Esau?" The voice replies, "I am." So Isaac blesses him: "Ah, the smell of my son is like the smell of a field blessed by God." But it is not Esau. It is Jacob in disguise.

Scene two: Jacob has fled to his uncle Laban's house. Arriving, he meets and falls in love with Rachel, and offers to work seven years for her father in order to marry her. The time passes quickly: the years "seemed like a few days because he loved her" (27:20). The wedding day approaches. Laban makes a feast. The bride enters her tent. Late at night, Jacob follows her. Now, at last, he has married his beloved Rachel. When morning comes, he discovers that he has been the victim of a deception. It is not Rachel. It is Leah in disguise.

Scene three: Judah has married a Canaanite woman and is now the father of three sons. The first marries a local girl, Tamar, but dies mysteriously young, leaving his wife a childless widow. Following a pre-Mosaic version of the law of levirate marriage, Judah marries his second son to Tamar so that she can have a child "to keep his brother's name alive" (38:8). Onan is loathe to have a son who will, in effect, belong to his late brother so he "spilled his seed" (38:9), and for this he too dies young. Judah is reluctant to give Tamar his third son, so she is left an *aguna*, "chained," bound to someone she is prevented from marrying, and unable to marry anyone else.

The years pass. Judah's own wife dies. Returning home from sheep-shearing, he sees a veiled prostitute by the side of the road. He asks her to sleep with him, promising, by way of payment, a kid from the flock. She asks him for his "seal and its cord and his staff" (38:18) as security. The next day he sends a friend to deliver the kid, but the woman has disappeared. The locals deny all knowledge of her. Three months later, Judah hears that his daughter-in-law Tamar has become pregnant. He is incensed. Bound to his youngest son, she was not allowed to have a relationship with anyone else. She must be guilty of adultery. "Bring her out so that she may be burnt," he says. She is brought to be killed, but she asks one favour. She tells one of the people to take to Judah the seal and cord and staff. "The father of my child," she says, "is the man to whom these things belong." Immediately, Judah understands. Tamar, unable to marry yet honour-bound to have a child to perpetuate the memory of her first husband, has tricked her father-in-law into performing the duty he should have allowed his youngest son to do. "She is more righteous than I," Judah admits. He thought he had slept with a prostitute. But it was Tamar in disguise.

This is the framework within which the meeting between Joseph and his brothers must be understood. The man the brothers bow down to bears no resemblance to a Hebrew shepherd. He speaks Egyptian. He is dressed in an Egyptian ruler's robes. He is called *Tzafenat Pa'neah*, an Egyptian name. He wears Pharaoh's signet ring and the gold chain of authority. They think they are in the presence of an Egyptian prince, but it is Joseph – their brother – in disguise.

Four scenes, four disguises, four failures to see behind the mask. What do they have in common? Something very striking indeed. It is only by *not being recognized* that Jacob, Leah, Tamar and Joseph *can be recognized*, in the sense of attended, taken seriously, heeded. Isaac loves Esau, not Jacob. Jacob loves Rachel, not Leah. Judah thinks of his youngest son, not the plight of Tamar. Joseph is hated by his brothers. Only when they appear as something or someone other than they are, can they achieve what they seek – for Jacob, his father's blessing; for Leah, a husband; for Tamar, a son; for Joseph, the non-hostile attention of his brothers. The plight of these four individuals is summed up in a single poignant phrase: "Joseph recognized his brothers, but they did not recognize him."

Do the disguises work? In the short term, yes; but in the long term, not necessarily. Jacob suffers greatly for having taken Esau's blessing. Leah, though she marries Jacob, never wins his love. Tamar had a child (in fact, wins) but Judah "was not intimate with her any more."[1] As for Joseph – his brothers no longer hate him, but now they fear him. Even after his assurances that he bears them no grudge, they still think he will take revenge on them after their father dies. What is achieved in disguise is never the love sought.

But something else happens. Jacob, Leah, Tamar and Joseph discover that, though they may never win the affection of those from whom they seek it, God is with them. That, ultimately, is enough. A disguise is an act of hiding – from others, and perhaps from oneself. From God, however, we cannot, nor do we need to, hide. "Man looks at the outward appearance, but the Lord looks at the heart" (1 Samuel 16:7). He knows our thoughts, hears our cry, answers our unspoken prayer. He heeds the unheeded and brings them comfort.

This is a matter of immense consequence when we compare Jewish and (Hellenistic) European thought. Strikingly, biblical Hebrew lacks a term with the precise range of meanings and resonances as the word "person." The Hebrew words *adam, ben-adam, ish* and *enosh* roughly translate as "human being, mortal, man, member of the species Homo sapiens." Often the precise meaning is given by context. There is however no exact equivalent of "person," with its senses of having a certain status within society, a bearer of legal rights (so that a rightless individual can be called a non-person), a body ("weapons concealed on his person") and

---

1. To be sure, there is one view in the Talmud (*Sotah* 10b) that holds that Judah was intimate with her again, in effect taking her as his wife, under the laws of *aguna* as then practiced (and reading the phrase *velo yasaf* to mean not "and did not do so again" but "and did not cease to do so.") However this is a distinctly minority interpretation.

so on. So, for example, the phrase "a personal God," which in English is a description of the God of Abraham, is almost impossible to translate into Hebrew without changing the meaning entirely.

The reason, as I mentioned in the essay, "A new Kind of Hero" (above, pp. 73–75), is that the word "person" entered English via the Latin "persona," meaning "a mask." It originally signalled the part played by an actor on the stage, in a culture – Hellenism – in which the theatre played a central part in the portrayal of the human condition. It then became a role played by the individual within society, because of the metaphor of society-as-theatre. It was then generalized to mean any individual within society. But it still bears traces of its theatrical origins ("He was one person at work, another at home"). We speak, in English, of the roles we occupy, the "games people play," the masks we wear (Jews wear masks only on Purim, as a parody of the non-Jewish phenomenon of courtly society, its dances and deceptions). It therefore becomes deeply problematic in Western philosophy, especially in Existentialism, as to what remains of "the self" once all the social roles have been subtracted.

Biblical Hebrew has no word for "person" precisely because it rejects the metaphors of society-as-theatre and self-as-part-played-upon-the-stage. This is no mere rejection: it goes to the very heart of Genesis's conception of the individual and the human condition. We are not the masks we wear; we are the individuals whose innermost thoughts are known to God. We are what lies behind the mask. That is one reason why the Torah systematically devalues sight in favour of sound, the voice and listening. We are not what others perceive us to be; we are what God knows us to be. The drama of the self is not played out on the stage of society; it is transacted in the inner dialogue between the individual and God.

Hence the centrality of these four narratives – of Jacob, Leah, Tamar and Joseph – in Genesis, the book of first principles. It is as if "appearances" – identities as the masks we wear – stand to genuine relationship as idolatry does to worship of the living God. Genesis has surprisingly little to say about idolatry (we only encounter it *en passant*, for example, when Rachel steals Laban's *terafim*) but a great deal to say about human interaction. It is as if it were preparing us for the larger biblical theme, the battle against idolatry, by signalling what is at stake in human terms. Just as idolatry involves worshipping an image of God instead of God Himself, so inauthentic human relationships involve mistaking someone's appearance for what they truly are, mistaking the mask for the self.

In the aftermath of the disguises of Jacob, Leah, Tamar and Joseph, there is no healing of relationship but there is a mending of identity. That is what makes them not secular narratives but deeply religious chronicles of psychological growth and maturation. What they tell us is simple and profound: those who stand before God need no mask, no disguise to achieve self-worth when standing before humankind.

Vayigash
ויגש

Vayigash begins with the climactic scene in which Joseph finally reveals himself to his brothers. Moved by Judah's impassioned plea for Benjamin's freedom, in return for which he declares himself ready to take Benjamin's place as a slave, Joseph discloses his identity and the estrangement of the brothers comes to an end. On Joseph's instructions, they return to Jacob with the news that his beloved son is still alive, and the family is reunited.

Three of the following essays are about the fundamental principles that underlie these events. The first is about *teshuva*, repentance; the second is about the seeming paradox that in Judaism the penitent is regarded as higher even than a perfectly righteous individual. The fourth is about forgiveness and why it is essential to the functioning of any human group, from a family to a society. The third offers an explanation of a feature of the Joseph story that puzzles most readers: why did Joseph not send a message to his father that he was alive? The suggested answer links the Joseph story to several others in Genesis, about the tragic misunderstandings that can emerge when human beings fail to communicate.

In Search of Repentance

The drama of Joseph and his brothers, which has thus far spanned two *parashot* and eight chapters, filled with tension and reversals of fate, now reaches its climax. Judah and Joseph face one another. Benjamin, the youngest of the sons, stands accused of theft and faces a lifetime of slavery. Judah makes an impassioned plea for his release. Yes, the missing silver cup has been found in his possession. Judah does not challenge the facts. Instead he throws himself on the mercy of the Egyptian ruler, of whose identity he is still unaware, and begs him to consider the impact Benjamin's imprisonment will have on his father. Jacob has already lost one beloved son. The shock of losing another will kill him:

> Now therefore, please let your servant remain here as your lord-ship's slave in place of the boy, and let the boy return with his brothers. For how can I go back to my father if the boy is not with me? No! Do not let me see the misery that shall come upon my father… (44:33–34)

These are the words that finally break Joseph's heart. Overcome with emotion, he commands all his attendants to leave, then turns to his brothers, and reveals his identity:

> Then Joseph could no longer control himself before all his atten-
> dants, and he cried out, "Have everyone leave my presence!" So
> there was no one with Joseph when he made himself known to
> his brothers. And he wept so loudly that the Egyptians and the
> house of Pharaoh heard. Joseph said to his brothers, "I am Joseph!
> Is my father still alive?" But his brothers were not able to answer
> him, for they were terrified at his presence. (45:1–3)

Their silence is eloquent. They are bewildered. The stranger turns out to be their brother. The ruler of Egypt is the boy who, years earlier, they had sold into slavery. The combination of shock and guilt paralyses them.

Breaking the silence, Joseph continues. He has yet another sur-prise for his brothers. He does not hold them guilty. There is no anger in his words. Instead he does the least expected thing. He *comforts* them. He forgives them. He speaks with a majestic graciousness:

> Then Joseph said to his brothers, "Come close to me." When they
> came close, he said, "I am your brother Joseph, the one you sold
> into Egypt. And now, do not be distressed and do not be angry
> with yourselves for selling me here, for God sent me ahead of
> you to preserve life. For two years now has there been famine
> in the land, and for the next five years there will not be plowing
> and reaping. But God sent me ahead of you to preserve for you
> a remnant on earth and to save your lives by a great deliverance.
> So it was not you who sent me here, but God." (45:4–8)

With this, the long story reaches closure. The estrangement, which began with the words, "[The brothers] hated him and could not speak peaceably to him" (37:4), is at an end. Joseph is, as he twice dreamed he would be, a ruler. His brothers have bowed down to him. He has sur-vived their attempt to kill him. He has risen from slavery to become the second most powerful man in the most powerful empire of the ancient world. But a central question remains. What *kind* of story is this? Is it a fairytale of rags to riches? A story of revenge? A tragedy of internal dissolution and family in-fighting? What are the deeper themes playing beneath the apparently simple surface? To understand the narrative, we must trace the sequence of events, trying to uncover the intent driving Joseph in the successive encounters with his brothers.

First, the brothers come before Joseph to buy grain. He recognises them but they do not recognise him. He then "speaks harshly," accusing them of espionage. He has them imprisoned for three days.

He then releases them, holding Shimon as a hostage, and tells them that they must bring Benjamin with them next time, to verify their story. Unbeknown to them, he has the money they had paid for the grain put back into their sacks. Discovering this, the brothers are unnerved. Something is happening to them, but they do not know what. They are returning without Shimon but with money instead. It does not make sense, but it does evoke in them a guilty conscience. Did they not, once before, sell (or at least plan to sell) one of their brothers for money. They tremble and ask "What is this that God has done to us?" (42:28).

Returning home, they tell their father what has happened, but Jacob refuses to let Benjamin return to Egypt with them. Eventually the food runs out. After much persuasion on the part of Judah, Jacob allows Benjamin to accompany the brothers back to Egypt. This time, Joseph greets them with warmth, releasing Shimon, inviting them to eat with him. After providing them with fresh supplies of grain, he sends them on their way. Now, however, he does more than place money in their sacks. He has his favourite divination cup placed in Benjamin's grain.

The brothers have left the city, relieved that the visit has been unexpectedly painless. No sooner have they gone than they are overtaken by Joseph's steward. Someone has stolen his master's silver cup. The brothers protest their innocence. The steward searches their bags, starting with the eldest. Finally they reach Benjamin's, and there, in his sack, is the cup. It is the brothers' worst nightmare come true. They knew that having once come home without Joseph, they cannot lose Benjamin as well. Judah has staked his life on it. He has told his father, "I myself will guarantee [Benjamin's] safety; you can hold me personally responsible for him. If I do not bring him back to you and set him here before you, I will bear the blame before you all my life" (43:9). So the brothers appear before Joseph once more, and the drama moves toward its climax.

There are several possible readings of the logic driving this drama that so puzzles the brothers – and the readers. The first, suggested by the Torah itself ("Then he [Joseph] remembered his dreams about them and said to them: You are spies" [42:9]), is that *Joseph was acting so as to fulfill his childhood dreams*, in which his family bowed down to him.

This, however, cannot be the case. *Before* Joseph acts like a stranger, we read "When Joseph's brothers arrived, they bowed down to him with their faces to the ground" (42:6), fulfilling his first dream. If the story were simply about the fulfilment of Joseph's second dream, he should have devised a strategy that would bring the whole family, including Jacob, to Egypt. Jacob and all his brothers would have bowed down to him, the dreams would be fulfilled, and Joseph could then reveal his identity. Nothing of this kind happens. Joseph's actions do not advance, but actually delay this outcome. It cannot be, then, that Joseph was acting simply to fulfil his dreams.

The second possibility is that Joseph is driven by an urge for revenge: he is making his brothers suffer as they once made him suffer. But this too is untenable. At every significant stage (42:24, 43:30, 45:1–2), Joseph turns aside to weep, careful not to let the brothers see him in this state. People engaged in revenge do not weep when executing vengeance. The Torah emphasizes his uncontrollable emotional response, repeating this detail three times, precisely to *exclude* the possibility that Joseph was acting out of desire to do to his brothers what they had once done to him. Those who repay evil with evil take satisfaction in so doing. Joseph takes no satisfaction at all. He is acting *against* his inclination and it causes him unbearable pain. The question therefore returns in full force. What is the logic of Joseph's carefully constructed plot?

One of the key concepts of Judaism – the theme of its holiest days from Rosh Hashana to Yom Kippur – is *teshuva*, a complex concept involving remorse, repentance and return. The abstract noun *teshuva* is post-biblical, but the idea it embodies is central to the Hebrew Bible. It is what the prophets call on Israel to do. It is what Jonah is sent to Nineveh to achieve. In a related sense it is what certain sacrifices (guilt and sin offerings) are intended to accompany.

Teshuva, as analysed by the sages and later by Maimonides, has certain key elements. The first is confession and acknowledgement of wrongdoing:

> How does one confess? The penitent says, "I beseech You, O Lord, I have sinned, I have acted perversely, I have transgressed before You, and have done such and such, and I repent and am ashamed of my deeds."[1]

The second is to commit oneself not to repeat the offence:

> What is this *teshuva*? It is that the sinner abandons his sin, removes it from his thoughts, and resolves in his heart never to repeat it, as it is said, "Let the wicked forsake his way, and the man of iniquity his thoughts." (Isaiah, 55:7)[2]

There is a further condition of complete repentance. As defined by Maimonides:

> What is perfect *teshuva*? This occurs when an opportunity presents itself for repeating the offence once committed, and the offender is able to commit the offence, but refrains from doing so because of the *teshuva* – not out of fear or failure of vigour.[3]

As soon as we understand these three points, the logic of Joseph's course of action becomes clear. The drama to which he subjects his brothers has nothing to do with the dreams, or with revenge. To the contrary, Joseph is not acting for himself but *for the sake of his brothers*. He is leading them – for the first time in recorded history – through the three stages of *teshuva*.

Recall what happened as a result of his intervention. His initial move was to accuse his brothers of a crime they had not committed (being spies), holding them in custody for three days, to see whether this

---

1. Maimonides, *Mishneh Torah*, Hilkhot Teshuva, 1:1.
2. Ibid., 2:2.
3. Ibid., 2:1.

would remind them of a crime they *did* commit (selling their brother into slavery). The effect is direct and unequivocal:

> They said to one another, "Indeed we are guilty [*aval ashemim anaḥnu*] because of our brother, for we saw the distress of his soul when he pleaded with us, and we would not listen. That is why this distress has come upon us." ...They did not realise that Joseph could understand them, since he was using an interpreter. (42:21–23)

Following the first encounter with Joseph, the brothers *confess and express remorse* for what they did. The first stage of *teshuva* has taken place.

The second takes place far away from Joseph, but he has so arranged matters that he will know whether it has happened or not. Joseph is holding Shimon as hostage.[4] He tells the brothers that he will be released only if they return with Benjamin. Knowing his father as he does, Joseph has calculated, rightly, that Jacob will only allow Benjamin to go if he is certain that his sons will not let happen to Benjamin what they let happen to Joseph. This indeed happens when Judah says to Jacob:

> "I myself will guarantee [Benjamin's] safety; you can hold me personally responsible for him. If I do not bring him back to you and set him here before you, I will bear the blame before you all my life." (43:9)

The second condition of repentance has been achieved: a commitment not to repeat the offence. Judah undertakes not to let happen this time what happened last time, namely that Jacob's sons returned without their youngest sibling whose safety they should have guaranteed.

The third act is a master-stroke. Joseph constructs a scene – one could almost call it a controlled experiment – to see if his brothers have

---

4. This is a significant detail. Shimon is the second oldest of the sons. By rights, Joseph should have held Reuben, the eldest. However, he knows that Reuben was the one brother who tried to save him. Shimon is therefore the eldest of those who conspired to kill Joseph.

indeed changed. They had once sold him into slavery. He now puts them in a situation in which they will have overwhelming temptation to repeat the crime by abandoning Benjamin to slavery. This is why he plants the cup in Benjamin's sack, arranges for him to be accused of theft, rules that his punishment will be to remain in Egypt as a slave, and tells the other brothers that they are free to leave.

Joseph, in effect, recreates the past. Benjamin, like Joseph, is a son of Rachel, and therefore likely to be envied and despised by the other brothers. The brothers' resentment of Joseph was heightened by the jealousy they felt at the sight of the many-coloured robe Jacob had given him. Joseph therefore creates once again a situation of inequality. When he sits the brothers down for a meal he arranges that they be seated in order of age, highlighting the fact that Benjamin is the youngest, and then ensures that "Benjamin's portion was *five times as much* as anyone else's" (43:34). There is only one explanation for this strange detail. Joseph is trying to make his brothers jealous of their youngest sibling.

As far as possible, the circumstances of their original crime have now been replicated. Their youngest brother, a child of Rachel, is about to be taken as a slave in Egypt. The brothers have reason to be jealous of him as they were of Joseph. This time they rise to the challenge. As Benjamin is about to be taken into custody, his brothers offer to join him in prison. Joseph declines: "Far be it from me to do such a thing! Only the man who was found to have the cup will become my slave. The rest of you go back to your father in peace" (44:17).

The moment of trial has now begun. Joseph has offered the brothers a simple escape route. All they have to do is walk away. It is then, when "Judah went up to him and said..." (44:18), that the story reaches its climax. Judah, the very brother who was responsible for selling Joseph into slavery (37:27), now offers to sacrifice his own freedom rather than let Benjamin be held as a slave.

The circumstances are similar to what they were years earlier, but Judah's behaviour is now diametrically opposite to what it was then. He has the opportunity and ability to repeat the offence, but he does not do so. Judah has fulfilled the conditions set out by the sages and Maimonides for "perfect *teshuva*." As soon as he does so, Joseph reveals his identity and the drama is at an end.

Not dreams, not revenge, but *teshuva* is what has driven Joseph all along. His brothers once sold him as a slave. He survived: more than survived, he has prospered. He knows (he says so constantly) that everything that has happened to him is somehow part of God's plan. His concern is not for himself but for his brothers. Have *they* survived? Do they realise the depth of the crime they committed? Are they capable of remorse? Can they change? The entire sequence of events between the brothers' first arrival in Egypt and the moment Joseph reveals himself to them, is an extended essay in *teshuva*, a precise rehearsal of what will later become normative Jewish law.

And it must happen at this precise point because – unbeknown to any of the participants – the family of Abraham is about to undergo exile in Egypt, prior to their becoming a nation under the sovereignty of God. That will place more demands on Israel than on any other people in history. God knows that they will often fail – they will sin, complain, worship idols, break His laws. That He accepts, though at times it gives Him great grief. God does not demand perfection: by giving us free-will He empowers us to make mistakes. All He asks is that we acknowledge our mistakes and commit ourselves not to make them again – in a word, that we be capable of *teshuva*. Judah, by undergoing Joseph's test, demonstrated that the children of Israel had become *ba'alei teshuva*, masters of repentance, capable of learning from, and growing through, their mistakes. Jewish history, starting with exile and exodus in Egypt, could now begin.

Penitential Man

The sequence from Genesis 37 to 50 is the longest unbroken narrative in the Torah, and there can be no doubt who its hero is: Joseph. The story begins and ends with him. We see him as a child, beloved – even spoiled – by his father; as an adolescent dreamer, resented by his brothers; as a slave, then a prisoner, in Egypt; then finally as the second most powerful figure in the greatest empire of the ancient world. At every stage, the narrative revolves around him and his impact on others. He dominates the last third of Genesis, casting his shadow on everything else. From almost the beginning, he seems destined for greatness.

Yet history did not turn out that way. To the contrary, it is another brother who, in the fullness of time, leaves his mark on the Jewish people. Indeed, we bear his name. The covenantal family has been known by several names. One is *Ivri*, "Hebrew" (possibly related to the ancient *apiru*), meaning "outsider, stranger, nomad, one who wanders from place to place." That is how Abraham and his children were known to others. The second is *Yisrael*, Israel, derived from Jacob's new name after he "wrestled with God and with man and prevailed." After the division of the kingdom and the conquest of the North by the Assyrians, however, they became known as *Yehudim* or Jews, for it was the tribe of Judah who dominated the kingdom of the South, and they who survived the Babylonian exile.

So it was not Joseph but Judah who conferred his identity on the people, Judah who became the ancestor of Israel's greatest king, David, Judah from whom the messiah will be born. Why Judah, not Joseph? The answer undoubtedly lies in the beginning of *Vayigash*, as the two brothers confront one another, and Judah pleads for Benjamin's release.

Yet this final confrontation can only be fully understood in the context of Judah's initial behaviour towards Joseph. It is Judah, in his first recorded words, who suggested selling Joseph into slavery:

> Judah said to his brothers, "What will we gain if we kill our brother and cover his blood? Let's sell him to the Ishmaelites and not harm him with our own hands. After all – he is our brother, our own flesh and blood." His brothers agreed. (37:26–27)

This is a speech of monstrous callousness. There is no mention of the evil of murder, merely a pragmatic calculation ("What will we gain"). At the very moment he calls Joseph "our own flesh and blood," Judah is proposing to sell him as a slave. Here there is none of the tragic nobility of Reuben who, alone of the brothers, sees that what they are doing is wrong, and makes an attempt to save Joseph. At this point, Judah is the last person from whom we expect great things.

However, Judah – more than anyone else in the Torah – changes. The man we see confronting Joseph all these years later is not the same personality as the one who spoke when Joseph was trapped in the pit. Then he was prepared to see his brother sold into slavery. Now he is prepared to suffer that fate himself rather than see Benjamin held as a slave. As he says to Joseph:

> Now therefore, please let your servant remain here as your lordship's slave in place of the boy, and let the boy return with his brothers. For how can I return to my father if the boy is not with me? No! Do not let me see the misery that shall come upon my father… (44:33–34)

It is a precise reversal of character. Callousness has been replaced with concern. Indifference to his brother's fate has been transformed into courage on his behalf. Judah is willing to suffer what he once inflicted on Joseph so that the same fate should not befall Benjamin. At this point Joseph reveals his identity. We know why. Judah has passed the test that Joseph has carefully constructed for him. Joseph wants to know if Judah has changed. He has.

This is a highly significant moment in the history of the human spirit. Judah is the first penitent – the first *ba'al teshuva* – in the Torah.

This did not happen in a sudden change of character. It was set in motion by another event that happened between these two meetings, namely the story of Tamar. Tamar, we recall, had married Judah's two elder sons, both of whom had died, leaving her a childless widow. Judah, fearing that his third son would share their fate, withheld him from her – thus leaving her unable to remarry and have children.

Once she understands her situation, Tamar disguises herself as a prostitute. Judah sleeps with her. She becomes pregnant. Judah, unaware of the disguise, concludes that his daughter-in-law must have had a forbidden relationship and orders her to be put to death. At this point, Tamar – who, while disguised, had taken Judah's seal, cord and staff as a pledge – sends them to Judah with a message: "The father of my child is the man to whom these belong."

Judah now understands the full significance of what had happened. He had placed Tamar in the impossible situation of living widowhood. He is the father of her child. And more – he also realises that she has behaved with extraordinary discretion in revealing the truth without shaming him. Tamar is the heroine of the story, but it has one significant consequence: Judah admits he was wrong. "She was more righteous than I," he says.

This is the first time in the Torah someone acknowledges their own guilt. It was also the turning point in Judah's life. Here was born the ability to recognise one's own wrongdoing, to feel remorse, and to change – the complex phenomenon known as *teshuva*. This is the beginning of the process that later leads to the great scene in *Vayigash*, where Judah is capable of turning his earlier behaviour on its head and doing the opposite of what he had once done before. Judah is *ish teshuva*, penitential man.

No sooner do we realize this than we understand the deep significance of his name. Its root, the verb *lehodot*, has two main meanings. It means "to thank," which is what Leah had in mind when she gave Judah, her fourth son, his name: "this time I will thank the Lord" (27:35). But it also means, "to admit, acknowledge." The biblical term *vidui*, "confession," – then and now part of the process of *teshuva*, and according to Maimonides, its key element – comes from the same root. Judah means "he who acknowledged his sin."

Acknowledging his sin, Judah also demonstrates one of the fundamental axioms of *teshuva*: "Rabbi Abbahu said: In the place where penitents stand, even the perfectly righteous cannot stand."[1] His proof text is the verse from Isaiah (57:19), "Peace, peace to him that was far and to him that is near," which puts one who "was far" ahead of one who "is near." As the Talmud makes clear, however, Rabbi Abbahu's reading is by no means uncontroversial. Rabbi Yohanan interprets "far" as "far from sin" rather than "far from God." The real proof is Judah.

Joseph is consistently known to tradition as *haTzaddik*, "the righteous." Judah is a penitent, the first in the Torah. Joseph became *mishneh leMelekh*, "second to the king." Judah, however, became the father of Israel's kings. Where the penitent Judah stands, even the perfectly righteous Joseph cannot stand. However great an individual may be in virtue of his or her natural character, greater still is one who is capable of growth and change. That is the power of penitence, and it began with Judah.

1. *Berakhot* 34b.

Does My Father Love Me?

It is one of the great questions we naturally ask each time we read the story of Joseph. Why did he not, at some time during their twenty-two-year separation, send word to his father that he was alive? For part of that time – when he was a slave in Potiphar's house, and when he was in prison – it would have been impossible. But certainly he could have done so when he became the second most powerful person in Egypt. At the very least he could have done so when the brothers came before him on their first journey to buy food.

Joseph knew how much his father loved him. He must have known how much their separation grieved him. He did not know, could not know, what Jacob thought had happened to him, but this surely he knew, that it was his duty to communicate with him when the opportunity arose, to tell his father that he was alive and well. Why then did he not? The following explanation,[1] is a tantalizing possibility.

The story of Joseph's descent into slavery and exile began when his father sent him, alone, to see how the brothers were faring.

---

1. I am indebted for this entire line of thought to Mr. Joshua Rowe of Manchester.

His brothers had gone to graze their father's flocks near Shechem, and Israel said to Joseph, "As you know, your brothers are grazing the flocks near Shechem. Come, I am going to send you to them."

"Very well," he replied.

So he said to him, "Go and see if all is well with your brothers and with the flocks, and bring word back to me." Then he sent him off from the Valley of Hebron. (37:12–14)

What does the narrative tell us immediately prior to this episode? It tells us about the second of Joseph's dreams. In the first, he had dreamt that he and his brothers were in the field binding sheaves. His stood upright while the sheaves of his brothers bowed down to him. Naturally, when he told them about the dream, they were angry. "Do you intend to reign over us? Would you rule over us?" There is no mention of Jacob in relation to the first dream.

The second dream was different:

Then he had another dream, and he told it to his brothers. "Listen," he said, "I had another dream, and this time the sun and moon and eleven stars were bowing down to me."

When he told his father as well as his brothers, his father rebuked him and said, "What is this dream you had? Will your mother and I and your brothers actually come and bow down to the ground before you?" His brothers were jealous of him, but his father kept the matter in mind. (37:9–11).

Immediately afterwards, we read of Jacob sending Joseph, alone, to his brothers. It was there, at that meeting far from home, that they plotted to kill him, lowered him into a pit, and eventually sold him as a slave.

Joseph had many years to reflect on that episode. That his brothers were hostile to him, he knew. But surely Jacob knew this as well. In which case, why did he send Joseph to them? Did Jacob not contemplate the possibility that they might do him harm? Did he not know the dangers of sibling rivalry? Did he not at least contemplate the possibility that by sending Joseph to them he was risking Joseph's life?

No one knew this better from personal experience. Recall that

Jacob himself had been forced to leave home because his brother Esau threatened to kill him, once he discovered that Jacob had taken his blessing. Recall too that when Jacob was about to meet Esau again, after an interval of twenty-two years, he was "in great fear and distress," believing that his brother would try to kill him. That fear provoked one of the great crises of Jacob's life. So Jacob knew, better than anyone else in Genesis, that hate can lead to killing, that sibling rivalry carries with it the risk of fratricide.

Yet Jacob sent Joseph to his other sons knowing that they were jealous of him and hated him. Joseph presumably knew these facts. What else could he conclude, as he reflected on the events that led up to his sale as a slave, that Jacob had deliberately placed him in this danger? Why? Because of the immediately prior event, when Joseph had told his father that "the sun and moon" – his father and mother – would bow down to him.

This angered Jacob, and Joseph knew it. His father had "rebuked" him. It was outrageous to suggest that his parents would prostrate themselves before him. It was wrong to imagine it, all the more so to say it. Besides which, who was the "moon"? Joseph's mother, Rachel, the great love of Jacob's life, was dead. Presumably, then, he was referring to Leah. But his very mention of "the sun and moon and eleven stars" must have brought back to his father the pain of Rachel's death. Joseph knew he had provoked his father's wrath. What else could he conclude but that Jacob had deliberately put his life at risk?

Joseph did not communicate with his father because he believed his father no longer wanted to see him or hear from him. His father had terminated the relationship. That was a reasonable inference from the facts as Joseph knew them. He could not have known that Jacob still loved him, that his brothers had deceived their father by showing him Joseph's bloodstained cloak, and that his father mourned for him, "refusing to be comforted." We know these facts because the Torah tells us. But Joseph, far away, in another land, serving as a slave, could not have known. This places the story in a completely new and tragic light.

Is there any supporting evidence for this interpretation? There is. Joseph must have known that his father was capable of being angered by his sons. He had seen it twice before.

The first time was when Shimon and Levi killed the inhabitants of Shechem after their prince had raped and abducted their sister Dina. Jacob bitterly reprimanded them, saying: "You have brought trouble on me by making me a stench to the Canaanites and Perizzites, the people living in this land. We are few in number, and if they join forces against me and attack me, I and my household will be destroyed"(34:30).

The second happened after Rachel died. "While Israel was living in that region, Reuben went in and slept with his father's concubine Bilhah – and Israel heard of it" (35:22). As we have seen earlier, according to the sages, Reuben merely moved his father's bed,[2] but Jacob believed that he had slept with his handmaid, an act of usurpation.

As a result of these two episodes, Jacob virtually broke off contact with his three eldest sons. He was still angry with them at the end of his life, cursing them instead of blessing them. Of Reuben, he said:

> Unstable as water, you will no longer excel, for you went up onto your father's bed, onto my couch and defiled it. (49:4)

Of his second and third sons he said:

> Shimon and Levi are brothers –
> their swords are weapons of violence.
> Let me not enter their council,
> let me not join their assembly,
> for they have killed men in their anger
> and hamstrung oxen as they pleased.
> Cursed be their anger, so fierce,
> and their fury, so cruel!
> I will scatter them in Jacob
> and disperse them in Israel. (49:5–7)

So Joseph knew that Jacob was capable of anger at his children, and of terminating his relationship with them (that is why, in the absence of

---

2.   Rashi to *Bereshit* 35: 22; *Shabbat* 55b.

Joseph, Judah became the key figure. He was Jacob's fourth son, and Jacob no longer trusted the three eldest).

There is evidence of another kind as well. When Joseph was appointed second-in-command in Egypt, given the name Tzafenat Pa'neah, and had married an Egyptian wife, Asenat, he had his first child. We then read:

> Joseph named his firstborn Menasheh, saying, "It is because God has made me forget all my trouble *and all my father's house.*" (41:51)

Uppermost in Joseph's mind was the desire to forget the past, not just his brothers' conduct towards him but "all my father's house." Why so, if not that he associated "all my trouble" not just with his siblings but also with his father Jacob? Joseph believed that his father had deliberately put him at his brothers' mercy because, angered by the second dream, he no longer wanted contact with the son he had once loved. That is why he never sent a message to Jacob that he was still alive.

If this is so, it sheds new light on the great opening scene of *Vayigash*. What was it in Judah's speech that made Joseph break down in tears and finally reveal his identity to his brothers? One answer is that Judah, by asking that he be held as a slave so that Benjamin could go free, showed that he had done *teshuva*; that he was a penitent; that he was no longer the same person who had once sold Joseph into slavery. That, as I have argued in the previous two essays, is a central theme of the entire narrative. It is a story about repentance and forgiveness.

But we can now offer a second interpretation. Judah says words that, for the first time, allow Joseph to understand what had actually occurred twenty-two years previously. Judah is recounting what happened after the brothers returned from their first journey to buy food in Egypt:

> Then our father said, "Go back and buy a little more food." But we said, "We cannot go down. Only if our youngest brother is with us will we go. We cannot see the man's face unless our youngest brother is with us."
>
> Your servant my father said to us, "You know that my wife

bore me two sons. One of them went away from me, and I said, 'He has surely been torn to pieces.' And I have not seen him since. If you take this one from me too and harm comes to him, you will bring my gray head down to the grave in misery." (44:27–31)

At that moment Joseph realized that his fear that his father had rejected him was unwarranted. On the contrary, he had been bereft when Joseph did not return. He believed that he had been "torn to pieces," killed by a wild animal. His father still loved him, still grieved for him. Against this background we can better understand Joseph's reaction to this disclosure:

> Then Joseph could no longer control himself before all his attendants, and he cried out, "Have everyone leave my presence!" So there was no one with Joseph when he made himself known to his brothers. And he wept so loudly that the Egyptians heard him, and Pharaoh's household heard about it. Joseph said to his brothers, "I am Joseph! Is my father still alive?" (45:1–3)

Joseph's first thought is not about Judah or Benjamin, but about Jacob. A doubt he had harbored for twenty-two years had turned out to be unfounded. Hence his first question: "Is my father still alive?"

Is this the only possible interpretation of the story? Clearly not. But it is a possibility. In which case, we can now set the Joseph narrative in two other thematic contexts which play a large part in Genesis as a whole.

The first is tragic misunderstanding. We think here of at least two other episodes. The first has to do with Isaac and Rebecca. Isaac, we recall, loved Esau; Rebecca loved Jacob. At least one possible explanation, offered by Abrabanel,[3] is that Rebecca had been told "by God," before the twins were born, that "the elder will serve the younger." Hence her

---

3. Abrabanel to *Bereshit* 25:28. Isaac loved Esau, Abrabanel argues, because he was the firstborn. Isaac believed, therefore, that he would inherit the divine blessing and covenant. From her oracle, Rebecca knew otherwise. On this reading, the drama unfolded because of a failure of communication between husband and wife.

attachment to Jacob, the younger, and her determination that he, not Esau, should have Isaac's blessing.

The other concerns Jacob and Rachel. Rachel had stolen her father's *terafim*, "icons" or "household gods," when they left Laban to return to the land of Canaan. She did not tell Jacob that she had done so. The text says explicitly, "Jacob did not know that Rachel had stolen the gods" (31:32). When Laban pursued and caught up with them, he accused Jacob's party of having stolen them. Jacob indignantly denies this and says "If you find anyone who has your gods, he shall not live" (31:32). Several chapters later, we read that Rachel died prematurely, on the way. The possibility hinted at by the text, articulated by a midrash and by Rashi,[4] is that, unwittingly, Jacob had condemned her to death.

In both cases, misunderstanding flowed from a failure of communication. Had Rebecca told Isaac about the oracle, and had Rachel told Jacob about the *terafim*, tragedy might have been averted. Judaism is a religion of holy words, and one of the themes of Genesis as a whole is the power of speech to create, mislead, harm or heal. From Cain and Abel to Joseph and his brothers ("They hated him and could not speak peaceably to him"), we are shown how, when words fail, violence begins.

The other theme, even more poignant, has to do with fathers and sons. How did Isaac feel towards Abraham, knowing that he had lifted a knife to sacrifice him? How did Jacob feel towards Isaac, knowing that he loved Esau more than him? How did Leah's sons feel about Jacob, knowing that he loved Rachel and her children more? *Does my father really love me?* – that is a question we feel must have arisen in each of these cases. Now we see that there is a strong case for supposing that Joseph, too, must have asked himself the same question.

"Though my father and mother may forsake me, the Lord will receive me," says Psalm 27. That is a line that resonates throughout Genesis. No one did more than Sigmund Freud to place this at the heart of human psychology. For Freud, the Oedipus complex – the tension between fathers and sons – is the single most powerful determinant of the psychology of the individual, and of religion as a whole.

Freud, however, took as his key text a Greek myth, not the

4. Rashi to *Bereshit* 31:32; *Bereshit Raba* and *Zohar* ad loc.

narratives of Genesis. Had he turned to Torah instead, he would have seen that this fraught relationship can have a non-tragic resolution. Abraham did love Isaac. Isaac did bless Jacob a second time, this time knowing he was Jacob. Jacob did love Joseph. And transcending all these human loves is divine love, rescuing us from feelings of rejection, and redeeming the human condition from tragedy.

Forgiveness

Judah has passed the test so elaborately contrived by Joseph. Twenty-two years earlier, it was Judah who had proposed selling Joseph into slavery. Now Joseph – still unrecognized by his brothers – has put him through a carefully constructed ordeal to see whether he is still the same person, or has changed. He has changed. Judah is now willing to become a slave himself so that his brother Benjamin can go free. This is all Joseph needs to know. Now, at last, he reveals his identity to his brothers in a moment of intense emotion.

The most important feature of the scene, however, is Joseph's complete forgiveness for what the brothers had done to him all those years before.

> "And now, do not be distressed and do not be angry with your-selves for selling me here, for God sent me ahead of you to pre-serve life. For two years now has there been famine in the land, and for the next five years there will not be plowing and reaping. But God sent me ahead of you to preserve for you a remnant on earth and to save your lives by a great deliverance. So it was not you who sent me here, but God." (45:5–8)

Joseph makes no reference to the brothers' plot to kill him or to the fact that they had sold him into slavery. He makes no mention of the lost years he spent, first as Potiphar's slave, then as a prisoner in jail. Not only does he forgive them, he does everything possible to relieve them from a sense of guilt. He tells them that they were not really responsible; that it had been God's plan all along; that it had been for the best, so that he could save lives during the years of famine, and so that he could act as their protector in the years to come. It is a moment of supreme generosity of spirit.

Nor is this the only such moment. Five chapters later, at the end of the book of Genesis, Joseph repeats the act of forgiveness. Jacob has died, and the brothers now fear that Joseph will take revenge after all. They are afraid that his apparent friendliness was merely a way of biding his time until their father was no longer alive (recall Esau's words: "The days of mourning for my father are near; then I will kill my brother Jacob" [27:41]). This is what Joseph says on this second occasion:

> "Don't be afraid. Am I in the place of God? You intended evil towards me, but God intended it for good, to bring to pass what is now being done, the saving of many lives. Therefore, do not be afraid. I will nourish you and your children." And he reassured them and spoke kindly to them. (50:19–21)

It is sometimes said that Judaism lacks the concept of forgiveness. Occasionally the claim is more specific: in Judaism, God forgives, people do not. This is simply not so. In Maimonides' words:

> It is forbidden for a person to be obdurate and not be appeased. On the contrary, one should be easily pacified and difficult to move to anger. When asked by an offender for forgiveness, one should forgive with a sincere mind and a willing spirit...forgiveness is natural to the seed of Israel.... [1]

---

1. Rambam, *Mishneh Torah*, Hilkhot Teshuva, 2:10.

Nor is it necessary for the offender to apologise:

> If one who has been wronged by another does not wish to rebuke
> or speak to the offender – because the offender is simple or con-
> fused – then if he sincerely forgives him, neither bearing him
> ill-will nor administering a reprimand, he acts according to the
> standard of the pious. [2]

In other words, if you judge that the offender will not apologise, because
he is the kind of person incapable of admitting or understanding that
he has done wrong, then you should forgive him anyway. You do not
have to, but it is *middat hassidut*, "the standard of the pious," to do so.

So it is not that God forgives, while human beings do not. On
the contrary, we believe that just as only God can forgive sins against
God, so only human beings can forgive sins against human beings. That
is why Yom Kippur atones for our sins against God, but not for our sins
against other human beings.[3]

The reason there is so little reference to interpersonal forgiveness
elsewhere in the Bible lies in the fact that, as mentioned in the Introduction (p. 5), the book of Genesis is about "first principles." It is here more
than anywhere else that the emphasis is on personal relationships, and
here that the themes of hostility, resentment, estrangement and reconciliation are explored in all their depth and pathos. Once the Torah has
established the principle of human forgiveness, which it does here in
the Joseph narrative, it does not need to repeat it elsewhere.

Note how profound the passage really is. Joseph does more than
forgive. He wants to make sure that the brothers, especially Judah, have
changed. They are no longer people capable of selling others into slavery.
For it would have been absurd for the victim to forgive while the crime
was still being committed or while the criminal was still unrepentant.[4]

2. Ibid., Hilkhot De'ot 6:9.
3. For a fascinating discussion of forgiveness, see Simon Wiesenthal, *The Sunflower:
   On the Possibilities and Limits of Forgiveness*, revised and expanded edition (New
   York: Schocken, 1997).
4. See Richard Swinburne, *Responsibility and Atonement* (Oxford: Clarendon, 1989).

Consider a modern equivalent, the "Truth and Reconciliation" process established in South Africa by Nelson Mandela: it could only come about once apartheid had been ended.

Nor is it Judah alone who has to change. So does Joseph. He has to rethink the entire sequence of events. He no longer sees it in terms of a wrong done against him by his brothers. He sees it as part of a providential plan to bring him to where God needs him to be ("So then, it was not you who sent me here, but God"). He thinks not only of the moment twenty-two years earlier when he was sold as a slave, but of its long-term consequences. Before he can come to terms with his brothers, Joseph has to come to terms with himself and his experiences. That is why forgiveness lifts the forgiver even more than the one who is forgiven.

But the real significance of this passage goes far beyond the story of Joseph and his brothers. It is the essential prelude to the book of Exodus and the birth of Israel as a nation. The book of Genesis is, among other things, a set of variations on the theme of sibling rivalry: Cain and Abel, Isaac and Ishmael, Jacob and Esau, Joseph and his brothers. The book begins with fratricide and ends with reconciliation. There is a clear pattern to the final scene of each of the four narratives:

1	Cain/Abel	Murder
2	Isaac/Yishmael	The two stand together at Abraham's funeral
3	Jacob/Esau	Meet, embrace, go their separate ways
4	Joseph/brothers	Forgiveness, reconciliation, coexistence

In the development of these four narratives, the Torah is making a statement of the most fundamental kind. Historically and psychologically, families precede society and state. If brothers cannot live together in peace, then they cannot form a stable society or a cohesive nation. Maimonides explains that forgiveness and the associated command not to bear a grudge (Leviticus 19:18) are essential to the survival of society: "For as long as one nurses a grievance and keeps it in mind, one may come to take vengeance. The Torah emphatically warns us not to bear a grudge, so that the impression of the wrong shall be quite obliterated and be no longer remembered. This is the right principle. It alone makes civilization and human relationships possible."[5]

Forgiveness is not merely *personal*, it is also *political*. It is essential to the life of a nation if it is to maintain its independence for long. There is no greater proof of this than Jewish history itself. Twice Israel suffered defeat and exile. The first – the conquest of the Northern Kingdom, followed a century and a half later by the destruction of the First Temple and the Babylonian exile – was a direct consequence of the division of the kingdom into two after the death of Solomon. The second – defeat at the hands of the Romans and the destruction of the Second Temple – was the result of intense factionalism and internal strife, *sinat hinam*.

When people lack the ability to forgive, they are unable to resolve conflict. The result is division, factionalism, and the fragmentation of a nation into competing groups and sects. That is why Joseph's forgiveness is the bridge between Genesis and Exodus. The first is about the children of Israel as a *family*, the second is about them as a *nation*. Central to both is the experience of slavery, first Joseph's, then the entire people. The message could not be clearer. Those who seek freedom must learn to forgive.

---

5. Rambam, *Mishneh Torah*, Hilkhot De'ot 7:8.

Vayeḥi
ויחי

With *Vayehi*, the book of Genesis, full of conflicts within the family, comes to a serene end. Jacob, reunited with his beloved Joseph, sees his grandsons, the only such scene in the Torah. He blesses them, then, on his death-bed, blesses his twelve sons. He dies and is buried in the cave of Makhpelah with his parents and grandparents. Joseph forgives his brothers a second time, and he himself dies, having assured his brothers that God will eventually bring the family back to the Promised Land. The long patriarchal narrative is at an end and a new period – the birth of Israel as a nation – is about to begin.

The first of the following essays looks at the values of truth and peace in Judaism, and which takes priority when they clash. The second analyzes the names of Joseph's sons and what they tell us about his state of mind when he named them. The third looks at the paradoxical idea that, through *teshuva*, we can change the past. The fourth shows how forgiveness is an essential part of the life of freedom, for it alone liberates us from being held captive by memory and resentment. Jewish time, defined by repentance and forgiveness, is the defeat of tragedy in the name of hope.

The White Lie

Keep far from falsehood" warns the Torah in Exodus (23:7), and throughout the ages, the complex of issues surrounding truth and falsehood have raised important ethical questions. Is it permitted to tell a white lie? If a murderer is at large, brandishing a gun, and his intended victim takes refuge in your house, are you obligated to tell the truth when the would-be killer knocks on your door and asks, "Is he here?" Immanuel Kant, the greatest philosopher of modern times, said Yes. We should always tell the truth, whatever the consequences.[1] For Kant, morality is a matter of universal rules that apply in all circumstances, so that permitting a lie in one case would involve permitting it in all cases, which would rob all communication of trustworthiness. Judaism says No. Not only is it permitted to tell a white lie to save a life, it is also permitted to do so for the sake of peace.

The sages derived this from two episodes, one in *Parashat Vayeḥi*.

---

1. Immanuel Kant, "On a supposed right to lie from altruistic motives," *Berliner Blätter*, September 1797; English translation in Sisela Bok, *Lying: Moral Choice in Public and Private Life* (New York: Pantheon, 1978), 267–72.

Jacob has died. The brothers fear that Joseph will now take revenge for the fact that they sold him into slavery. They devise a stratagem:

> And they sent a message to Joseph, saying, "Your father left these instructions before he died: 'This is what you are to say to Joseph: I ask you to forgive your brothers the sins and the wrongs they committed in treating you so badly.' Now please forgive the sins of the servants of the God of your father." When their message came to him, Joseph wept. (50:16–17)

There is no evidence that Jacob ever said these words attributed to him. The sages therefore assume that what the brothers said was in fact a lie. They conclude: "It is permitted to change [i.e. to tell a white lie] for the sake of peace."[2]

They find evidence for this principle in a second source as well. When three visitors come to Abraham in his old age and announce that in a year's time Sarah will bear a child, Sarah laughs, saying to herself: "After I am worn out, will I now have pleasure, and my husband is old?" (18:12). God tells Abraham that Sarah disbelieves, but tactfully leaves out part of her reasoning: "Why did Sarah laugh and say, 'Will I really have a child, now that I am old?'" (18:13). There is no reference to Sarah's remark about her husband being old. Thus, the sages conclude that even God Himself may "change [the truth]" for the sake of peace.

Both sources are necessary. If we only had the evidence of Joseph's brothers, we could not infer that what they did was correct: Perhaps they were wrong to lie. And if we only had the evidence of God's words to Abraham, we could only infer that a half-truth is permitted, not an actual lie: God does not say anything false – He merely omits some of Sarah's words. Both together serve to establish the rule. Peace takes precedence over truth.

To understand a civilization, it is necessary not only to know the values and virtues it embraces, but also the order of priority among them. Many cultures value freedom and equality. The difficult question is: which takes precedence? Communism values equality more than free-

2. *Yevamot* 65b.

dom. Laissez-faire capitalism values freedom more than equality. They share the same ideals, but because they assign them different places in the ethical hierarchy, they result in completely different societies.

Truth and truthfulness are fundamental values in Judaism. We call the Torah "the law of truth" (Malachi 2:6). The sages define truth as the signature of God.[3] Yet truth is not the highest value in Judaism. Peace is.

The reasons for this are twofold. First is the extraordinary value Judaism attributes to peace. The nineteenth-century historian, Sir Henry Sumner Maine, said: "War is as old as mankind. Peace is a modern invention."[4] He had much evidence to support him. Virtually every culture until modern times was militaristic. Heroes were mighty men of valour who fought and often died on the field of battle. Legends were about great victories in war. Conflict – whether between the gods, the elements, or the children of light against the children of darkness – was written into the human script.

Against this backdrop, the prophets of ancient Israel were the first in history to see peace as an ideal. That is why the words of Isaiah, echoed by Micah, have never lost their power:

> He will judge between the nations and will settle disputes for many peoples. They will beat their swords into plowshares and their spears into pruning hooks. Nation will not take up sword against nation, nor will they train for war anymore. (Isaiah 2:2–4)

This vision of a world at peace was not centuries but millennia ahead of its time.

At the same time, Judaism took a more subtle view of truth than did the philosophers of antiquity. In logic, a sentence is either true or false. There is no third alternative. In Judaism, by contrast, truth is many-faceted and elusive. Of the disputes between the schools of Hillel and Shammai, the Talmud says, "These and those are the words of the

---

3. *Shabbat* 55a.
4. Cited at the beginning of Michael Howard, *The Invention of Peace: Reflections on War and International Order* (London: Profile, 2001).

living God."[5] Indeed, some believe that, though now the law is in accord with the school of Hillel, in the Messianic Age it will follow the view of Shammai.[6] Ultimate truth forever eludes us. God, the ultimate reality, is "beyond our understanding."[7] Maimonides held that we can only know what God is not; not what He is.

There is such a thing as truth in the eye of the beholder. The school of Hillel held that one should always say at a wedding, "The bride is beautiful and gracious." But what if she isn't, asked Shammai? Will you tell a lie? In the eyes of her husband, she is beautiful, answered Hillel.[8]

There is a remarkable midrash that speaks about the creation of humankind:

> Rabbi Shimon said: When the Holy One, blessed be He, came to create Adam, the ministering angels formed themselves into groups and parties, some of them saying, "Let him be created," whilst others urged, "let him not be created." Thus it is written, *Love and Truth fought together, Righteousness and Peace combated each other* (Psalms 85; 11): Love said, Let him be created, because he will dispense acts of love; Truth said, Let him not be created, because he is compounded of falsehood; Righteousness said, Let him be created, because he will perform righteous deeds; Peace said, Let him not be created, because he is full of strife. What did the Lord do? He took Truth and cast it to the ground. Said the ministering angels before the Holy One, blessed be He, Sovereign of the Universe! Why do You despise Your seal? Let Truth arise from the earth! Hence it is written, "Let truth spring up from the earth." (ibid. 12)[9]

5. *Eruvin* 13b.
6. This idea was generally maintained by the sixteenth-century exponents of Lurianic Kabbala. The rulings of the school of Shammai were generally stricter than those of the school of Hillel. Hence, the law follows Hillel in the present age when spirituality is weak; it will follow the more demanding rules of Shammai when the spirit has won its victory over physical instincts in the Messianic Age.
7. Job 36:26.
8. *Ketubot* 17a.
9. *Bereshit Raba* 8:5.

Human beings, said the angels, are a mixture of faults and virtues. They do good deeds of loving-kindness and righteousness. But they are also prone to conflict and violence, and all too often they tell lies. Thus the angels were divided – two against two – as to whether human beings should be created at all. God, according to the midrash, decided the case by disregarding the objection of the angel of truth: He "cast it to the ground." Nonetheless, God did not abandon the claim of truth. He said "Let truth spring up from the earth."

The midrash, in the deceptively simple way that it teaches its deepest and most subtle insights, is suggesting that truth on earth can never aspire to the pristine clarity of truth in heaven. We see "as through a glass, darkly."[10] We see from one perspective, not all. Often our judgments are clouded by emotion. At times our limited understanding leads us to think we have understood all there is to understand. It takes courage and imagination, as well as humility, to admit how little we know. So, by casting truth to the ground, God was in effect saying: Let us not judge human beings as if they were angels. Enough that they aspire to truth and search for it. That is what it means for truth to "spring up from the earth."

Perhaps, though, the midrash is suggesting something deeper as well, for it speaks of God casting down truth, not peace. Yet the angel of peace, like the angel of truth, objected to the creation of humankind. How then was the claim of peace answered? Perhaps the divine response to truth also constituted an answer to the complaint of peace. It is when human beings believe that they possess absolute truth – truth as it is in heaven – that they fight their most savage wars. Crusades and jihads were waged in the name of truth. So were the terrors that followed the French Revolution and the brutalities of Stalinist Russia. Isaiah Berlin devoted much of his intellectual energy to arguing that "Few things have done more harm than the belief on the part of individuals or groups… that he or she or they are in *sole* possession of the truth."[11]

The way to peace is to realise that our grasp of truth is partial, fragmentary, incomplete. That is the human condition. Truth matters,

10. In Aramaic, *Be'ispaklaria she'einah me'ira*: *Yevamot* 49b, *Sanhedrin* 97b. This seems to be the source of the famous phrase used by Paul in 1 Corinthians 13:12.
11. Isaiah Berlin *Liberty*, (Oxford: University Press, 2002), 345.

but peace matters more. That is Judaism's considered judgement. Many of the greatest crimes in history were committed by those who believed they were in possession of the truth while their opponents were sunk in error. To make peace between husband and wife (Abraham and Sarah) and between brothers (Joseph and Jacob's other sons), the Torah sanctions a statement that is less than the whole truth. Dishonesty? No. Tact, sensitivity, discretion? Yes. That is an idea both eminently sensible and humane.

Forgetfulness and Fruitfulness

The drama of younger and older brothers, which haunts the book of Genesis from Cain and Abel onwards, reaches a strange climax in the story of Joseph's children. Jacob/Israel is nearing the end of his life. In the only scene involving grandparents and grandchildren in the entire book, Joseph visits him, bringing with him his two sons, Menasheh and Ephraim. Jacob asks Joseph to bring them near so that he can bless them. The Torah describes what follows next in painstaking detail:

> Joseph took them both, Ephraim in his right hand toward Israel's left, and Menasheh in his left hand towards Israel's right, and brought them near him. But Israel reached out his right hand and put it on Ephraim's head, though he was the younger, and crossing his arms, he put his left hand on Menasheh's head, even though Menasheh was the firstborn…. When Joseph saw his father placing his right hand on Ephraim's head it displeased him; so he took hold of his father's hand to move it from Ephraim's head to Menasheh's head. Joseph said to him, "No, my father, this one is the firstborn; put your right hand on his head." But

his father refused and said, "I know, my son, I know. He too will become a people, and he too will become great. Nevertheless, his younger brother will be greater than he, and his descendants will become a group of nations." He blessed them that day, saying: "In your name will Israel pronounce this blessing: 'May God make you like Ephraim and Menasheh.'" So he put Ephraim ahead of Menasheh. (48:13–14, 17–20)

It is not difficult to understand the care Joseph took to ensure that Jacob would bless the firstborn first. Three times throughout his life, his father had set the younger before the elder, and each time it had resulted in tragedy. Jacob, the younger, had sought to supplant his elder brother Esau. In choosing a wife, he had favoured the younger sister Rachel over Leah. And he favoured the youngest of his children, Joseph and Benjamin, over the elder Reuben, Shimon and Levi. The consequences were catastrophic: estrangement from Esau, tension between the two sisters, and hostility among his sons. Joseph himself bore the scars: thrown into a well by his brothers, who initially planned to kill him and eventually sold him into Egypt as a slave. Had his father not learned? Or did he think that Ephraim – whom Joseph held in his right hand – was the elder? Did Jacob know what he was doing? Did he not realise that he was risking extending the family feuds into the next generation?

Why, in any case, did Jacob favour Ephraim over Menasheh? He had not seen his two grandchildren before. He knew nothing about them. None of the factors that led to the earlier episodes were operative here.

We cannot be sure of the explanation. Here, as so often in the Torah, the narrative is undetermined, leaving it to us, the reader, to flesh out the details. In the rabbis' wonderful phrase: "the text itself cries out: Expound me!"[1] In this case, we know that Jacob knew only this about his grandsons: their names, Menasheh and Ephraim. This was enough to persuade him to bless Ephraim before Menasheh. For encoded in Joseph's sons' names is the story of his years of exile away from Jacob.

---

1. Solomon Buber, comp., *Tanḥuma, Vayeshev* 13; see Rashi to Bereshit 1:1; 37:20.

When Joseph finally emerged from prison to become chief minister of Egypt, he married and had two sons:

> Before the years of the famine came, two sons were born to Joseph by Asenat, daughter of Potiphera, priest of On. Joseph named his firstborn Menasheh, saying, "God has made me forget [*nasheh*] all my trouble and all my father's household." The second son he named Ephraim, saying, "For God has made me fruitful [*fara*] in the land of my affliction." (41:50–52)

With the utmost brevity the Torah intimates an experience of exile that was to be repeated many times across the centuries. At first, Joseph felt relief. The years as a slave, then a prisoner, were over. He had risen to greatness. In Canaan, he had been the youngest of eleven brothers in a nomadic family of shepherds. Now, in Egypt, he was at the centre of the greatest civilization of the ancient world, second only to Pharaoh in rank and power. No one reminded him of his background. With his royal robes and ring and chariot, he was an Egyptian prince (as Moses was later to be). The past was a bitter memory he sought to remove from his mind. Menasheh means "forgetting."

But as time passed, Joseph began to feel quite different emotions. Yes, he had arrived; he had achieved the power and greatness of which he had dreamed in his youth. But this people was not his; nor was its culture. To be sure, his family was, by any worldly terms, undistinguished, unsophisticated. Yet they remained his family. They were the matrix of who he was. Though they were no more than shepherds (a class the Egyptians despised), they had been spoken to by God – not the gods of the sun, the river and death, the Egyptian pantheon – but God, the Creator of heaven and earth, who did not make His home in temples and pyramids and panoplies of power, but who spoke in the human heart as a voice, lifting a simple family to moral greatness.

By the time his second son was born, Joseph had undergone a profound change of heart. To be sure, he had all the trappings of earthly success – "God has made me fruitful" – but Egypt had become "the land of my affliction." Why? Because it was exile. There is a sociological observation about immigrant groups, known as Hansen's Law: "The second generation seeks to remember what the first generation sought to forget."[2] Joseph went through this transformation very quickly. It was already complete by the time his second son was born. By calling this child Ephraim, he was remembering what, when Menasheh was born, he was trying to forget: who he was, where he came from, where he belonged.

On this reading, Jacob's blessing of Ephraim over Menasheh had nothing to do with their ages and everything to do with their names. He knew that the stay of his family in Egypt would not be a short one. Before leaving Canaan to see Joseph, God had appeared to him in a vision:

> Do not be afraid to go down to Egypt, for I will make you into a great nation there. I will go down to Egypt with you, and I will surely bring you back again. And Joseph's own hand will close your eyes. (46:3–4)

He knew, in other words, that this was the start of the long exile that God had told Abraham would be the fate of his children, a vision the Torah describes as accompanied by "a deep and dreadful darkness"(15:12). Knowing that these were the first two children of his family to be born in exile, knowing too that the exile would be prolonged and at times difficult and dark, Jacob sought to signal to all future generations that there would be a constant tension between the desire to forget (to assimilate, acculturate, anaesthetise the hope of a return) and the promptings of memory (the knowledge that this is "exile," that we are part of another story, that ultimate home is somewhere else).

The child of forgetting (Menasheh) may have blessings. But greater are the blessings of a child (Ephraim) who remembers the past and future of which he is a part.

2. Marcus Lee Hansen, *The Problem of the Third Generation Immigrant* (Rock Island, IL., Augustana Historical Society, 1938), 9.

The Future of the Past

The scene that brings the book of Genesis to a close is intensely significant. Years before, Joseph had forgiven his brothers for selling him into slavery, telling them "Now, do not worry or feel guilty because you sold me. Look: God has sent me ahead of you to save lives" (45:5). Evidently, though, they only half believed him. Could he really forgive an act of cruelty that had altered the whole course of his life? Their feelings of guilt had not gone away, and they come back to haunt them when Jacob dies.

It seems clear from the earlier story of Esau that sons were not allowed to take revenge against their brothers in the lifetime of their father. Esau says, "The days of mourning for my father will be here soon. I will then be able to kill my brother Jacob" (27:41). That is the possibility the brothers contemplate in the case of Joseph. They fear that he may want to take revenge but has waited until the death of Jacob. They are anxious that his words of forgiveness in the past may not have been sincere. He may simply have been biding his time, waiting for the appropriate moment (as later happened, for example, in the case of Amnon and Absolom).

After Jacob's death, the brothers come to Joseph and say, "Your father left these instructions before he died: 'This is what you are to say to Joseph: I ask you to forgive your brothers the sins and the wrongs they committed in treating you so badly.' Now please forgive the sins of the servants of the God of your father" (50:16).

The sages realised that this testament from Jacob had never taken place – had it been true, there would be some reference to it in the narrative.[1] Yet Joseph takes his brothers' words seriously – not because he believes them, but because the very fact that they say this indicates that they are still feeling anxious and guilty. His response is majestic in its generosity:

> "Don't be afraid," said Joseph. "Am I in place of God? You intended to harm me but God intended it for good, to accomplish what is now being done, the saving of many lives." (50:19–20)

As we have already discussed, this final scene is the resolution of one of the central problems of the book of Genesis: the continuing theme of sibling rivalry. A book replete with tensions, hatred, and competition ends with forgiveness. This closing is essential to the biblical drama of redemption, for if brothers cannot live together, how can nations? And if nations cannot live together, how can the human world survive? Only now, with the reconciliation of Joseph and his brothers, can the story move on to the birth of Israel as a nation, passing from the crucible of slavery to the constitution of freedom as a people under the sovereignty of God.

Yet there is something more, and different, at stake in Joseph's remark, and it is this I wish to explore here. It concerns the most paradoxical of all rabbinic statements about *teshuva*.

One of the most colourful characters of the Talmud was the third-century sage known as Resh Lakish. Resh Lakish was originally a highway robber and gladiator. Tradition reports that he encountered the great scholar, Rabbi Yohanan, bathing in the Jordan. Rabbi Yohanan persuaded him to give up his lawless ways and join him in the house of

---

1. See the essay, "The White Lie," p. 331.

study. Resh Lakish repented and became Rabbi Yohanan's disciple and colleague (and also his brother-in-law: he married Yohanan's sister).

The Talmud reports that, despite relinquishing his earlier life, Resh Lakish occasionally used his physical strength to good ends. On one occasion he rescued a rabbinic colleague, Rav Imi, who was being held captive by a group of kidnappers. Another time, he went into a town where Rabbi Yohanan had been robbed and brought back his stolen possessions. But he is best known as one of the most famous of *ba'alei teshuva*, penitents, of the Talmudic era. Perhaps speaking from his own experience, he coined several aphorisms about *teshuva*, two of which are reported in the tractate of *Yoma* (86b):

> Resh Lakish said: Great is repentance, because through it deliberate sins are accounted as unintentional, as it is said, "Return, O Israel, to the Lord your God, for you have stumbled in your iniquity" (Hosea 14:2). "Iniquity" means a deliberate sin, yet the prophet calls it "stumbling" [i.e. unintentional]. Resh Lakish also said: Great is repentance, because through it deliberate sins are accounted as though they were merits, as it is said, "When the wicked man turns from his wickedness and does what is lawful and right, he shall live thereby" (Ezekiel 33:19).

The two statements, the second stronger than the first, are reconciled in the Talmud: the first applies to repentance from fear (of punishment), the second to repentance from love (of God and the good). But despite their similarities, they are strikingly different. The first makes sense. When we acknowledge our wrongs, we signal that we regret having done them. We retrospectively disassociate ourselves from them. The acts remain, but the intent does not. To that extent we turn them from deliberate sins to actions that we now wish we had not done. They become, as it were, unintentional.

The second statement, by contrast, is virtually unintelligible. By signalling our remorse, we at best declare that now, on reflection, we did not mean to do what we did. We cancel the intention. What we cannot do is cancel the deed. It has been done. It is part of the past. It cannot be changed. How then can deliberate sins be transformed into their opposites – into merits, into good deeds?

Nor does Resh Lakish's quotation from Ezekiel prove his point. If anything, it proves the opposite. The prophet is speaking about a person who, having undergone *teshuva*, now does good instead of evil – and it is because of his good deeds, not his earlier evil ones, that "he shall live." What the verse shows is that good deeds can overcome a previous history of wrongdoing, not that they can turn wrong into right, bad into good, deliberate sins into merits.

I have hinted in previous essays, however, that the source of many of the sages' principles of *teshuva* are not derived from the proof texts cited by the Talmud itself, but from the story of Joseph and his brothers – the key biblical narrative of repentance. The reason the sages did not cite this as their source is twofold: first, the Joseph story is narrative, not law; second, it precedes the covenant at Mount Sinai, and therefore only serves as a valid precedent if some confirmation can be found in the post-Mosaic literature.

Resh Lakish's statement about sins and merits is such a case. Almost certainly its source lies in the words Joseph speaks to his brothers in the closing chapter of Genesis: "You intended to harm me but God intended it for good." This is the paradigm that stands at the basis of Resh Lakish's argument. The brothers had committed a deliberate sin by selling Joseph into slavery; they (or at least Judah, the instigator of the decision to sell Joseph) had done *teshuva*. The result is that – through divine providence ("God intended it") – their action is now reckoned "for good."

Not only is this the source of Resh Lakish's principle, it also enables us to understand what it means. Any act we perform has multiple consequences, some good, some bad. When we intend evil, the bad consequences are attributed to us because they are what we sought to achieve. The good consequences are not: they are mere by-products, happenstance, unintended outcomes.

Thus, in the case of Joseph, many positive things happened once he had been brought to Egypt. He became master of Potiphar's household, a prison administrator, an interpreter of dreams. Later he became second-in-command of Egypt, overseer of its economy, and the man who saved the country from ruin during the years of famine. None of these consequences could be attributed to his brothers, even though they would not have happened had the brothers not done as they did. The reason is that the brothers neither foresaw nor intended this set of outcomes. They meant to sell Joseph as a slave, and that is what they did.

However, once the brothers had undergone complete repentance, their original intent was cancelled out. It was now possible to see the good, as well as the bad, consequences of their act – and to attribute the former to them. Stripped of their initial aim, the act could instead be defined by what part it played in a providential drama whose outcome was only now fully apparent in retrospect. To paraphrase Shakespeare's Mark Antony, the good they did would live after them; the bad was interred with the past (*Julius Caesar*, act III, scene 2.). That is how, through repentance, deliberate sins can be accounted as merits, or as Joseph put it: "You intended to harm me, but God intended it for good." This is a hugely significant idea, for it means that by a change of heart we can redeem the past.

This still sounds paradoxical, for we tend to take for granted the idea of the asymmetry of time: The future is open, but the past is closed. Before us lie a series of paths. Which we take depends upon our choice. Behind us lies the history of our previous decisions, none of which we can undo. We cannot go back in time. That is a logical impossibility. We can affect what is yet to be; but, in the words of the sages, "What has been, has been,"[2] and we cannot alter it. With or without repentance, the past is surely immutable. All of this is true, but it is not the whole truth. The revolutionary idea behind Joseph's and Resh Lakish's words is that there are two concepts of the past. The first is what happened. The second is the significance, the meaning, of what happened.

In ancient Israel a new concept of time was born. This did more than change the history of the West; in a sense, it created it. Until Tanakh, time was generally conceived as a series of eternal recurrences, endlessly repeating a pattern that belonged to the immutable structure of the universe. The seasons – spring, summer, autumn, winter – and the lifecycle – birth, growth, decline and death – were a reiterated sequence

2. *Pesaḥim* 108a.

in which nothing fundamentally changed. This is variously called cyclical, or cosmological, or mythic time. There is a powerful example of it in Tanakh itself, in the book of Ecclesiastes:

> Generations come and generations go,
> but the earth remains forever.
> The sun rises and the sun sets,
> and hurries back to where it rises...
> All streams flow into the sea,
> yet the sea is never full.
> To the place the streams come from,
> there they return again...
> What has been will be again,
> what has been done will be done again;
> there is nothing new under the sun. (Ecclesiastes 1:4–9)

This conception of time produces a deeply conservative philosophy of life. It justifies the status quo. Inequalities are seen as written into the structure of the universe. All attempts to change society are destined to fail. People are what they are, and the world is what it is always been. At best this view leads to resignation, at worst to despair. There is no ultimate meaning in history. As the author of *Ecclesiastes* says:

> "Meaningless! Meaningless!"
> says the Teacher.
> "Utterly meaningless!
> Everything is meaningless." (Ecclesiastes 1:2)

The Jewish understanding of time that emerges from Tanakh, in contrast, was utterly revolutionary. For the first time people began to conceive that God had created the universe in freedom, and that by making man in His image, He endowed him too with freedom. That being so, he might be different tomorrow from what he was today, and if he could change himself, he could begin to change the world. Time became an arena of change. With this, the concept of history (as opposed to myth) was born.

Many great thinkers have written on this theme, including the historian Arnold Momigliano[3] and the anthropologist Mircea Eliade.[4] Here is how the British historian J.H. Plumb puts it in his book, *The Death of the Past*:

> The concept that within the history of mankind itself a process was at work which would mould his future, and lead man to situations totally different from his past, seems to have found its first expression among the Jews…. With the Jews, the past became…an intimate part of destiny and an interpretation of the future…. The uniqueness of this concept lay in the idea of development. The past was no longer static, a mere store of information, example and events, but dynamic, an unfolding story…. This sense of narrative and of unfolding purpose bit deeply into European consciousness.[5]

And what applies to nations, applies also to individuals. We live life forwards, but we understand it backwards. The simplest example of this is autobiography. Reading the story of a life, we see how a deprived childhood led to the woman of iron ambition, or how the early loss of a parent shaped the man who spent his later years pursuing fame in search of the love he had lost. There is an air of inevitability about such stories, but it is an illusion. The deprived childhood or the loss of a parent might equally have led to a sense of defeat and inadequacy. What we become depends on our choices, and we are (almost) always free to choose this way or that. But what we become shapes the story of our life, and only in hindsight, looking back, do we see the past in context, as part of a tale whose end we now know. In life considered as a narrative, later events change the significance of earlier ones. It was the gift of Judaism to the world to discover time as a narrative.

That was what Resh Lakish knew from his own experience. He

---

3. Arnold Momigliano, "History and the Concept of Time," in *History and Theory: Studies in the Philosophy of History*, Beiheft 6 (Middletown, CT: Wesleyan University Press, 1966), 18–19.
4. Mircea Eliade, *Cosmos and History: The Myth of The Eternal Return* (New York: Harper, 1959).
5. J.H. Plumb, *The Death of the Past* (Harmondsworth: Pelican, 1973), 56–57.

had been a highway robber. He might have stayed one. Instead he became a *ba'al teshuva*, and the very characteristics he had acquired in his earlier life – physical strength and courage – he later used to virtuous ends. He knew he could not have done so had he had a different past, a life of study and peace. His sins became merits because in retrospect they were an essential part of the good he eventually did. What had happened (the past as past) did not change, but its significance (the past as part of a narrative of transformation) did.

That too was the profound philosophical-spiritual truth Joseph conveyed to his brothers. By your repentance – he intimated to them – you have changed the story of which you are a part. The harm you intended to do ultimately brought about good. So long as you stayed the people prepared to sell a brother into slavery, none of that good could be attributed to you, but now you have transformed yourself through *teshuva*, and so have transformed the story of your life as well. By your change of heart you have earned the right to be included in a narrative whose ultimate outcome was benign.

We now see the profound overarching structure of the book of Genesis. It begins with God creating the universe in freedom. It ends with the family of Jacob on the brink of creating a new social universe of freedom which begins in slavery, but ends in the giving and receiving of the Torah, Israel's "constitution of liberty."[6] Israel is charged with the task of changing the moral vision of mankind, but it can only do so if individual Jews, of whom the forerunners were Jacob's children, are capable of changing themselves – that ultimate assertion of freedom we call *teshuva*. Time then becomes an arena of change in which the future redeems the past and a new concept is born – the idea we call hope.

---

6. The phrase belongs to F.A. Hayek, *The Constitution of Liberty* (Chicago: University of Chicago Press, 1960).

Jewish Time

Different cultures tell different stories. The great novelists of the nineteenth century, for example, wrote fiction that is essentially ethical. Jane Austen and George Eliot explored the connection between character and happiness. In this, they were greatly influenced by the Bible, and there is a palpable continuity between their work and the book of Ruth. Charles Dickens, following in the tradition of the prophets, wrote about society and its institutions, and the ways in which they can fail to honour human dignity and justice.

By contrast, today's fascination with stories like *Star Wars, Batman, Spiderman* and their many variants is conspicuously dualistic. There is a force of evil, separate from and independent of, God and the good. Evil is "out there" in the universe, not just "in here" within the human heart. These stories are closer to myth than monotheism.

Jack Miles, in his *God: A Biography*, draws the distinction by way of a comparison between Sophocles's *Oedipus Rex* and Shakespeare's *Hamlet*.[1] Oedipus is doomed from the beginning of the story. The Delphic oracle has spoken; Oedipus's fate is sealed; the more he acts to

1. Jack Miles, *God: A Biography* (New York: Simon and Schuster, 1995), 397–98.

avoid it the more tightly enmeshed in it he becomes. Watching Oedipus is cathartic. We are purged of our emotions of fear, sorrow and grief and become reconciled to our mortality.

The drama of *Hamlet*, however, lies within the mind, the soul, of Hamlet himself. The conflict is not between human intention and blind fate, but between the two forces at work in Hamlet's character, "the native hue of resolution" versus "the pale cast of thought." Hamlet's battle, like Jacob's wrestling match with the angel, is with himself. Tanakh, as Miles concludes, "is far nearer in spirit to *Hamlet* than to *Oedipus Rex*." It is a literature, not of fate but of freedom.

There is, however, one aspect of Tanakh, systematically evident in the narrative of Genesis, that is rare to the point of uniqueness. It is a *story without an ending* which looks forward to an open future rather than reaching closure. This defies narrative convention.[2] Normally we expect a story to create a tension that is resolved in the final page. That is what gives art a sense of completion. We do not expect a sculpture to be incomplete, a poem to break off halfway, a novel to end in the middle. Schubert's *Unfinished Symphony* is the exception that proves the rule.

Yet that is what the Bible repeatedly does. Consider the *Ḥumash*, the five Mosaic books. The Jewish story begins with a repeated promise to Abraham that he will inherit the land of Canaan. Yet even when we reach the end of Deuteronomy, the Israelites have still not crossed the Jordan. The *Ḥumash* ends with the poignant scene of Moses on Mount Nebo (in present-day Jordan) seeing the land – to which he has been journeying for forty years but is destined not to enter – from afar.

Nevi'im, or *Prophets*, the second part of Tanakh, ends with Malachi foreseeing the distant future, understood by tradition to be the messianic age:

> See, I will send you the prophet Elijah before the coming of the great and awesome day of the Lord. He will turn the hearts of the fathers to their children, and the hearts of the children to their fathers..." (Malachi, 3:24)

2. See Frank Kermode, *The Sense of an Ending: Studies in the Theory of Fiction* (New York: Oxford University Press, 1967).

Nevi'im, which includes the great historical as well as prophetic books, thus concludes neither in the present or the past, but by looking forward to a time not yet reached. *Ketuvim, Writings*, the third and final section, ends with King Cyrus of Persia granting permission to the Jewish exiles in Babylon to return to their land and rebuild the Temple. After thirty-nine books, and more than a thousand years in real time, we are almost back where we began, with Abraham in Ur of the Chaldees about to begin his journey to the Promised Land.

Torah, Nevi'im, Ketuvim: none concludes with an ending in the conventional sense. Each leaves us with a sense of a promise not yet fulfilled, a task not yet completed, a future seen from afar but not yet reached. The paradigm case – the model on which all others are based – is the ending of the book of Genesis in this *Parashat Vayeḥi*.

Recall that the story of the people of the covenant begins with God's call to Abraham to leave his land, birthplace and father's house and travel "to a land which I will show you" (12:1). Yet no sooner does Abraham arrive than he is forced by famine to go to Egypt. That is the fate repeated by Jacob and his children. Genesis ends not with life in Israel but with a death in Egypt:

> Then Joseph said to his brothers, "I am about to die. But God will surely come to your aid and take you up out of this land to the land He promised on oath to Abraham, Isaac and Jacob." Then Joseph made the sons of Israel swear an oath and said, "God will surely come to your aid, and then you must carry my bones up from this place." So Joseph died at the age of a hundred and ten. And after they embalmed him, he was placed in a coffin in Egypt. (40:24–26)

Again, a hope not yet realised, a journey not yet ended, a destination just beyond the horizon.

In great works, form and content work together, each reinforcing the other in an indissoluble whole. The unfinished nature of Genesis links to the theme which ends the Joseph story: *forgiveness*. Hannah Arendt, in *The Human Condition*, offers a profound insight into the connection between forgiveness and time. Human action, she argues, is potentially tragic. We can never foresee the consequences of our acts, but once done, they cannot be undone. We know that:

> ... he who acts never quite knows what he is doing, that he always becomes "guilty" of consequences he never intended or even foresaw, that no matter how disastrous the consequences of his deed, he can never undo it ... All this is reason enough to turn away with despair from the realm of human affairs and to hold in contempt the human capacity for freedom.[3]

What transforms the human situation from tragedy to hope, Arendt argues, is the possibility of forgiveness:

> Without being forgiven, released from the consequences of what we have done, our capacity to act would, as it were, be confined to one single deed from which we could never recover.... Forgiving, in other words, is the only reaction which does not merely re-act but acts anew and unexpectedly, unconditioned by the act which provoked it and therefore freeing from its consequences both the one who forgives and the one who is forgiven.[4]

Atonement and forgiveness are the supreme expressions of human freedom – the freedom to act differently in the future than one did in the past, and the freedom not to be trapped in a cycle of vengeance and retaliation. Only those who can forgive can be free. Only a civilization based on forgiveness can construct a future that is not an endless repetition of the past. That, surely, is why Judaism is the only civilization whose golden age is in the future.

It was this revolutionary concept of time based on human freedom that Judaism contributed to the world. Many ancient cultures believed in cyclical time, in which all things return to their beginning. The Greeks developed a sense of tragic time, in which the ship of dreams

---

3. Hannah Arendt, *The Human Condition* (Chicago: University of Chicago Press, 1958), 233.
4. Ibid., 237, 241.

is destined to founder on the hard rocks of reality. Europe of the Enlightenment introduced the idea of linear time, with its close cousin, progress.

Judaism believes in something else, neither endless repetition nor inevitable progress, but *covenantal time*, the story of the human journey in response to the divine call, with all its backslidings and false turns, its regressions and failures, yet never doomed to tragic fate, always with the possibility of repentance and return, always sustained by the vision with which the story began, of the Promised Land, the new society, the place where justice and compassion triumph over the evil that lurks within the human heart, where human virtue and divine blessedness meet in the consummation of the covenant that we call redemption. As Harold Fisch has put it: "The covenant is a condition of our existence in time... We cooperate with its purposes never quite knowing where it will take us, for 'the readiness is all.'" In a lovely phrase, he speaks of the Jewish imagination as shaped by "the unappeased memory of a future still to be fulfilled."[5]

Tragedy gives rise to *pessimism*. Cyclical time leads to *acceptance*. Linear time begets *optimism*. Covenantal time gives birth to *hope*. These are not just different emotions. They are radically different ways of relating to life and the universe. They are expressed in the different kinds of stories people tell. Jewish time always faces an open future. The last chapter is not yet written. The messiah has not yet come. Until then, the story continues – and we, together with God, are its co-authors.

5.   Harold Fisch, *A Remembered Future: A Study in Literary Mythology* (Bloomington: Indiana University Press, 1984), 11, 19.

About the Author

A global religious leader, philosopher, author and moral voice for our time, Rabbi Lord Jonathan Sacks served as chief rabbi of the United Hebrew Congregations of the Commonwealth between September 1991 and September 2013.

Described by HRH The Prince of Wales as "a light unto this nation" and by former British Prime Minister Tony Blair as "an intellectual giant," Rabbi Sacks is a frequent academic lecturer and contributor to radio, television, and the press in Britain and around the world. He holds sixteen honorary degrees, including a Doctor of Divinity conferred to mark his first ten years in office as chief rabbi, by the then Archbishop of Canterbury, Lord Carey.

In recognition of his work, Rabbi Sacks has won several international awards, including the Jerusalem Prize in 1995 for his contribution to Diaspora Jewish life, The Ladislaus Laszt Ecumenical and Social Concern Award from Ben-Gurion University in Israel in 2011, the Guardian of Zion Award from the Ingeborg Rennert Center for Jerusalem Studies at Bar-Ilan University, and The Katz Award in recognition of his contribution to the practical analysis and application of Halakha in modern life in

Israel in 2014. He was knighted by Her Majesty The Queen in 2005 and made a Life Peer, taking his seat in the House of Lords in October 2009.

The author of twenty-five books, Rabbi Sacks has published a new English translation and commentary for the Koren Sacks Siddur, the first new Orthodox siddur in a generation, as well as powerful commentaries for the *Rosh HaShana, Yom Kippur,* and *Pesaḥ Maḥzorim.* A number of his books have won literary awards, including the Grawemeyer Prize for Religion in 2004 for *The Dignity of Difference,* and National Jewish Book Awards for *A Letter in the Scroll* in 2000, *Covenant & Conversation: Genesis* in 2009, and the *Koren Sacks Pesaḥ Maḥzor* in 2013. His Covenant & Conversation commentaries on the weekly Torah portion are read in Jewish communities around the world.

After achieving first-class honours in philosophy at Gonville and Caius College, Cambridge, he pursued post-graduate studies in Oxford and London, gaining his doctorate in 1981, and receiving rabbinic ordination from Jews' College and Yeshivat Etz Chaim. He served as the rabbi for Golders Green Synagogue and Marble Arch Synagogue in London, before becoming principal of Jews' College.

Born in 1948 in London, he has been married to Elaine since 1970. They have three children and several grandchildren.

www.rabbisacks.org / @RabbiSacks

The fonts used in this book are from the Arno family